Praise for

"From the Bible to the _____
Song of Solomon, the journey or quest has been a staple motif of Western literature. _Motiba's Tattoos_ is a welcome addition to that list."
—_The Washington Post_

"The history of the Gujarati diaspora is one of the great unwritten narratives of premodern globalization. Mira Kamdar gives us a loving and poignant account of this story."
—Amitav Ghosh, author of
The Calcutta Chromosome and _Shadow Lines_

"Evocative descriptions of the sights, sounds, smells, and tastes of India."
—_The Seattle Times_

"The remains of her exotic world that Kamdar salvages are not only a glowing historical account of the life and times of her gifted and graceful grandmother but a tribute to the endowment one generation offers to another."
—_The Oregonian_

MIRA KAMDAR is a senior fellow of the World Policy Institute at New School University. She has written for the _Los Angeles Times_, the _Chicago Tribune_, and _World Policy Journal_. Currently at work on a novel, she divides her time between New York City and Vancouver, Washington.

Motiba's Tattoos

A Granddaughter's Journey from America
into her Indian Family's Past

Mira Kamdar

Ⓟ

A PLUME BOOK

For Alexander and Anjali: Jai Mataji!

PLUME
Published by the Penguin Group
Penguin Putnam Inc., 375 Hudson Street, New York, New York 10014, U.S.A.
Penguin Books Ltd, 27 Wrights Lane, London W8 5TZ, England
Penguin Books Australia Ltd, Ringwood, Victoria, Australia
Penguin Books Canada Ltd, 10 Alcorn Avenue, Toronto, Ontario, Canada M4V 3B2
Penguin Books (N.Z.) Ltd, 182–190 Wairau Road, Auckland 10, New Zealand

Penguin Books Ltd, Registered Offices: Harmondsworth, Middlesex, England

Published by Plume, a member of Penguin Putnam Inc. This is an authorized reprint of a hardcover
edition published by PublicAffairs, a member of the Perseus Books Group. For information address
PublicAffairs, 250 West 57th Street, Suite 1321, New York, New York 10107.

First Plume Printing, September 2001
10 9 8 7 6 5 4 3 2 1

All photographs courtesy of the author and the author's family.

Portions of this work were originally published in different form in *World Policy Journal* as
"Bombay / Mumbai: The Postmodern City." Vol. XIV, No. 2, Summer 1997, pp. 75–88, and
"Rangoon: A Remembrance of Things Past." Vol. XVI, No. 3, Fall 1999, pp. 89–109.

The Library of Congress has catalogued the PublicAffairs edition as follows:
Kamdar, Mira.
Motiba's tattoos: a granddaughter's journey into her Indian family's past / Mira Kamdar.
  p. cm.
  ISBN 1-891620-58-4 (hc.)
     0-452-28269-1 (pbk.)
1. Kamdar, Mira. 2. Gujarati Americans—Biography. 3. East Indian American women—Bibliography.
4. Racially mixed people—United States—Biography. 5. East Indian Americans—Ethnic identity.
6. Kamdar family. 7. Grandmothers—Kathiawar Agency— Biography. 8. Kathiawar Agency—
Biography. 9. Kathiawar Agency—Social life and customs—20th century. I. Title.
E184.G84 K36 2000
973.04'914'0092—dc21
[B]   00-039010

Printed in the United States of America
Original hardcover design by Victoria Kuskowski

Contents

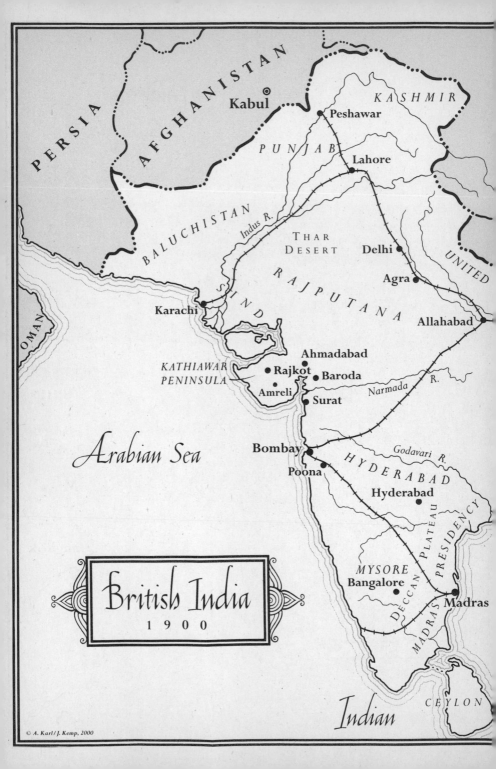

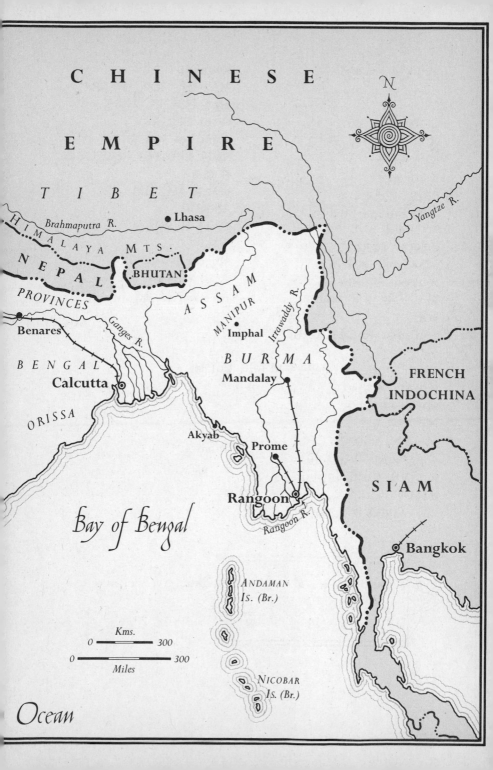

અતોભ્રષ્ટ તતોભ્રષ્ટ

ખાસ્સા સમય પછી
બે દાયકાને જાગૃત કરતી
નજરે ચઢ્યો
૪ x ૬ નો
ફેમિલી ફોટોગ્રાફ.
વીસમી સદીના ઉત્તરાર્ધની
ત્રણ પેઢીની
વર્ણસંકર ફેશનમાં
કેવાં ઊપસી આવે છે
ગાંધીજીના જમાનાને
પ્રતિબિંબિત કરતા બાપાજી
અને
મુંબઈ જેવા આધુનિક શહેરમાં
હવે
ગુજરાતી માતાની ઐતિહાસિક પ્રતિકૃતિ જેવાં બા.
ભાઈઓ, ભાભીઓ
એમનો સમુદાય...
અને વચ્ચે હું-
અતોભ્રષ્ટ તતોભ્રષ્ટ.
સૌની આંખો ઝીણી કરતી
ચોપાસથી પ્રવેશી પ્રકાશતો
તડકો-
એય જડપાયો છે ફોટામાં
અને
ક્યાંક ક્યાંક ડોકાય છે
ફોટો જીવે ત્યાં સુધી
તાજું જ દેખાવાનો પ્રયત્ન કરતી ફૂલોની ક્યારીઓ..

પશ્ચાદ્‌ભૂમાં
અડધું જૂનુ, અડધું નવું ઘર-
સ્થળે સ્થળે રંગ ઊખડેલું..
મનના રસ્તા પર
એકબીજાને અથડાઈ
પસાર થતા અનેક વિચારો સાથે
મેં ફોટાને
ખાનામાં મૂકી દીધો.
અંધારામાં
દીવાસળી ઝબૂકે
એમ
બધું તાદૃશ થયા પછીય
કેટલી અલ્પજીવી હોય છે
આ સ્મરણની ઋતુ..!

પન્ના નાયક

Family Portrait

After a long time
I came across
my family portrait
bringing back
two decades, three generations.

How my father stands out—
a man reflecting Gandhi's times!
And my mother—
an authentic Gujarati lady
In these modern days of Bombay!
Brothers, with their wives and
children
and I amongst them—
neither there, nor here!

The glaring sun
trying to shut everyone's eyes
has also entered the photograph.
And peeping in are the flowers
trying to look fresh
as long as the portrait lives.
In the background
the house with some peeling plaster
looks a little old, a little new...

I put away the picture.
Many thoughts cross my mind.

In the flash of a lighted match
darkness clears for a moment
and one sees
things as they are
and yet how short-lived
is the season of memory

——PANNA NAIK

Introduction

My grandmother's tattoos were one of the great mysteries of my childhood. Etched onto her chin, her cheeks, and her forearms were thin lines, dots, and crosses of a blackish blue-green. The marks were purely abstract. There was no pictorial element to hint at a meaning. No one ever explained to me how my grandmother came to have these tattoos, why she wore them, or what they meant. Certainly, I never dared to ask. I simply took them to be mute signs of the unknowable world out of which she came.

As I grew older, I became aware of another mystery related to my grandmother: no one knew her real name. Even she claimed not to know it. She was known within the family as "Ba" (mother). I always called her "Motiba" (grandmother). Outside the immediate family, she was called "Baluben." I knew that "ben" meant "sister," a common term of affectionate respect. "Balu," I was told, was simply a nickname, with no meaning or sense to it. It was what she had always been called, and no more. Later, one of my aunts told me my grandmother's real name was "Jayakunver," or "Victorious Princess." This name seemed too grand and impersonal to belong to my tiny grandmother. In any case, no one, least of all she herself, ever used it. Motiba's anonymity bothered me. It compounded her mystery. One of the most important persons in my life was in many ways a cipher.

It's not that I didn't know anything about her. I knew that her father had been very rich and that she came from significantly more money than my grandfather did. In marrying him, she had made the poorest match of her family. A visit to any one of her relatives was a visit to a level of comfort and luxury well above that enjoyed in the home she'd made with my grandfather. I remember as a child paying a call on an old uncle of hers. His slightly moldering mansion was tucked away in a large private garden in the exclusive Malabar Hill section of Bombay. The salon where we met him had enormous high ceilings, polished floors of black and white marble, and heavily carved teak furniture. The cool quiet was broken only by the gentle, rhythmic sound of a great fan that turned slowly overhead. As we left, he pressed a stainless steel pocketknife in the shape of a finely scaled fish into my hand. The fish could be worn as a pendant without anyone knowing it contained a sharp little knife under its skin. It bore the imprint TATA STEEL on one of its sides. As he placed the small knife in my palm, he said, "Remember, money can be made and lost, but an education can never be taken from you." Awed by the apparent wealth of this man, I found it hard to interpret the wisdom of his words. I supposed he meant that education could be a sort of consolation prize if you didn't have money. If you couldn't be rich, at least you could be smart. I still have the knife.

What I knew best about Motiba were all the things about her that didn't need to be told to me. The graceful beauty of her long, tapered hands, for example: hands that soothed a feverish forehead as no one else's could; hands that coaxed every last drop of juice out of an orange; hands that could roll out a perfectly round *chapati* in less than a minute flat. Motiba spoke no more than five or ten words of English. As a child, I spoke very little Gujarati, her native tongue. So we conversed in a sort of private, pidgin language all our own. Mostly, our communication took place in a continuum of pure emotion, punctuated by soothing clicks of the tongue or shushing of the lips. One pronouncement I will always associate with my grandmother is a sort of kissing sound she would make, pursing her lips together and sucking a little air in. Repeated, this could mean encouragement, as in, "Come on, finish the last of your milk." Uttered just once, it could mean that some activity was over, as in, "Okay, now give me the glass."

These exchanges invariably took place in the kitchen, the one room in the house that was off-limits to men. In this exclusively female zone, Motiba reigned supreme. The men in the family were more or less kept in the dark about exactly what went on in the kitchen. My sense, even as a child, was that as long as food was delivered when and as expected to the dining room, the men had no call to interfere. In the kitchen, *saris* were allowed to slip immodestly off heads, and all manner of gossip was bandied about with impunity. Much of the work of mixing, chopping, and kneading took place on the floor. Children ran freely in and out, picking their way through an obstacle course of rolling pins, trays of vegetables, bowls of condiments. Sometimes there were upsets, as on the occasion when my then–eighteen-month-old sister Devyani caught the overhanging lip of a beaten brass charger with her foot and sent a couple of quarts of *dokhla* batter right onto the floor. It had taken over twenty-four hours for the batter to ferment to the proper consistency. There was no way to quickly whip up a substitute. Motiba darted over to the site of the accident, scooped up the spilled batter with her bare hands, put as much of it as possible back into the bowl, and said, "What the men don't know won't hurt them."

Meal preparation consumed hours of Motiba's time, but in the lulls after breakfast and, especially, after lunch, my grandmother relaxed in her kitchen. I can see her sitting cross-legged on the kitchen floor, her small frame backlit by sunshine leaking into the room from the blistering Bombay afternoon outside. The servants have finished the washing up, and the kitchen has been restored to order, cleanliness, and calm after the messy hubbub of three women cooking a ten-course meal for fourteen family members. Motiba is speaking to me in Hindi, saying, "*Hum nehin jayenge. Hum Bharat mein rehenge.*" Invoking her status as a respected elder addressing a much younger person, she uses the Hindi version of the "royal we," saying, "We are not going. We are staying in India." We've been talking about my aunt's proposal that Motiba emigrate to America, where her later years can be graced by a more comfortable lifestyle. She bobs her head from side to side in that curious Indian gesture that can mean either "Yes" or "No" or even "Yes and No." Tears stream down her cheeks. Motiba is weeping not because she's upset about the prospect of moving to America but because she is engaging in one of her favorite pastimes. In front of her on the floor is a bowl of tiny green chilies, their small size inversely proportionate to the wallop they pack. Motiba selects one of these emerald jewels, lifts it delicately by the stem, and dips it into a small bowl of coarse salt. Then she pops the whole thing into her mouth, biting it off just where the stem emerges from the dangerous flesh. Fresh tears spring from her eyes. *"Bahu saras chhe! Bahu saras chhe!"* she exclaims in Gujarati. "It's so good! It's so good!" I sit gape-mouthed in front of her, marveling that such pain can bring so much pleasure. *"Joie chhe?"* she asks me, smiling impishly through her tears and extending one of the lethal little green devils in my direction. "No, no! It's too hot!" I say, leaping up and jumping back several feet. She laughs, wipes her tears away with the back of her hand, and tells me that when I grow up my tastes will change.

* * *

Motiba stood no more than five feet two inches tall. Her figure in old age was as lithe as when she was a young girl. In the years I knew her, she always dressed in a plain white cotton *sari,* worn "Gujarati style" with the *paalav* drawn up from the back to drape in front over the right shoulder. A huge ring of keys, one for each of the vigilantly locked cupboards in the house, was securely tied into a knot formed by a corner of her *sari* and then tucked in at the waist. Her blouses were custom-made with a secret little pocket sewn on the inside between her breasts. This was where Motiba kept her money when she went out shopping, sure that no pickpocket would be so bold as to attempt to dislodge her currency from that intimate spot. She was extremely skilled at reaching into that pocket and deftly extracting from her cleavage only the amount needed for the transaction at hand.

Like most old Gujarati ladies, Motiba wore her hair parted in the middle and braided into a single tress that was wound up into a bun at the nape of her neck. Her hair had whitened and thinned with age so that she was left with a thin little braid that formed a tiny bun when she put it up in the morning. Motiba wore no jewelry, other than two bangles of twenty-two-carat gold, the soft metal worn thin and smooth. She wore these only because not to do so would have been interpreted as an insult to her status as a married woman. Although this plainness was a mark of dignity in old age and an indication of Motiba's disdain for the material world at a point in her life when she wished to focus on spiritual matters, it is also true that she been forced to sell much of her jewelry to provide dowries for her husband's sisters. She was promised that better times would bring her more and even richer jewels, but better times never came. In old age, my grandmother was a diminished, rather stripped-down version of her former self.

Motiba's ears offered physical evidence of the era when she had been rich and adorned. At the lobes were large holes, stretched long by the weight of the heavy gold earrings that had hung there for years. A line of smaller holes ran all the way up the outer edges of both ears, emptied now of the gold rings and studs set with precious stones that had once graced them. The left plane of her nose was pocked in the center by a hole that had held a magnificent ruby and pearl nose ring on her wedding day, replaced by a simple diamond solitaire she wore for years after. Motiba hadn't always been so plain. Once a luxuriant black mane of hair had flowed down her back to her knees, the rest of her person covered with gold and jewels. As a little girl, I naturally took young Motiba, beautiful and rich as I always imagined her to be, as my role model.

One day, when she was well into her eighties, my petite grandmother suddenly and unaccountably swelled up. She complained of stomach pain and was administered various digestive remedies. After some months, when it was too late to save her, she was diagnosed with inoperable uterine cancer. Motiba spent the last weeks of her life in constant, blinding pain. I desperately wanted to go to her to say good-bye. But it was not to be. While her womb was killing her, mine was harboring the first flutterings of my daughter's life. "Not during this trimester," said my doctor, "If you get sick there, you could lose the baby." Agonizing over a choice between my grandmother and my own child, I decided I could not risk making the trip. From my apartment in New York, I called Hinduja Hospital in Bombay. "Motiba," I said, sobs threatening to overwhelm my already-halting command of the language, "so much love goes to you from my heart." I uttered this in Hindi, a language we both knew imperfectly but the only one we shared. She was then beyond words and could produce only a sort of high-pitched, urgent whine. I told her why I couldn't come. Motiba had given birth to six babies and lost one. She had nourished them all with her milk and had even suckled an orphaned nephew in an era when formula and bottles were unknown and babies who couldn't get a mother's milk did not survive. As heartbreaking as the situation was, I knew that Motiba understood.

Once it was decided there was nothing medical science could do for her, Motiba was released from the hospital. As if she had been holding on just long enough to get home, she passed away in her bed a mere fifteen minutes after crossing the threshold of the apartment where she had lived for over twenty-five years. Motiba's tattoos, those signs from another world indelibly etched onto her body, vanished in the flames that consumed my grandmother the next day at the neighborhood electric crematorium.

What was the meaning of Motiba's tattoos? I sought out the family elders. I began asking questions. It seems they were beauty marks, permanent ornaments. One of my aged aunts suggested that Motiba had them applied at a religious festival by an itinerant tattoo artist. This might have been done as part of her preparation for marriage. Before her wedding, Motiba would also have had holes pierced all the way up the side of each ear to hold multiple sets of gold earrings. She would have had her body hair waxed and then been rubbed down with milk and sandalwood paste so her skin would be smooth and soft. A Marwari specialist was certainly summoned to the house to trace elaborate paisley swirls on her hands and feet with *mehndi,* or henna paste. On her wedding day, in addition to the heavy gold and jeweled nose ring, Motiba wore an elaborate ornament of worked gold along the centered part of her hair. Her physical adornment was not a statement of personal style. Motiba was a precious gift from her family to her husband's family. Every element of her presentation was dictated by the strict traditions of her community, of which she was, entirely and firstly, a member. The style and placement of her tattoos marked her as a daughter of her community. They also protected her against the evil eye. Part beauty mark, part brand, part talisman, Motiba's tattoos were a legacy of the tribal values she carried literally inscribed on her person into the modern age.

From New York's East Village to Portland, Oregon's, Saturday Market, tattooing, body piercing, and *mehndi* are all the rage. *Mehndi*, or "henna tattooing" as it is commonly called, has become a popular party activity for teenagers. Young people use *mehndi* and other forms of "body adornment," such as piercing, to make custom statements of personal style. Though Motiba indulged with pleasure in all these practices, it would never have occurred to her, or to any young person in her time and place, to tattoo a little butterfly on her rear because it looked cute, to pierce her lower lip because it was hip, or to engage in a little collective *mehndi* painting at a party because charades had gone out of fashion.

How can the world into which Motiba was born at the dawn of the twentieth century possibly be understood from our world at the century's end? Hers was an agrarian and pastoral world, where tribe and territory were everything, and people were deeply rooted to their homeland. They took their rural, feudal values with them into the mercantile imperial world of British India. But even this world, a fundamentally nineteenth-century world, was on the cusp of changing forever. The last traces of Motiba's world are nearly extinct. Anyone who has sat and watched the sun set knows that the last rays are the ones that disappear the most quickly. At the very end, what remains of the glow seems to gather itself and rush out of sight. So it is that the last traces of premodern life in India—a country whose name is often coupled with "timeless" or "eternal"—are disappearing at an accelerating rate. Much of what

existed of "eternal India" even a few years ago is no more. What little remains will soon be gone.

I have "Generation X," twenty-something female cousins in
Bombay who call their mother for help when they need to wear a
sari to a wedding or other fancy occasion. Having worn Western
clothes their entire lives, they don't know how to wrap the six
yards of continuous silk around their bodies. Theirs is a world of
international brands: Calvin Klein, Benetton, Guess?, Dolce &
Gabbana. Members of the young urban Indian generation, those
who can afford it as well as those who can't, identify much more
with their contemporaries in a global consumer culture emanating
from the West than with their Indian parents and grandparents.
And why shouldn't they? After all, their world bears hardly any
resemblance to that of the generations that preceded them.

On a recent trip to Kathiawar, the region of India where Motiba
was born, I had a sudden epiphany about the extent to which the
world in which people of our class live has become globalized. We
were in a car traveling to a private country club for a family party.
My husband and I had our two children, six and two years, with us
and also two little cousins, a six-year-old from London and a ten-
year-old Kathiawari native from Rajkot. The children were debat-
ing the relative merits of the different programs offered on the
Cartoon Network. One thought *Johnny Quest* was really cool.
Another preferred *Dexter's Laboratory*. Though my children and
their cousins lived thousands of miles away from each other on
three different continents, they all spoke English (differently
accented English but English all the same), the lingua franca of this

turn-of-the-century's global culture, and all watched the same cartoon channel in their different time zones. My husband and I
exchanged a look. Our children were indeed growing up in world
quite different from the one in which we were children, much less
the one in which Motiba had been a child two generations earlier.
It's hard to imagine, beyond the basic humanity we all share, what
little-girl Motiba had in common in 1913 with her contemporaries
in London or New York.

* * *

Our family's story is part of the history of the Indian diaspora in the
twentieth century. In the first half of the century, Motiba's father
and then her husband sought their fortunes in Burma, then an
extension of British imperial India. After World War II, when things
became very difficult for the Indian merchant community in
Burma, my father was sent to study in the United States. He arrived
in 1949, and became one of the first American-trained Indian engineers in the country. He ended up marrying an American citizen. It
was the only way he could stay in the United States in those days,
when strict laws severely limited immigration from Asia. My
mother was a true Western girl, who grew up on a farm in Oregon,
broke and trained her own wild mustang named Cheetah, and com-
peted in rodeos. My father's employment in aerospace—his first
job was with Boeing—and my parents' "mixed marriage" were
made possible by deep changes in the global economy and the
beginnings of profound shifts in social mores in America. Motiba
was wary at first of these changes, not wanting her son to leave

India, threatening a hunger strike upon learning the news of his marriage to a "meat-eating daughter of peasant farmers" in America. Soon enough, however, Motiba became quite fond of my mother, her only foreign daughter-in-law. She also spent the last decade or two of her life jetting around the world visiting various offspring in the global diaspora. Motiba had family in Singapore, Tokyo, Los Angeles, Chicago, New York, London, and Nairobi. Still a devout Jain, she only flew airlines that could provide her with a "Hindu vegetarian" meal, something most do. Yet, many of the grandchildren she visited on these trips ate at McDonald's, wore clothes from the Gap, watched CNN, and kept in touch via e-mail.

My siblings and I represent the ultimate erasure of Motiba's world. American-born, none of us speaks Gujarati, Motiba's native language. We don't even look Indian, since our mother is Danish American. Once, when I arrived in Bombay after a twenty-some-hour trip, I decided to change some money before leaving the airport. I presented the man behind the foreign exchange counter my passport and proceeded to endorse a traveler's check. The man looked carefully at my passport, then looked up at me, then looked back at the passport, then looked back at me, repeating this process of comparative scrutinization several times until I asked, "Is there something wrong?" "But, madam," he exclaimed, "you look like a foreigner!" "I am a foreigner," I replied. "You're holding an American passport in your hand." "But, madam," he protested, "you have an Indian name!" "It's my father's name. My father is Indian." After some additional minutes of incomprehension over the apparent disjunction of name with appearance, the man finally cashed my check. He just didn't get the most essential thing about a passport from the United States of America: it reveals nothing in and of itself about the ethnic or national origin of the bearer.

Half Indian, half Scandinavian, I am a product of geographical and cultural extremes, of a bifurcated provenance so unlikely, I often feel I could only have come into existence in twentieth-century America. There is perhaps no land more the opposite of Kathiawar than where I was born in the Pacific Northwest. Kathiawar is ancient, the Pacific Northwest is—as least as far as Western Civilization is concerned—brand new. Kathiawar is feudal and tribal, the Pacific Northwest is home to defiant individualists. Kathiawar is dry, baked, brown, flat. The Pacific Northwest is wet, cool, green, rent by the majestic peaks of the snow-clad Cascade range. There are a very few scraggly thorn-protected trees in Kathiawar. Despite the devastations of clear-cutting, the Pacific Northwest is still a land of primeval forests, the home of the world's only temperate rain forest.

Some of Motiba's great-grandchildren are blond. "I wonder what your grandmother thinks of all these White great-grandkids?" an in-law once asked. I don't know. I shall never know, exactly, what she thought of it all. But there are hints: memories, snatches of conversation, offhand remarks small by themselves but betraying wholly unsuspected perspectives. The difficult task is to interpret these, to piece them together, to create sense and narrative out of the necessarily fragmented and unconscious nature of family memory.

Since her death, I have been haunted by memories of my Motiba, and by speculation about the many mysteries of her life. It was only after she was gone that I realized how little I knew about her; how many questions I had that she will never be able to answer. Born in the early 1900s, she died in the 1990s. Her life spanned the twentieth century and, in many ways, traced its main trajectory, a vector that proceeded from the rural to the urban; from the local to the global; from a cohesive identity to a vague cosmopolitanism. The story of my grandmother's life and the lives of her descendants is the story of leaving home, of losing one's tribe. It is the story of diaspora, of the transition from rootedness to rootlessness, of moving until you no longer know who you are and have forgotten who you once were. It is a story that is very much hers—and mine—and yet it is a story that is not ours alone. With infinite variation, this story can be told about millions of people all over the world, people who began in 1900 in a rural village and ended up hard on the year 2000 in one of the planet's metropolises. The generation born at the beginning of the twentieth century comprises the last emissaries of a world that is now almost entirely extinct; a world that will never be the same again.

My grandmother's favorite aphorism was a quote from the Jain saint Rajachandra, Mahatma Gandhi's friend and mentor, and her own father's guru. It goes like this: *Apurva aavo avasar kyare aavashe?* "When will that special occasion come that never came before?" Of course, my grandmother believed in reincarnation, so most of life experienced as the present was, for her, merely another version of an eternally and tiresomely recycled past. The moment, "that never came before" is the moment of freedom from the stubbornly present past. It is the moment of *moksha,* of liberation of the soul from the unending cycles of rebirth and death. For my Indian grandmother, the past is what one spends one's whole life striving permanently to escape by achieving *moksha.* For me, unmoored in the wake of the twentieth century, the past is something I desperately wish that I could catch hold of, but it tends to slip, like the multicolored powders of Motiba's *rangoli*—delicate designs traced in welcome on the threshold that will be erased by the first person who enters—in a steady stream through my fingers.

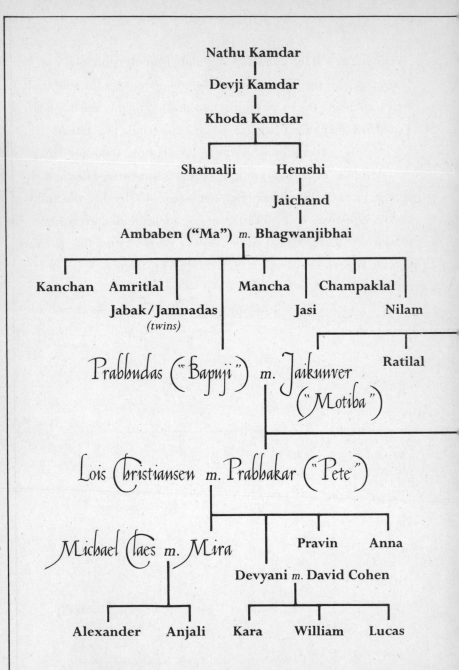

Kamdar–Khara
FAMILY TREE

Nadji Khara
|
Karshanji Khara
|
Jakalben *m.* Bhagwanjibhai Khara

Premchandbhai   Nanchandbhai

Hariben *m.* Muljibhai *m. (2nd)* Samratben

Mangalji   Jaya   Manubhai   Shashikant
                        m.   ("Shashimama")
Anoopchand   Dhiraj   *m.*
                    ("Dhirajmami")   Pravina

Vinayak   Chitra   Usha
("Vinukaka") *m.* Mehta
                    Dilip   Dipti
                ("Dipukaka") *m.* Kothari
Paresh   Viren

Shilpa
Mehta *m.* Ketan   Dhaval   Amit

Priya   Bipin
          Bhayani *m.* Bharati ("Bharatiphaiba")

Prashant   Samit *m.* Rakhee Kapadia

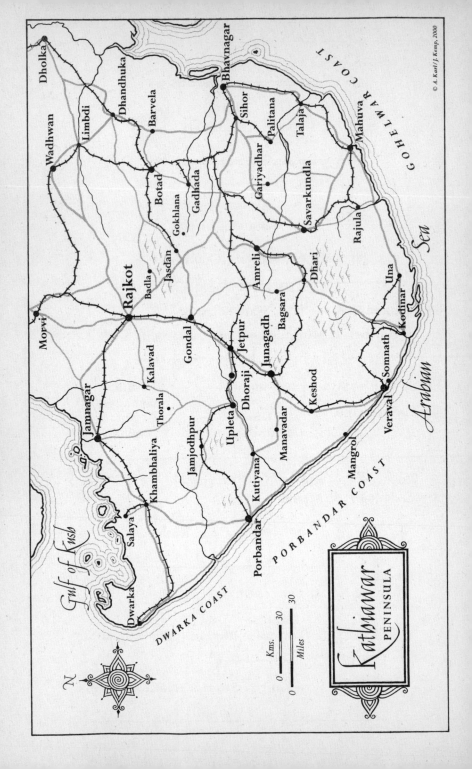

1

Kathiawar

Dad, who are we?
We are Kathis, people who come from someplace else.

My ancestors were keepers of cows and she-buffalos. These animals were regarded more as members of the family than as livestock. Motiba's mother-in-law, like most housewives of her time and place, kept a water buffalo in a room inside the family compound. Ma milked her buffalo every morning and evening, fed her, watered her, and gave her special treats from the kitchen. She doted on her buffalo, and the animal returned her affection in full. The liters and liters of rich buffalo milk that flowed daily from Ma's cow nourished the family both directly and indirectly, for Ma transformed cream from the many liters of milk the family could not consume into clarified butter, *ghee,* and sold it to neighbors whose cows were less generous than hers.

The bond between Ma and her buffalo cow was deep. Indeed, the beast would not allow anyone else to come near it. Yet, a time came when Ma was too feeble to care for her cow. The animal had to be sold. Knowing of the cow's affection for their mother, Ma's sons decided that it would be best if Ma stayed completely out of sight when the new owner came to take the animal away. But when this person, a neighbor in the same town, arrived to claim the hapless beast, the she-buffalo refused to budge. She dug her splayed hooves into the earthen floor of her chamber, stuck her neck out defiantly, and turned her great brown eyes toward the house where

Ma lay resting. One after another, the men of the house emerged to put their muscle into the effort. Soon, five grown men were pulling and heaving with all their might, but the she-buffalo wouldn't budge. With her eyes rolling wildly in their sockets and with snorts and exhalations of breath, the cow held fast.

At last, Ma was sent for. She got herself out of bed with some effort and hobbled over to the stubborn beast. Speaking to the animal in Gujarati, she explained that she'd simply become too old to milk her anymore; that the cow had to go. Her new owners were honest people, personally known to Ma, and they would take good care of her. Then, in front of the cow, Ma performed *aarti* and *puja,* ritual ceremonies usually reserved for deities, or, on certain special occasions, people, to honor and bless the animal. She then applied a *tilak,* a smear of saffron-colored pigment, to the buffalo's forehead. The moment this ceremony was completed, the animal allowed itself to be led away quite peaceably by its new owner. Ma returned to her cot. The she-buffalo did well in her new home.

* * *

My family comes from Kathiawar, a region of India where the ancient Hindu sanctity of cows and milk is respected as perhaps nowhere else. Kathiawar is the home of the Hindu god Krishna, and nothing is dearer to Krishna than cows and all that comes with them. As a child, the mischievous godling was fond of stealing butter and milk and downing them when no one was looking. When he became a young man, Krishna's attention shifted to the cows' companions, winsome milkmaids who fell irresistibly in love with

Ambaben ("Ma") Kamdar and Bhagwanjibhai.

the blue-skinned, flute-playing god who could multiply himself into as many Krishnas as it took to make love to each one of them in the manner that gave her most pleasure. Milk was considered to be such a sacred substance when Motiba was a girl that its sale was prohibited by ancient custom. It is for this reason, as much as those imposed by the hot climate, that every family kept its own cow, consuming the fresh milk every day and turning the cream from any extra milk into *ghee. Ghee* would keep without refrigeration. More important, *ghee* could be sold.

In the house where Motiba was born, a prize milch cow was also kept inside the walled family compound, its pen right next to the room where Motiba spent her first days of life. A small portion of every dish served at every meal to the family was offered to this cow as a token of deep respect and affection. Unlike Ma's household, lucky enough to be blessed by a single productive she-buffalo, Motiba's family was a prosperous one and owned a large number of cows and buffalos. Her father's family had inherited quite a bit of land, and on the land family members raised cows, not for milk or meat, which would have gone against their religious beliefs, but for *ghee*.

Motiba was born in Gokhlana, a small village in Kathiawar. On the western edge of the Indian subcontinent in the modern state of Gujarat, Kathiawar has been overrun by various marauding hordes from time immemorial. The legends and traditions that Motiba absorbed as part of her acculturation into the life of her people were saturated with the hard-won reflexes of surviving in a tough land. Kathiawar has been claimed at various times in its long history by Greeks, Persians, Scythians, Huns, Satraps, Guptas, Vallabhis, and Central Asian Muslims. In addition to outright imperial forays by this impressive list of invaders, the peninsula has been traversed by a dizzying array of nomadic tribes, including Rabaris, Chaoras, Ahers, Mers, Jethvas, Walas, and Kathis. It is after the Kathis that Kathiawar, "land of the Kathis," is named.[1]

The Kathis were a distinctly predacious tribe, famed for the quality and swiftness of their horses and the beauty of their women. Fiercely independent, they lived primarily by raiding the more sedentary, work-loving folk around them, caring little whether these were traders in town or village farmers. The Kathis carried on in this fashion for centuries, leading Colonel Alexander Walker to observe as recently as 1808, when he was the

British agent in Kathiawar, that the Kathis were "distinguished only for rapacious habits and robbery" and further that "to this mode of life they attach neither disgrace nor reproach. On the contrary, they boast of their devastations and rapine."[2] As to where they came from, another British administrator, Colonel J. W. Watson, was of the view that "the cradle of their race is unknown." Watson, the foremost nineteenth-century British historian of Kathiawar and the founder of a museum in the Kathiawari city of Rajkot that bears his name, was of the opinion that the Kathis were descended from a "Khatti" people he cites as mentioned in ancient Assyrian inscriptions. Watson further speculates that these "Khattis" were the Hittites of the Old Testament,[3] a conclusion that seems utterly fantastic.

Whether of Kathi origin or not, on both my grandmother's and grandfather's sides of the family, our history is deeply tied to that of the Kathis, and that history is fundamentally a history of people and cows. The Kathis were cattle rustlers first, then herdsmen, and only after the ownership of cows had required them to settle down, rulers. They were, in short, domesticated by their cattle. My ancestors worked for countless generations as administrators and landlords for the local Kathi princes. Though there are no surviving historical records, it is probable that the land Motiba's family owned had been received by one of her ancestors as a gift for service rendered to one of the local Kathi rulers.

When asked where they are from, members of my family now comfortably settled in London or Chicago are far more likely to reply, with considerable pride, that they are Kathiawari than that they are from India. India is an abstract political entity; modern, secular, a mere ideal. Kathiawar is home.

* * *

Kathiawar is the axe-head—shaped near-peninsula that juts into the Arabian Sea on the western side of the Indian subcontinent. For several thousand years, its extensive coastline, many ports, and strategic location made it the first stop, after the steppes of Central Asia and the deserts of Sindh, on the way to all the riches of India. More anciently known as Saurashtra, Kathiawar was for much of its history an important nexus for trade and an inevitable prize for invaders of all stripes. In his early nineteenth-century *History of Gujarat,* C. F. Bayley has this to say about Kathiawar:

> The peninsula of Kathiawar, known to the ancient Hindus as Saurashtra and to the Muhammadans as Sorath, had been the object of Muslim desire ever since the first establishment of their power in Gujarat during the reign of Ala-ud-din Khalji of Delhi. The glowing eulogy of this province, recorded by Sikander, will, perhaps, furnish the secret of this desire: "And what a country is Sorath! As if the hand of heaven had selected the cream and essence of Malwa, Khandesh, and Gujarat, and had made a compendium of all the good people of the world, and had picked out the noblest and most vigorous men from the three countries named, and collected them together unto one standard, as a touchstone of the countries of the world."[4]

Fragments of cloth woven in Saurashtra over 3,000 years ago have been found in the tombs of the ancient Egyptians. According to Bayley, the Greeks knew Saurashtra as *Saurastrene,* "the good land," and their chroniclers describe many specific ports and cities in Saurashtra where trading opportunities were to be had. Alexander the Great invaded Saurashtra in 327 B.C. and established a Greco-Bactrian empire in nearby Punjab before returning to Greece. The Greeks knew the Indian emperor Chandragupta Maurya, who reigned over Saurashtra from 322 to 297 B.C., calling him *Sandrocotus.* In Junagadh, a city about 100 kilometers southwest of Gokhlana, there lies a great stone inscribed in the second century B.C. with edicts dictated by the emperor Ashoka, India's peace-loving king. Four centuries later, Ashoka's reign in Kathiawar had been replaced by that of the Satrap, or *kshatrapa,* kings, invaders from pre-Islamic Persia.

There is evidence that these Persian kings may have been Motiba's remote ancestors. Only nine kilometers from Gokhlana, near Jasdan, the *kshatrapa* kings left behind a stone inscription proclaiming in ancient Prakrit that it dates from the year 127 Bhadrapada (175 A.D.). Known as the "Jasdan stone," the carved inscription details the genealogy of the *kshatrapa* royal line. The last king named is "Khara," my grandmother's family's unusual name.[5] Thirty kilometers from Gokhlana on the other side of Jasdan, a nineteenth-century monument commemorates the spot where the local king's *diwan,* or chief administrator, died defending the nearby village of Bhadla from attack. Actually, there are two identical monuments, one where the man's body fell and one nearby where his severed

head fell. On the side of one of the monuments, there is a marble
plaque inscribed with the declaration, "Here lies the Khara *surdindada*." A *surdindada* is a family member whose life has been cut
short before its time. The Khara *surdindada* was one of Motiba's
brave ancestors, a faithful retainer who died at his prince's side.
Even now, when not a single Khara remains in residence in
Gokhlana, the inhabitants of the village are quite aware of the connection between these roadside memorials thirty kilometers distant from where they live and the Khara family that once lived in
Gokhlana. There are even a few family-minded Kharas who make
regular trips from Bombay to Kathiawar to pay their respects to this
long-deceased ancestor.

A single antique inscription and a monument by the side of a
one-lane road are flimsy evidence upon which to base an ancestral
claim, but India is an ancient land. It is at least plausible that my
grandmother's family was settled in and around Gokhlana for as
long as 1,800 years. In any case, it is safe to say that they lived there
for many generations, until the forces of the twentieth century
propelled them within a few short decades over oceans and continents to every corner of the earth.

* * *

My Motiba, Jayakunver Khara, whose name means "Victorious
Princess" and who may have been descended of kings, was born in
a mud-walled eight-by-twelve-foot room directly under a bare,
red-tiled roof held aloft by the twisting limbs of the unmilled tree
limbs used for the rafters. The walls and floor of the room were

smoothly plastered with an ochre-colored paste of dung, a constant supply of which was provided by the cow tethered just outside the door. The room opened, as did the rooms on either side, onto an open gallery that ran the full length of the house and above which the roof overhung, protecting the interior of the house both from the searing heat that can reach 120 degrees or more in the hot season and the torrential rains of monsoon. At one end of the gallery was a built-in tiled counter on which clay jars of drinking water were kept along with a supply of copper tumblers. The capillary action of the clay causes the water-filled jars to sweat, thereby effectively cooling the temperature of the water inside while the clay imparts a fresh, earthy taste that makes the water extremely refreshing. A ready supply of fresh, cool water is no trivial thing in hot, dusty Kathiawar.

The house was one of a cluster of similarly constructed homes in which each of the five brothers of Motiba's grandfather's generation lived with his respective household. The family was organized along typically Indian "joint family" lines, with brothers living and working together in a single corporate economic unit. Bhagwanjibhai, the second of the five Khara brothers, had three sons, Nanchandbhai, Muljibhai, and Premchandbhai. (The suffix *bhai* means "brother" and is used as an honorific. Any Indian would feel that the name of a peer or a superior was oddly naked if not outright disrespectful without *bhai* attached to it for a male or *ben,* "sister," for a female.)

Motiba was the first of five children born to Muljibhai and his wife Hariben. The others were three boys, Ratilal, Mungalji, and

*Bhagwanjibhai and Jakalben Khara, Motiba's paternal grandparents,
in hand-painted 1920 studio portraits.*

Anoopchand, and a sister, Jaya. At the time of Motiba's birth, her
father was still living under his own father's roof. Upon marriage,
he and his brothers had each been granted a private room in the
paternal house. Years later, even after the brothers had left the village and built grand primary and secondary residences for themselves and their respective families, they would live in close
proximity to one another, and pool their financial resources in common business enterprises for the rest of their lives.

When Motiba was born in 1908, life in Gokhlana and its immediate environs was still innocent of even the most basic innova-

tions of the nineteenth century. The British had labored furiously during the half century prior to Motiba's birth to bring the steam engine, the railroad, and the telegraph—those artifacts of modernity that most transformed life in the nineteenth century—into the region. They had done this for their own imperial purposes, of course, mainly with a view to getting as much cotton out of Kathiawar and down to the docks of Bombay as possible. In 1908, as today, the railroad reached as near to Gokhlana as the town of Amreli, some forty-five kilometers to the southwest, but Gokhlana itself remained accessible only by oxcart, camel cart, horseback, or foot. The journey in and out of the village had to be made on dirt paths of hard-packed, rutted earth, scored and gouged with the traces of the last passages made on them when the rains of the previous monsoon had dried up. These were covered by a layer of superfine dust during the dry season and became impassable mires of mud during the three-month monsoon of June, July, and August.

* * *

A few years before her death, Motiba began to talk about Gokhlana. She had not been back to the village since she'd left as a five-year-old and felt a sudden need to connect with the place where she was born. She just wanted to see the village one last time. By the time one of her daughters was able to take her, she was too sick to make the trip. After Motiba's death, I resolved that I would go to Gokhlana in her stead. I conscripted my father and Dhirajben Khara to go with me. We have always called Dhirajben "Dhiraj-

mami." The suffix "mami" means "mother's brother's wife." Dhirajmami is Motiba's brother Manubhai's widow. She grew up in
Amreli, just a few miles from Gokhlana. I would be traveling into
the heart of peasant Kathiawar, and I needed native guides.

We hired a driver and a car, one of India's ubiquitous and
frozen-in-time white 1940s-era Ambassador sedans, and set off
from Rajkot one early winter morning. The sky was low and gray,
and had a metallic quality that, unusually for that time of year,
threatened rain. It was cool enough for me to want a sweater, yet
the coolness contained the certitude of a warm afternoon. None of
us had ever been to Gokhlana. In fact, no member of the Khara
family had been there in over eight decades. It seemed a mythic
place. We'd heard about it our whole lives, but did it really exist?

My father sat up front next to the driver who, a typical small-
town youth, found quite amusing his city-folk passengers' wish to
pay money to be taken to some tiny village lost in the countryside.
Dhirajmami and I sat in the back. I've always been tremendously
fond of Dhirajmami. She has a regal, elegant bearing that is softened by smiling eyes and great personal warmth and charisma. She
manages to be both dignified and sweetly adorable at the same
time. I was happy to have her along because my father's excitement
about the prospect of going to Gokhlana was surpassed only by his
anxiety about what his American-born daughter might see there.

Dhirajmami had brought along goodies for the trip: jugs of cold
boiled water; tins of wafer-thin crisp rounds of wheat *khakhara;*
bunches of tiny bananas; and boxes of *chickee,* a Rajkot specialty
resembling peanut brittle. Her homemade *chickee* was made from

sesame seeds and pure *gol,* raw sugar. She plied my father and me with these treats at regular intervals, and out of anticipation more than hunger, we snacked our way down the highway. We were all surprised when after only an hour or so, we'd reached the ancient Kathi town of Jasdan. From here, we had to ask directions. Gokhlana was too small to appear on any published map, and our driver had never heard of it. It seemed that most of the residents of Jasdan had never heard of it either, for the first few people we asked sent us in wrong directions. Finally, we found someone who knew the road. The excitement was palpable as we began our way down the final stretch. None of us spoke. We were too absorbed in taking in every detail of the landscape outside the windows of the old Ambassador as it lurched its way through the outskirts of the last, gradually thinning Jasdan slum. Feral pigs scurried out of our way, their filth-stained bellies nearly dragging on the ground. A couple of mangy pariah-dogs barked at the passing car in a desultory sort of way before returning to matters of local dog social life. Then we were beyond the town, smoothly rolling forward through a vast countryside that stretched out dustily to a faraway horizon under the glowering sky.

Curiously, the road from Jasdan to Gokhlana had just been paved with a fresh ribbon of pitch-black asphalt exactly one lane wide with no shoulder. I have never seen, in all my travels across the length and breadth of India, such a perfectly smooth, virginally black expanse of road. For hours, we had been bounced unmercifully within inches of the ceiling and against the sharp outcrops of the door handles and window knobs as the creaky old Ambassador jolted its way, apparently strutless and shockless, over the potholes of the highway

and along the rutted track through the slum. Our suddenly smooth
ride on this wonder of a new road lent an unreal quality to the final
approach to the ancestral village. As there were no other cars, our
driver nosed the Ambassador right down the center of the pavement. It seemed as if the road had been specially unfurled upon the
never-ending dust of Kathiawar to welcome us to Gokhlana.

When we were just a few kilometers from the village, we had to
stop to allow a flock of sheep that was being herded down the middle of the road be guided off the pavement. To conserve fuel, the
driver killed the Ambassador's rumbling engine. Suddenly, we were
immersed in deep quiet, an odd sensation in India where the constant din of the street—competing Hindi film songs, the nasal cries
of itinerant vendors, the warning bells of three-wheeled rickshaws
weaving their way through a sea of pedestrians—is the norm. The
only sounds here were those of the light, quick clippity-clop of the
sheep's hooves on the pavement and the tinkling of the bells at their
necks. The shepherds were wiry, sun-creased men of an indetermi-
nate age in absolutely traditional Kathiawari peasant dress. They had
huge turbans wrapped around their heads. Quarter-sized gold ear
studs wobbled at the tops of their ears and thick gold loops dangled
from their earlobes. They wore tight-chested frock coats of white
muslin with a gathered skirting extending from just under the
armpits to their waists. Their jodhpurs were also of white muslin,
billowing loosely from waist to knee and then skin tight around the
calves. On their feet they wore great clogs of leather and wood.
They had quite an air of "don't tread on me" as they walked resolutely past the car, remaining perfectly poker-faced before the

unlikely sight of alien people in the neighborhood traveling in, of all means of conveyance, a private car. Centuries of surviving foreign invaders had bred extreme wariness around strangers into these men. We greeted them. They returned the greeting tersely without changing their expression or moving their heads.

* * *

My father spied a bush of *chaniya bor,* or "chickpea berries," and called for Dhirajmami and me to get out of the car to taste some. He was quite excited to see these small beanlike berries, as they

Stopping to let sheep pass on the road to Gokhlana.

recalled days of youth roaming the Kathiawari countryside. *Chaniya bor* is a desert plant that grows wild in the region. It is a favorite free snack for shepherds, playing children, or very poor hungry people.

A hard stone the size of a pea is surrounded by a thin layer of tart, yellow-green fruit. There is very little flesh around the pit, and you have to sort of work the little berry off the hard center with your teeth and then spit the pit out. Though your mouth tends to pucker up with the tartness, you also quickly hanker for another.

We stood by the side of the road eating *chaniya bor,* waiting for the sheep to pass. To the west were round, old hills, scarred by gullies ricocheting down their bare brown slopes to join little streams crisscrossing the gently sloping plain. Despite a low, gray sky pregnant with rain, there was a desert feeling of vastness. The visual sweep of the landscape was uninterrupted by much in the way of trees. Almost every inch of the plain was cultivated, and we could make out square after square of furrowed field, each one surrounded by a wall of gnarled cactus, the huge thorns an effective barrier against hungry livestock. Most of the fields were full of cotton, and the cotton was ripe, so that the dull green of the fields looked a bit like a fabric of dotted Swiss. The country appeared empty at first, but slowly it became clear that it was full of people bent over the plants, quietly collecting the fat, white bolls of cotton. Dust suspended permanently in the dry air softened the edges of things, lending a dreamlike quality to a view in which actions seemed to take place in slow motion. The air smelled of the earth, warm and musky, and of the moisture-laden clouds. This was where Motiba came from. Each of her early childhood days had this landscape as a backdrop, these smells, these soft sounds.

After the sheep passed, we got back into the car and drove into Gokhlana. The village appeared suddenly out of the surrounding fields. If we hadn't known it was there and if the road didn't lead right into it, we might have missed it, so perfectly did it blend into the landscape. At the edge of the village, the pavement stopped, and we threaded our way slowly over a pitted dirt path that wound around mud-plastered houses and between sump holes filled with waste to a small sort of dirt plaza in front of the village temple. The village elders were sitting around the base of an old mango tree, all dressed alike in the manner of the shepherds we'd passed, all sporting great white handlebar mustaches. Everyone assembled in the village square stared at us, remaining perfectly motionless and expressionless as we got out of the car. My father approached the venerable group under the tree. No one moved. Not a single man got up to greet him. Then my father, in perfect Kathiawari dialect, said simply, "This is our village. Our family is Khara and we used to live here. Can you show us our old house?"

The old men broke out into broad smiles; clapped my father on the back; and began, all at the same time, to chatter excitedly. Responding to some mysterious telepathy, people began pouring into the square: there were men, mostly old, the able-bodied ones being out in the fields or with the livestock, and barefoot children. The women kept inside their houses, certainly dying of curiosity but too modest to emerge from the safety of their domestic enclosures. In a nearby lane, a man and a woman were working together, laying sheaves of sorghum out to dry on the roof of their home. The man, wearing a brilliant hot-pink shirt, smiled broadly, puffed out his chest, twirled his great black mustache, and asked us to take his picture as he heaved stalks of grain up onto the roof for the woman to catch and lay out in neat rows. The woman pulled her _sari paalav_ down all the way in front of her face so that we couldn't see her anymore and turned her back to us, her shoulders shaking with laughter.

An ad hoc committee of the elders formed to show us around Gokhlana. Three tiny dirt lanes radiated out from the village square. There was the one we had come in on, a lane that was more or less a continuation of that one in the opposite direction, and a third one that went off at roughly a ninety-degree angle to the junction of the first two. From these three lanes, no more than six feet wide, even tinier paths branched off to private homes and courtyards. The lanes were lined with indecipherable walls, inset at regular intervals with elaborately sculpted wooden doors with heavy round iron pulls and dead bolts.

To the visitor, Gokhlana presents a coy face. The high, plastered mud walls are of the same color as the dirt of the lanes and the surrounding land. The village is a mazelike warren of narrow alleys, each one bisected by open drains that are mere furrows in the dirt guiding wastewater away from the houses. Above each door along any of the walls is painted a likeness of the god Ganesh, whose presence for Hindus is auspicious at entries and beginnings. These doors open onto private, walled courtyards around which, or to one side of which, are built the houses. Nearly every courtyard is shaded by carefully watered and tended fruit trees—mango, papaya, _chikoo,_ lime—the produce of which supplies the family with fresh fruit in season and the makings of fiery pickles that can be eaten year-round. Sometimes there are flowering plants, such as hibiscus or

bougainvillea. This explosion of greenery and color cannot be suspected from outside the high, dull walls. To step through one of
these doors and into the garden is to pass from a desert world of
unrelenting brown dust into a world of water and color. It is not
unlike that startling moment in *The Wizard of Oz* when the black and
white of Kansas gives way to the technicolor of Oz.

"Here was the elder Khara's house. And here, across from it,
was Bhagwanjibhai Khara's house," indicated one of our self-
appointed guides, pointing to the door of my great-great-grand-
father's compound. We stepped over the threshold, bending
down to pass through a low carved wooden door. On the other
side was a narrow open courtyard. An open verandah ran along
one side of it, overhanging the series of small, unconnected
rooms that made up the house. The family that now lives there,
local Brahmins, is descended from the one that received the
house as a gift from Motiba's father, Muljibhai Khara, my great-
grandfather. The eldest member of this Brahmin family remembered when the Kharas lived here. He remembered Motiba when
she was a little girl, and he showed us the room where she was
born. With the exception of a couple of bare light bulbs and the
framed posters of Krishna and Hanuman that had replaced the
images of Jain *tirthankaras,* "realized souls," nothing about the
house had changed since the days when Motiba lived there as a little girl. The family invited us in, calling "*Aavo. Aavo.*" They insisted
we sit down. "*Beso. Beso.*" And so we sat on the springy, cow-
dung–plastered floor and took in the feel of the room where
Motiba first entered this world.

There was a new baby in the family, just four months old. A traditional wooden cradle painted in bright yellow, blue, and red sat in a
corner of the room. As a baby, Motiba was certainly rocked to sleep
in a similar cradle. The current baby's mother sat down near me,

On the porch in front of the room where Motiba was born.

cross-legged on the floor, artfully inserted the baby behind her *sari*
without revealing a thing of her person, and proceeded to nurse it.
Everyone smiled. At the back of the room, embroidered quilts were
stacked high upon a great wheeled dowry chest known as a *patara*. A
small picture of young Krishna playing his flute hung next to the
quilts. Otherwise, the room was bare. Outside, fat drops of rain
began to fall upon the floury dust, making pockmarks in the dirt so

that soon the courtyard took on the appearance of a soft, brown
lunar landscape. The air filled with the peculiar odor of dust in the
rain. We sat there together for a while, my father's emotion betrayed
by his nervously working jaw. Dhirajmami smiled at everyone,
charming them with her sophisticated yet approachable air. The rain
stopped. Not five minutes into the shower they'd been promising all
morning, the clouds broke up. Suddenly, it was very hot.

* * *

The world Motiba entered in Gokhlana in 1908 was a premodern
world, where the texture of life had changed little in centuries.
Fields were still cultivated—as some are even today by the poorest farmers—with wooden plows, drawn by teams of oxen guided
along the furrows by a single, turbanned, bare-legged farmer.
Almost all of the family's food was produced locally. Naturally, the
family could provide for all its dairy needs. They used the money
they earned selling *ghee* to buy grains, dried beans and lentils, rice,
sugar, salt, and spices. Everything was purchased in its most basic
"unprocessed" form. This meant unrelenting work for the women
of the family, who were in charge of food preparation. With no
refrigeration and a hot climate, fresh milk had to be consumed
immediately. By boiling it at regular intervals throughout the day,
one could forestall the souring process long enough to keep the
milk from turning for a few hours, but eventually it would sour. So,
most of the milk was churned into buttermilk and butter; cooked
down into creamy sweets; or turned into yogurt, the shelf life of
which was also no more than twenty-four hours.

Wheat was ground into flour with a hand-held stone pestle in a
mortar set right into the floor, and only enough was ground at any
one time to produce the flour needed for the meal being prepared.
Some form of unleavened wheat bread was served with every meal,
so batches of wheat kernels had to be ground several times a day. For
breakfast, there might be *thepla,* oily and very thin cakes seasoned
with turmeric and fresh, slightly bitter *methi* leaves, or *bhakhari rotis,*
thick, wheaty cakes tender on the inside with a crisp, golden surface
slathered in fresh butter. For lunch and dinner, there were always
chapatis, tender, pliant rounds ripped piece by piece into edible
spoons to scoop up the curries and sauces. Festive occasions called
for *puris,* perfectly puffed hollows of wheat deep-fried several at a
time and served in great piles, still piping hot. Many dishes were
made from batters of fermented rice or *dal* or a combination of
both. These preparations required planning a day or two ahead, so
that the grains could attain the proper consistency through fermen-
tation, producing a frothy, light batter that was then poured into
molds and steamed to form square cakes of *dhokla* or doughnut-
holed *wada.* Many dishes and snack foods were made from *chana,* or
chickpea flour. This also had to be ground, then made into doughs
or batters, then baked on the open hearth or fried in oil. Fruits and
vegetables were harvested from the family garden plot every day or
purchased from the local farmers or from itinerant vendors. Every
morning the women had to consider the day's menu and decide just
what would be needed. Without refrigeration, nothing would keep
longer than twelve hours or so. Any uneaten cooked food was fed to
servants or given to animals. There was no such thing as leftovers.

The men ate first, served by the women, who each kept her head and face carefully covered by the *paalav* of her *sari* as a sign of modesty and respect. This practice of covering the head and face, known as *laaj,* is now almost entirely extinct in my family, but it was very much alive when Motiba was young. The women worked as a team, one in the kitchen rolling balls of dough into flat rounds; one grilling or frying as required; and one serving the men piping hot fresh breads, one at a time, as they came off the fire. Then the children were fed. The women ate last, in the kitchen. All eating was done sitting cross-legged on the floor with the diner leaning over a large rimmed metal plate called a *thali.* Small mounds of drier vegetable mixtures would be placed directly on the *thali,* whereas soups and curries with a lot of sauce were served in small bowls called *kachori.* The meal inevitably ended with rice and *dal* or *kadhi,* a yogurt-based soup. Yogurt *(dahi)* or buttermilk *(chaas)* was served with every meal. All meals were strictly vegetarian. The only animal product consumed was milk.

The Kharas were vegetarians because they were Jains, not Hindus like the rest of the families in Gokhlana (who may or may not have been vegetarians). Jains believe that all life is precious, that all living things suffer, and that the taking of any life is a horrible sin. The central doctrine of Jainism is *ahimsa,* "nonviolence." Jains trace the origins of their religion back to the Indus Valley civilization of over 3,000 years ago. The name of the religion derives from the word *jina,* meaning "conqueror." Jains are conquerors of the weaknesses of the flesh, victors over the phenomenal world of *samsara.* They do not believe in gods such as those in the Hindu pantheon but worship the example of twenty-four *tirthankaras*—which literally means "forders"—exemplary individuals who have made it beyond *samsara* to achieve *moksha,* or liberation from the relentless cycle of existence and all its attendant sufferings. The basic way to attain *moksha,* Jains believe, is to abjure from doing any violence to any living thing, to respect the life force, or *jiva,* present in everything in the world. Fasting and remaining motionless in meditation are two typical means to this end. Many Jain folktales from Kathiawar feature sainted individuals who fasted themselves to death. My father, who loves to debate the finer aspects of Jain theology, is fond of initiating such discussions with the statement, "My basic problem is that I eat." To eat is necessarily to consume some form of *jiva,* the animating life force of existence.

The Jain ethos of self-denial is nowhere in India more palpable than in Gujarat, a "dry" state where vegetarian cuisine is the norm. Jain doctrine has influenced the policies of some of India's most famous non-Jain rulers, such as the Hindu king Ashoka and the Mughal ruler Akbar, notably convincing them to pass edicts forbidding animal slaughter and to exempt Jain pilgrims from paying tolls when traveling to sacred sites. Because their religious beliefs prohibit them from practicing agriculture—imagine the many insect and plant lives one might accidentally take tilling the soil— Jains have traditionally been merchants, bankers, moneylenders, jewelers, diamond dealers, and administrators. Though technically outside Hinduism, and therefore outside the caste system, most Jains in Kathiawar have been assimilated into the *bania,* or merchant, caste. Their influence with the ruling class has historically resulted as much from their wealth as from the legitimate attractions of their doctrine. But it was Jain doctrine alone, particularly the philosophy of nonviolence, that was to have the profoundest influence on Kathiawar's most famous native son and political leader, Mohandas Karamchand Gandhi, India's Mahatma. And Gandhi, in turn, had a profound influence on my Jain family.

When did the Kharas become Jains? No one can say. But the community of Kathiawari Jains was, and still is, a close-knit one. It is a community that takes care of its own, and within which *khaandaan* and *amiraat,* nobility of birth and character, count—or at least used to count—even more than money. Motiba was born into a community that is extremely conscious of its difference from mainstream Hinduism. She was nourished as much on stories of the lives of the *tirthankaras* as on a strictly vegetarian cuisine. The rituals she learned, the prayers she uttered, the temples she visited were almost all distinctly Jain. After her father became a rich man, he spent substantial sums of money supporting Jain philanthropies, such as boarding houses for young religious students. Muljibhai Khara was also close to the Jain sage Rajachandra, the young Gandhi's guru. A picture of the extremely thin (from all that fasting) Rajachandra seated cross-legged in deep meditation always hung in the Khara house. In early childhood, Motiba absorbed a veneration for the teachings of Rajachandra that would last her entire life.

* * *

Motiba's early years in Gokhlana were typical of any little girl's in those days in rural Kathiawar. Childhood was, and in many cases still is, the freest time in an Indian woman's life. She does not yet require the strict shelter and control demanded of nubile women. In Hindu and Jain society of Motiba's era, girls were not considered to be real members of the family. They were merely "on loan" from God until such time as they could be delivered whole and pure into the "real" family of their future husband. I once heard someone refer to this as "growing flowers for someone else's garden."

The prevailing wisdom was that it was best to take no chances with the virtue of sexually mature girls. For girls of Motiba's class and generation, the carefree phase of life came to a sudden and crushing halt at puberty. The rule in the Khara family, according to one of Motiba's surviving cousins, was that no female member of the family should be seen outside the house after the age of twelve. At age twelve, the girls were made to drop out of school and come inside the house for good. They entered into *purda*—the word simply means "curtain"—a state of absolute invisibility to anyone outside the immediate family circle. If they needed anything, it was delivered to the house. Jewelers came to the house. Fabric merchants came to the house. Tailors came to the house. All manner of vendors came to the house. The practice of *purda* was widespread in the Muslim community, but it was also something the Kharas, and other prosperous Jain and Hindu families, adopted from the ruling Rajputs, feudal princes who were fanatical about the purity of their women. Keeping the women locked up was a powerful statement of superior social class. Only women of inferior social class were free to move about in the world.

None of the women in my family was happy about being yanked out of school and locked up in the house at the age of twelve. For Motiba, this heartbreaking moment came even earlier, at the age of nine, following the premature death of her mother. She often told me and other of her grandchildren how much she lamented giving up her studies in the fourth grade; how, though she was intelligent, she couldn't become educated; and how important it was for us to achieve that which was forbidden to her. She never got over this trauma. Neither did her sister-in-law. Motiba's future husband was bright enough to win a full scholarship for his studies at the new English-medium school established in the Kathiawari town of Jetpur by the local Kathi ruler. His younger sister, Jasi, my Jasiphaiba, or Aunt Jasi, was also extremely bright, the only other child in the family to win a full scholarship, in her case to attend the first school for girls opened in Jetpur. But at age twelve, she too was made to quit school. She was eighty-three years old when she told me this, and as she spoke, her voice rose and trembled with emotion. "I was just as smart as he was!" she cried. Jasiphaiba's revenge was to make sure that her own daughter got as full an education as possible, eventually completing a doctoral degree in social work.

Motiba made the most of her little-girl freedoms while she could. She romped in the fields of wheat, sorghum, pulses, and cotton that surrounded the clustered earthen houses of Gokhlana. She went barefoot most of the time, tripping across the fields and over irrigation ditches. One of her favorite treats was fresh-cut stalks of sugar cane, which she chewed thoroughly to extract every last drop of sweet juice. As a little girl, she was allowed to fly kites and play catch and marbles. With the other little girls in the village, she played at cooking with a miniature set of cookware made of unfired terra-cotta. They also sang songs, particularly wedding songs, accompanying themselves with silver bells, beating out the time with *dandia* sticks. "You are all so sweet, it just makes me feel like singing," began one popular song of the day.

What Motiba remembered the most about her early years in Gokhlana were the plays, known as *bhavais,* given by itinerant performers who earned their living traveling from village to village. There were reenactments of stories from the great Hindu epic tales of the *Ramayana* and the *Mahabharata,* and from the folk tales of Kathiawar and neighboring Rajasthan. Every village had its own versions of regional folk plays, and these were performed on holidays. As acting by women was considered to be barely one step away from prostitution, all the female roles in these plays were performed by men. When Motiba was a little girl, the most famous of these actors was Jai Shankar Sundari, *sundari* meaning "beautiful woman." Jai Shankar Sundari, based in the big city of Ahmedabad, set the fashion of the day for women in small towns and villages throughout Gujarat, and the women in Gokhlana kept up with these trends as best they could.

One of Motiba's strongest memories of her days in Gokhlana was of a visit to the village by a troupe of itinerant tight-rope walkers. Motiba was only three or, at most, five years old. The performers strung a rope between the poles and made their way, step by teetering step, over the heads of the enthralled villagers. Motiba was as awestruck as any of the local spectators. She truly belonged to an age now extinct, the pretelevision age, when all performance was live. Life in Gokhlana today has changed little from what it was when Motiba lived there, with one portentous exception: on the roof of the house next to the one in which Motiba was born is a new television satellite receiver dish. It has been put to practical use by the lady of the house, who has neatly laid hand-printed patties of cow dung out to dry around its base.

When my father, Dhirajmami, and I visited Gokhlana, we were invited by the village elders to have tea in the best room in the village: the room directly under the roof of the dung-adorned satellite dish, where the only television set in town sat protectively shrouded by an embroidered coverlet. Every available male in Gokhlana pressed into that room, squatting on his haunches and staring at us as we sipped scalding hot fresh tea—very strong, very milky, and very sweet—out of a hodgepodge collection of old chipped saucers. With considerable pride, the village elders took pains to make sure we noticed, acknowledged, and praised the presence of the television set in their midst; ultimate proof of Gokhlana's progress since our ancestors lived in the village a century before.

* * *

But it was not in Gokhlana that I got the strongest sense of the world of my grandmother's girlhood. This happened during a trip she and I made together, just the two of us, to visit the *kuldevi,* or clan goddess temple, of the Kamdars, Motiba's in-laws. Thinking back on that trip, I realize that Motiba was initiating me, her granddaughter, into the world of the family's women, which is also the world of the ahistorical past, the past that exists as ritual, belief, and symbol; the past that flows in the blood, that is expressed in ways we are barely conscious of, more feeling it than knowing what it is; the past that keeps a distinct people together as a tribe through the predations of flight, war, famine, or even prosperity. Motiba's own family, the Kharas, were rather strict in their adherence to the Jain teachings of Rajachandra and his acolytes. They had little patience with non-Jain beliefs, including the worship of ancient clan goddesses. Motiba's in-laws, the Kamdars, were different, and my grandfather in particular maintained a strong attachment to the family's clan goddess. Yet, it was clear that Motiba was quite happy to take me to visit the Kamdar *kuldevi* temple. My grandfather, Prabhudas Kamdar, had recently passed away. Perhaps Motiba thought the time was right to introduce me to the land of my forefathers.

Motiba and I flew together from Bombay to Rajkot, the de facto capital of Kathiawar. Rajkot felt clean, spacious, and blessedly dry after the oppressive stink of Bombay. We stayed at the home of Lilaben Desai, the widow of one of my grandfather's dearest childhood friends. Though there is no blood relation between the two families, we have always referred to Mrs. Desai as "Kaki," or "Auntie," more specifically, "father's brother's wife," and she has always treated us like daughters and granddaughters. In India, it is typical for close friendships to be understood as family relationships, with all the affection and responsibility that such relationships imply. Kaki's house is a traditional Kathiawari home built around an interior courtyard behind a walled garden riotous with the fuchsia tones of bougainvillea in permanent bloom. In the open well on one side of the courtyard lives a turtle to whom scraps of *chapati* are fed every day. Visiting children inevitably find the turtle the most fascinating feature of the house, and spend long minutes squatting near the well waiting for the creature to surface and seize a piece of bread in its jaws. Heavy wooden doors with sculpted motifs and iron pulls open out onto the inner and outer courtyards and divide the rooms. The floors are of huge slabs of dark gray slate, polished smooth by the patter of innumerable bare feet over many years. Motiba and I slept on communal beds in the "women and children's room" under vast mosquito nets and thick quilted *rajaais*. It was winter, and the temperature fell into the forties at night. Motiba, used to the even, damp heat of Bombay, shivered with cold. She wore her white cotton *sari* and the new mohair sweater I'd brought her from America to bed, changing into a fresh *sari* in the morning after a hot bath.

Kaki's son Arunbhai drove us to the *kuldevi* temple, some ninety kilometers west of Rajkot. We started off on a paved road, a state highway, actually, of two theoretical lanes, where we had constantly to dodge camels and oxcarts, stray dogs and cows, and herds of goats. The unrelentingly parched land was punctuated by scrubby trees along the sides of the road, clumped in the villages we passed and beside farmhouses. There were acacias, palms, *gul mohurs,* and the occasional banyan tree. The paved road and our car were the only traces of industrial or postindustrial life on the countryside. Proud, stiff-backed farmers dressed like those in Gokhlana—calf-hugging pants and pleated smocks of unbleached muslin, their heads wrapped in turbans of brilliant pink, yellow, or red—strode across the fields or guided hump-backed oxen pulling hand-hewn wooden plows through the furrows. Groups of women resplendent in elaborately mirrored and embroidered skirts and red tie-dyed half-*saris* walked resolutely along the road with impossibly large loads of sticks, water jugs, or sacks of harvested grain on their heads, their faces entirely veiled by their *saris* in full *laaj*. Every once in a while, we'd pass one of the remaining nomadic tribes camped in a hollow, the women and dusty-haired children occupied around their minuscule tents, the men out on the range with their flocks. Now and again, this scenery was punctuated by a bright square of corn or wheat, and we could hear the jerk-jerk-jerking sound of a diesel-powered pump filling the field with water from the underground currents of a nearby streambed. An entire flock of Sarus cranes, each one standing at least four feet tall, suddenly rose into the air out of a field of yellow mustard, tucking their long legs beneath them and flying slowly away on great, gray wings.

After about two hours, we turned off the main road onto a gravel lane. We were now very close to Thorala, the village where the Kamdar *kuldevi* temple resides. The landscape had a peaceful, permanent quality. It had probably looked just like this for centuries. Every once in a while, groups of wild peacocks and hens darted among the bushes. Families of quail scurried across the road in front of the slow-moving car, the babies keeping right up with their mother in a neat, undulating line. We passed shepherds, mostly young boys, with their herds of goats, sheep, and cattle doing the kinds of things shepherds spend most of their time doing: sitting under the shade of a bush tracing designs in the dust with a stick; roaming about with their staves, lashing out every now and then at a branch or a rock, perhaps a lizard. Naturally, the car got their attention. They stood and stared as we passed, registering a visit to the village by one of those rich people attached to the temple.

Another dusty and bone-rattling quarter of an hour brought us to the end of the road. We had to leave the car, and proceeded on foot down a narrow path. A stream trickled around the curve of a broad, flat riverbed, clearly showing how forcefully the monsoon floods had rent the now-dry banks. Unlike India's urban rivers, thick with raw sewage and toxic waste, this water was absolutely transparent. Downstream, two little girls were busy beating articles of wet clothing clean upon a rock. White storks and red-breasted herons fished patiently in the shallows. Motiba and I waded into the river to cross. Then, she did something I have never forgotten, not only for what it was but for the utter naturalness with which she did it: in the midst of the stream, Motiba drew up her *sari,* and in one smooth movement, squatted, peed, deftly washed herself with a couple of scoops of water from her left hand, then stood up letting her sari back down and continued on her way across the stream. At that moment, I saw the girl my grandmother had been, growing up in rural India, performing this very set of motions in the middle of a country stream probably thousands of times, so that seventy-odd years later when a trickle of water presented itself after a long car ride, the impulse and the movements to accomplish it came automatically.

I was shocked. It would never occur to me, versed as I am in modern—and very American—notions of sanitation and environmental consciousness to pee directly into a clear creek in which clothes are being washed downstream. And I would never unself-consciously expose myself like that. I would do what any American woman my age would do under the circumstances: head for a bush! In that moment, I glimpsed how wide the gulf of experience and perspective between my life and my grandmother's was, how radically different were our relationships to our bodies and to our environments. I also realized, for the first time in my life, that my grandmother didn't wear underwear, something I'd never thought about before.

Shortly after climbing out of the streambed, we entered the village, an immaculate collection of small lanes and mud-and-thatch dwellings. The village women called to us. "*Aavo, ben, aavo. Aavo dikri.*" "Come, sister, come on," they said. "Come, daughter." We were deep enough into the country and far enough from the tourist circuit that these women saw me not as a light-skinned foreigner but as a daughter of the family who ran the village *kuldevi* temple. They invited us into their spotless, cow-dung–plastered homes, lined with rows of shiny brass pots and decorated with inset mirrors and raised geometric motifs. They made us tea with fresh buffalo milk, very strong and very sweet, tinged with a taste of earth from the unfired clay saucer in which it was served. The women were handsome, with perfect white teeth. They were nearly covered with heavy silver ornaments, right down to the thick bracelets around their ankles and the rings on their naked toes. I noticed they all had tattoos similar to my

grandmother's. Yet these were real village women, and my grandmother was a jet-set Bombayite who had arrived by air-conditioned
car and had children in America and a Sony Trinitron in her living
room. We sat there sipping saucersful of hot, sweet tea and smiling.
Motiba made loud slurping sounds so the women would know how
much she was enjoying the drink. She engaged them in a rapid-fire
conversation in the local dialect. I could barely follow the gist of the
exchange, but smiled and bobbed my head from side to side. This was
Kathiawar as my ancestors must have lived it, and Motiba, after
decades of cosmopolitan life and travels to the capitals of Asia,
Europe, and North America, felt right at home.

* * *

The Kamdar *kuldevi* is Ashapura Devi, the "goddess capable of
realizing all hopes." She is a powerful yet benevolent deity in the
form of a beautiful mother seated side-saddle upon a she-camel.
True to the maternal ideal, she is tender and generous toward her
children yet utterly ferocious when it comes to protecting them
from harm. The priest at our *kuldevi* temple tells the story of the
difficult migration our clan undertook, fleeing before the wrath
of conversion-bent Muslims down from the steppes of Central
Asia, over the deserts of Sindh and Kutch, before arriving, finally,
in Kathiawar. "In the desert, there was no water. Mataji provided
water to our tribe. We survived. The Muslims couldn't find any
water, and they all died." Such are the legends the priest recites
about the nurturing and protection Ashapura Devi offered to our
tribe in an us-against-them world.

Until just twenty years ago, our *kuldevi* was worshipped in the form of some ovoid orange-painted stones that, according to legend, had been carried from place to place along the route of the tribe's migrations in an old wooden baby's cradle. Stones such as these are ancient iconographic representations of the mother-goddess, thought to represent the goddess's life-giving and nurturing breasts. Though no one in my family has ever mentioned it, I have read that Ashapura Devi is a goddess sought out by women who wish to conceive children, hence, perhaps the baby cradle used to carry the deity. Other orange-painted stones represent specific female ancestors who committed *sati*—self-immolation—rather than be despoiled by Muslims or other marauders, or simply to express their devotion to a deceased husband (or their fear of the life that awaited them as a widow). The Kamdar *kuldevi* temple is a shrine both to female power in the form of the mother-goddess and to female self-sacrifice, the source of that power.

Today, the baby cradle full of sacred stones sits at the feet of a gorgeous marble image of Ashapura Devi in an elaborate temple complex, but when my father was a child, it was housed in a small mud-and-thatch shrine. In those days, the village elders were personally known to my grandfather. Out of respect, he called the men *bapu,* "father," a term of respect, and the women *ba,* "mother." The villagers of Thorala are *garasias,* people of royal descent or who were rewarded by grants of land for loyal service to one of the Rajput kings or Kathi princes. As such they were to be treated with the highest respect. They had a reputation of being prone to violent disputes among themselves, a result of their war-loving nature.

Bapuji's father, my great-grandfather Bhagwanjibhai Kamdar, an experienced manager, would resolve all pending differences whenever he came to the village.

As recently as the 1930s, family members used to travel from Jetpur to Thorala by bullock cart. They would leave at three in the morning and arrive three hours later, at dawn. The day before, my grandfather would send, also by bullock cart, huge barrels of *laddus,* sweets, and *ganthiya,* snacks of fried chickpea batter. They would offer these special foods to the goddess; pray to her; perform any rituals that needed to be performed; and then, once the food had received her blessing, distribute it to the villagers. In those days, my grandfather and the other senior-most members of the family served the villagers with their own hands as a token of the great esteem in which they held those who lived in proximity to the goddess. The food was placed on sections of banana leaf. The villagers provided fresh *maakhan,* butter; *bajari rotlo,* millet flatbread; and hot pickles. Only after all the village elders had been served would the children in our family get to eat. Until then, they were expected to sit quietly and respectfully on the sidelines. After everyone had eaten, tea was served in throwaway unfired clay cups. The local men leaned back to smoke the *bidis* my grandfather had brought for them. Then the family piled into the bullock carts and made its way back to Jetpur.

Once, when Dipukaka, as I call him, my father's youngest brother Dilip (*kaka* means "uncle" or more specifically, "father's brother"), was a child, the family attempted one of these trips to Mataji's temple, but on the last stretch of road to the village, the bullocks balked, for no apparent reason, at continuing. There was nothing that could be done to force or cajole them to go forward. Finally, though they were very near to Thorala, the family members decided to go home and try again the next day. Mataji, it was felt, did not want them to come just then. The next day they set off once again. When they came to the spot on the road where the bullocks had refused to advance the day before, the same beasts paid no mind, placidly continuing their pace. When they arrived in the village, they discovered that there had been a dispute the day before between some of the villagers that had come to such a bad end that several had been killed. Had the family members arrived in the middle of the fight when passions were running high, they too might have been in danger. Everyone in the party went straight to the temple to thank Mataji for looking out for them and for keeping them out of harm's way. In Kathiawar, everything is interpreted as a sign freighted with meaning. Nothing happens by chance.

Later, in the 1940s, the family made the trip to Mataji in a fleet of Buick and Plymouth sedans owned by "a good and faithful Muslim family" of taxi drivers. Dipukaka claims that no matter how often they made the trip, the drivers of these cars would always get lost somewhere between Jetpur and Thorala. They would make a wrong turn, overshoot the turn off the main road, take the wrong dirt track after they left the main road—something—before finally finding the way to the village. This was interpreted to mean that the family must never take Mataji for granted.

Bapuji successfully bequeathed his devotion to the clan goddess to his children, who all, some more assiduously than others, make the effort to take the trip to Thorala. There are specific occasions when a trip to seek the goddess's blessing is required, such as when the firstborn son's hair gets its first cutting at age five, or when a newly married couple comes to perform a ritual before the goddess without which they cannot consummate their marriage. When my brother Pravin was born in 1961, Bapuji sent my mother a letter with strict instructions that his hair was not to be cut until he was five years old and could be brought to Thorala to have it shorn during the proper ceremony. My brother's thick hair was soon hanging down right in front of his face. Only after my mother wrote to report that she was receiving regular compliments on her new little "girl" did Bapuji relent and give her permission to have the baby's hair cut in Seattle. He never insisted on the hair-cutting ceremony again, and the tradition, impractical in this modern world, is now lost. One may, of course, come to pay *darshan* to the goddess any time, as I do whenever I happen to be in India. We always bring along *prasaad,* food that will be blessed by the goddess, including *laddus,* candy-coated peanuts, and fresh coconuts that the priest breaks up as he intones his prayers.

The intimate ceremony of ritual feeding that once bound the Kamdar family to the villagers of Thorala has long ceased. Now, as our car pulls away from the village to carry us back to Rajkot so we can catch our flight to Bombay, and then on to New York or London, we can see the temple priest distributing the *prasaad* to the village children who, far from looking like the descendants of feudal lords, look the way scrawny poor children do all over India. The cow-dung-plastered walls and deep front porches of the traditional homes that

graced Thorala's narrow lanes when Motiba and I were there have
been replaced by concrete block structures devoid of personality
and, it would appear, comfort. The villagers no longer wear traditional dress. The men are all in trousers with their collared shirts
untucked, machine-knit caps on their heads in place of the bright
turbans they used to sport. The married women wear proper *saris* of
nylon or machine-printed cotton in the "national dress" style with
the *paalav* draped over their left shoulder rather than in the Gujarati
style, in which the *paalav* is worn draped over the woman's bodice.
The young girls are all in cheap frocks or even nightgowns. It seems
puzzling at first that the women in this remote village should wear
their *saris* as women do in New Delhi and not as they do in any nearby
city or town in Kathiawar. Then one notices the television satellite
dishes sitting atop three of the new concrete bungalows: obviously,
the women of remote Thorala, who rarely, if ever, make the three-
hour trip to the nearest town, are aping fashions they can now see on
television in their own home. Soon every trace of life as it has been
lived in this village for hundreds of years will have vanished.
Teenagers who've seen *Baywatch* and the latest music videos from
Bombay find little appeal in traditional life and dress.

Out of devotion to Mataji, our *kuldevi,* our family has directly
contributed to the erasure of all that is traditional in this village.
There is now an official Kamdar *mahadevi,* or "great goddess,"
temple management committee. The committee has built a new
dharmashala across from the temple with Western-style toilets,
raised bed frames, a mirror, and even an electric clock in each
guest room. But for the villagers' welcoming cries of *"Jai Mataji,"*

"Long live the Mother-Goddess," the village of Thorala that Motiba took me to see on an enchanted afternoon twenty years ago has ceased to exist.

* * *

The Kamdars may well have come by their devotion to Ashapura Devi through service to the kingly Jadeja Rajput clan, whose members worship the goddess as their own *kuldevi*. Our surname derives from my forefathers' hereditary occupation as estate managers, or *kamdars* of the local rulers. Our ancestral home was located in the town of Jetpur in a lane known as *kamdar seri*. *Kamdar seri* is directly opposite and runs perpendicular to the now-crumbling palace of the Kathi princes of Jetpur. My grandfather's father, Bhagwanjibhai Kamdar, was, like his father before him and his father's father, a *kamdar*. During his career, he worked for the princes, or *darbars,* of Bilka, Chittal, and Jetpur states. But Bhagwanjibhai was the last *kamdar* in the family. Incredibly, he gave up his potentially lucrative post in the early 1900s to become a relatively ill paid schoolteacher. At the time, a feudal system of government was extremely well entrenched in Kathiawar. It depended almost entirely on the extraction of tithes and taxes from the people by the local petty princes, who each passed his required share of revenue up the food chain to the next level of ruler. Bhagwanjibhai's revolutionary departure preceded by some fifty years the formal elimination of this system in favor of democratic rule under an independent India. How my great-grandfather came to renounce the occupation of his forefathers is a remarkable story.

Once a year, as a condition of keeping his fiefdom, the *darbar,* or petty ruler, of Bilka had to pay *khandani,* a form of rent, to the ruler of Junagadh state, of which Bilka was a dependency. His *kamdar,* Bhagwanjibhai, known by his descendants simply as Adah, or grandfather, was, as usual, charged with safely delivering the *khandani* to Junagadh. Late in the evening, after the *darbar* had finished his dinner and evening entertainments, he summoned Adah to the palace. There, in the penumbra of one of the palace rooms, the *darbar* carefully counted out 2,000 rupees for the *khandani* and gave them to his faithful *kamdar.* Adah went home, tucked the money away in his usual hiding place, and went to sleep. Intending to get a good start on his journey, he rose early the next morning. Just to be on the safe side, he decided to recount the money. There were, indeed, twenty bills, but he discovered to his stupefaction that the *darbar* had given him twenty bills of 1,000 rupees instead of twenty bills of 100 rupees. Adah held in his hand 18,000 more rupees than he was required to deliver. His monthly salary as *kamdar* was a mere fifteen rupees. The 18,000 rupees he held in his hands represented an unimaginable fortune. Adah did not think twice about what he had to do. With great dispatch, he saddled his horse and galloped off to the *darbar*'s palace. Naturally, the *darbar* was still sleeping at such an early hour. His servants were loath to disturb him, but Adah insisted that the prince be awoken immediately. He had a matter of the utmost urgency that demanded the attention of the *darbar* and the *darbar* alone. After some minutes, the *darbar* emerged, rumpled and cross, demanding to know what business his *kamdar* could possibly have that merited his being disturbed.

Adah showed him the 20,000 rupees and pointed out the error that had been made. Then Adah asked that the correct 2,000 rupee sum be counted out so that he could get on his way without further delay. The *darbar* was impressed by the rare honesty of his *kamdar*. He offered him a substantial raise and suggested it was time his *kamdar* played a larger role in the management of his estate. This could only have been a tempting proposition for a father of five children. Adah asked permission to think over the new terms of his employment, and then he set off without further delay to deliver the *khandani* to Junagadh. Upon his return he accepted the *darbar's* proposal. But, a *kamdar* was required to do whatever his prince asked, good or bad. The *darbar* having a new level of confidence in his *kamdar*, began asking Adah to perform certain tasks that the honest man found morally repugnant. Eventually, Adah could no longer stand the turmoil in his soul. He resigned his post.

Perhaps Adah's moral repugnance came from the Jetpur princes' weakness for women. There were twelve princely brothers in Jetpur, all—according to my family—with an eye for pretty women. They considered any woman resident in their territory to be fair game, and imposed a local version of feudal Europe's *droit de cuissage*. The princes used a balconied window high on the palace walls to espy young women going down to the river to fetch water. They would select for their pleasure the ones that caught their fancy. (This was certainly one good reason to keep all girls over the age of twelve locked up in the house!)

Of course, it may be that the princes' conduct with the fairer sex was not what particularly offended Adah. His own family had suffered an unspeakable tragedy at the hands of one of the Jetpur princes. Adah's uncle was killed when, as a little boy, he was playing outside his house in *kamdar seri*. The prince was inside the palace, up on the second floor, near a window that opened onto the street, cleaning his hunting rifles. Suddenly, one of the guns went off. The bullet struck the playing child, killing him instantly. When this story is recounted, it is always implied that this tragedy may have resulted more from some callous target practice than from an accidental firing, though there was never any proof that it was anything other than a tragic accident.

The killing of this child was such a shock to the family that over a century after the event, Ganeshbapa, as the long-dead child is called, continues to be actively mourned and remembered. Loathe to abandon those dear to him, Ganeshbapa returned to visit the family in the form of a cobra for many years after his death. He would always appear in the same corner of the house. Members of my family swear that this was a corner from which there was no exit and into which there was no entry, proof, they say, that it was no ordinary snake that came to call. In his cobra form, Ganeshbapa would sway from side to side if he wished to communicate his approval of something and would advance and then turn around and retreat if he wished to communicate his disapproval of something. Ganeshbapa always appeared to the head of the family first. This individual would respond by immediately performing the pious gesture of bending his head and rubbing his temples with the knuckles of his closed hands, then offer the snake a saucer of milk (that most sacred substance). Properly acknowledged, Ganeshbapa would disappear, and the family would know that a student's performance on an upcoming exam had been blessed, or that one of the girls had been careless and gone into the kitchen when she was having her period. In this way, Ganeshbapa watched over the welfare of the family.

The shrine to Ganeshbapa used to be in the ancestral family home in *kamdar seri*. When the family left Jetpur and gave the home in *kamdar seri* away, the shrine was moved to the *kuldevi* temple in Thorala. Inside the *kuldevi* temple, there is a niche with an orange-painted stone in it that represents the little boy Ganesh. His memory is honored every time a family member visits the temple by the burning of incense and the saying of prayers. In front of the stone icon is a collection of tiny brass cobras, their heads raised. In the absence of a real home in Kathiawar, the *kuldevi* temple has become the Kamdar family's spiritual home. It is the only spot we remain anchored to the soil of Kathiawar, where the blood of our ancestors was spilled.

* * *

Like his father, my grandfather lived his life, as much as possible, according to a strict moral code of conduct. He was known his whole life as a *pukka,* or true, Gandhian. We never called him *adah* or even *dada,* common words for "grandfather." We always called him Bapuji, an affectionate term meaning "respected father" that was the same pet name used by those in Gandhi's entourage to express their affectionate regard for the Mahatma. Even Jawaharlal Nehru referred to Gandhi as Bapu. As a lad of eighteen, my grandfather was

so inspired by the Mahatma and intoxicated by the leader's movement for India's independence known as *Satyagraha,* "the insistence
on truth," that he wrote to Gandhi and asked permission to join the
him as a disciple at Sabarmati Ashram near Ahmedabad. Gandhi had
called on all families to sacrifice one son to the cause of freedom. My
grandfather volunteered to be that one. Gandhi replied, accepting
his enrollment and summoning him to come in a week's time. Ma,
Bapuji's mother, was beside herself with grief. Since Adah had given
up his post as *kamdar,* the family had barely gotten by on the meager
salary of five rupees a month he collected for his services as a local
elementary school teacher. True, the *ghee* Ma made from the milk of
her prize water buffalo and sold by word of mouth to housewives in
the neighborhood helped a little. But my grandfather had brilliantly
completed his studies and was thought to have great promise in life.
Though Bapuji was the third and not the eldest son, Ma viewed him
as the family's best prospective "earning member," the individual on
whom she placed her hopes for an easier life.

According to my grandfather's younger sister, Jasiphaiba, when
Gandhi's reply came to the house, Ma went on a sort of strike, refusing to eat and spending her days and nights, along with the rest of the
family, crying and lamenting my grandfather's impending departure
and the family's certain ruin. Her husband drafted a letter to the
Mahatma explaining the family circumstances and begging him to
disinvite his son. The morning Bapuji was supposed to leave for
Sabarmati Ashram, a second letter from Gandhi arrived at the house
admitting the merit of the parents' concerns and conceding that the
young man might do better to stay at home. My grandfather had to

acquiesce. It was a decision he regretted his entire life. He never forgave himself for not having the courage to sacrifice family duty to *Satyagraha*. Bapuji always felt that he had weakly given in to family attachment when a higher calling should have claimed him.

Within a year of this close call, Adah and Ma saw to it that my grandfather was married. They must have decided that they'd better catch their son in the sweet chains of domestic responsibility as quickly as possible before another moment of idealistic madness seized him. Even though the Kamdars were living in reduced circumstances, everyone in the Kathiawari Jain community respected Adah for having resigned his post for moral reasons. His family had the reputation of being people of *khaandaan* and *amiraat,* of noble birth and character. The intelligence and good looks of their son Prabhudas were well known, his support for Gandhi and *Satyagraha* admired.

When Motiba married him in 1924, Prabhudas Kamdar was a headstrong youth of nineteen who had as fully as possible embraced the teachings of the *guru* his family had not allowed him to join: Mahatma Gandhi. Born in 1905, Bapuji was ten years old when Gandhi returned to India from South Africa to begin his movement for India's independence from British rule. A Gujarati by birth, Gandhi published his fiery tracts in both the English- and Gujarati-language versions of his magazine, *Young India.* Bapuji, who attended the first English-medium school in his native town of Jetpur, read Gandhi in both English and Gujarati during his formative teenage years and was extremely aware of the Mahatma and his movement. By the time he reached young

adulthood, my grandfather had become a full-fledged supporter
of Gandhi's cause.

Muljibhai Khara heard that Bhagwanjibhai and Ambaben Kamdar were looking for a match for their son. He was impressed by the
reports he had about the family and the boy. He had become quite
an ardent supporter of Gandhi himself, and the boy's reputation as
a supporter of *Satyagraha* pleased him. This might be the right young
man for his daughter Jayakunver. Muljibhai went to Jetpur and met
Bhagwanjibhai. The Kharas were by now quite wealthy people.
Bhagwanjibhai made it clear that his family had little to offer in
terms of material comfort, but Muljibhai protested that his daughter would bring a substantial dowry and that his foremost criterion
in a son-in-law was quality of character. The match was agreed
upon. Motiba, who was all of fifteen years old, was not told about
her impending marriage until the week before the ceremony.

Naturally, the Kharas wanted to put on a wedding for their eldest daughter that reflected their now substantial wealth. Hundreds
of people were to be invited. Special foods were ordered from
caterers as far away as Bombay and Calcutta. Multiple sets of jewelry in twenty-two-karat gold, set with diamonds, Burmese rubies,
and pearls were ordered from the family jewelers. In all, Motiba
was given eighteen *tolas* of gold by her father. (A *tola* is equal to
11.66 grams.) A trousseau of sixty *saris* in the finest silks imported
from China, Japan, and Europe was collected. Alas, Motiba would
never get to wear any of the silks in her magnificent trousseau.

Gandhi had made the wearing of *khadi*, crude cotton cloth hand
woven in India, central to his independence movement. In his 1909

Hind Swaraj, he attributed India's impoverishment under British rule to the economics of cloth, and he applauded the voluntary return to the wearing of Indian dress—something theretofore thought terribly backward by the educated Indian elite—by members of the Bengali *swadeshi,* or self-rule, movement. When he returned to India in 1915 from South Africa, he did so in the dress of a Kathiawari peasant, and he made spinning cotton and weaving cloth a centerpiece of life at Sabarmati Ashram. All through the early 1920s, Gandhi exhorted India's people to wear *khadi* as a patriotic act. Gandhi described the "*khadi* spirit" as one of "self-sacrifice" and "fellow feeling with every human being on earth." According to Gandhi, it was a national and even a religious duty to wear *khadi.* Foreign cloth was synonymous with temptation, evil, luxury, and sin. To wear imported, machine-made cloth was to sell out your (Indian) self.

Somehow Bapuji learned about Motiba's extensive trousseau of silks. He sent a message to the Khara family that he would never accept a bride who came with clothing made of imported cloth. He let it be known that he himself would wear nothing other than locally produced *khadi.* If his bride was not willing to do likewise, the wedding need not take place. Three days before the wedding, Motiba's splendid trousseau was disassembled and returned, to be exchanged for a trousseau of cheap *khadi.* (Apparently, one or two non-*khadi saris* were snuck in, pieces that were simply too fine to let go. For years, they remained folded away at the bottom of her heavy teak dowry chest.) In the end, Motiba, the eldest daughter of what had become a very wealthy family, was married in the crudest of handwovens. Yet, because of the tenor of the times,

Bapuji's eccentric demand only served to raise the esteem in which his father-in-law held him. In fact, Muljibhai Khara, who could have worn any clothing he liked, even custom-made suits from Savile Row, took to wearing *khadi* himself. He was the only one of the three Khara brothers to do so. It seems his idealistic son-in-law exerted some influence over the successful man in this regard.

Bapuji didn't stop the Gandhian business with *khadi*. At the end of the wedding ceremony, he untied the silk cord that had been ceremonially knotted between himself and his new bride to signify their union, led my fifteen-year-old grandmother by her end of the cord over to his mother, and said, "You wanted a daughter-in-law? Here she is." He then announced his intention to take a vow of religious celibacy, to practice *brahmacharya*. This is something Gandhi himself had done in 1906, and that he encouraged his disciples to do. In 1924, the year my grandparents were married, Gandhi wrote that to become *brahmachari* meant to "search after Brahma," or God, through control "of all the senses at all times and at all places in thought, word, and deed." *Brahmacharya* went well beyond sexual denial to encompass all desire. Gandhi wrote that true "*brahmacharis* are perfectly sinless. They are therefore near to God."[6] Gandhi had embraced *brahmacharya* twenty years into his marriage and after the birth of five children, however. For my grandfather to proclaim this on his wedding day at the age of nineteen was a far more radical act than even that undertaken by the Mahatma.

What my fifteen-year-old grandmother made of all this can only be imagined. When I asked my grandmother before she died what it had felt like to be married at fifteen years of age to a man she had never even seen before, she seemed puzzled by my question. "You are born, then you marry, then you die," she answered. I insisted, finding her experience totally incomprehensible. After all, when I was fifteen I was living the decadent Southern California lifestyle of the post-pill 1970s. The freedom to do as I pleased was near total, notwithstanding my parents' efforts to control me. It came out that, for Motiba, the moment of her arranged marriage had been anticipated her whole life. She had been prepared for such an event for years. Her main concern was to "do a good job" for her in-laws. She was entirely conscious that her relationship with her husband's parents was much more important than her relationship with him. She was being married *into* a family, not *to* a husband. As she spoke about her "training," I suddenly understood that my grandmother approached marriage at the age of fifteen the way a freshly minted M.B.A. approaches an entry-level job with a reputable multinational: she had gotten a good assignment, an opportunity to prove what she was worth in the area of expertise for which she'd been prepared: marriage.

In addition to finding herself married to a man who spurned all physical pleasure, Motiba experienced a distinct and sharp decline in lifestyle. She had been raised in the lap of luxury, with an army of servants and attendants to look after her every need. She was used to wearing fine clothes and costly jewels, and had never had to cook, clean, or otherwise help out around the house. In the much more modest Kamdar home, the cooking and many of the other household tasks were done by the women of the family. This included physically demanding chores, such as fetching water from the river. Today, the river in Jetpur is so incredibly filthy and polluted, it is hard to imagine it as anything but the open sewer and toxic waste dump it has become. In 1924, however, decades before the town would experience a boom in the textile-dyeing business that would destroy its ecology, it must have been much cleaner, for my grandmother and her then—nine-year-old sister-in-law, my Jasiphaiba, used to fetch water from it every day. Jasiphaiba told me that they would always take a certain path that was rather steep in parts, requiring them to hike up their _saris_ and tuck them in so as not to trip over them. When they reached the river, they would again adjust their _saris_ so they wouldn't get wet as they waded out a bit where the current ran faster and where, they believed, the water was cleaner. They would take the clay water jars, dip them in the water, and slosh them back and forth to clear the surface of any debris, then fill them, lift them up upon their heads, and turn back to make the return trip. I can imagine my beautiful grandmother with her lithe young legs sparkling with damp as she stepped out of the river and began her way up the dirt path toward the town, letting her _sari_ down as soon as it was practical with one hand as the other steadied the heavy jar on her head. Most of the year, it would have been so hot and dry that a trip to fetch water with the inevitability of getting somewhat wet would have been a welcome errand.

Jasiphaiba, who lived with my grandmother during those early years of marriage at her in-laws' house, confirms the legend of my grandmother's saintly demeanor under the circumstances. Apparently, Motiba never once uttered the smallest complaint, never gave the slightest sign that she was unhappy about any of the changes in her life. Like an Indian version of Snow White, so noble was the character of the beautiful and rich young Motiba that she smilingly went about performing tasks of household drudgery that were clearly below the station to which she'd been born. After all, it was her duty to do so. It was her fate to go to her husband's house, even if her husband wanted nothing to do with her. A vow of celibacy on the part of one of the partners in a marriage on the day of the wedding would be grounds for annulment in most cultures. But not in India. Even today, when divorce has begun to make a hesitant and very recent inroad on tradition, marriages are generally considered unsunderable, no matter the circumstances.

Motiba's new husband was never an easy man to live with. He later became a patriarch whose grown children trembled in fear whenever he called them. Bapuji always kept aloof from the rest of the family, with the exception of any small children who happened to be about, on whom he doted. If there was a sticky matter to be put before him, my slight grandmother would be sent into the room where Bapuji spent his days listening importantly to the BBC and the *Voice of America*. She was the only one who was not afraid to confront him. I remember very starkly the night I awoke at the age of nine in darkness and in fear to feel the whole apartment in Bombay shaking violently, a thunderous roar drowning out all but the piercing screams coming from my own throat. I saw my grandfather standing in the frame of our bedroom door and instantly thought he had become so angry about something that, all-powerful as I believed him to be, he had seized hold of the house in a rage. In fact, we were in the throws of a devastating earthquake in which thousands perished. My grandfather was bracing himself in the door frame so as not to fall, and had come to warn us or help us. But this was only clear to me later, after the dust had settled, and that eery post-earthquake silence had begun to be broken by the sounds of quiet weeping and of people finding each other safe in the shattered night.

Just what Bapuji's mother and wife thought of Gandhi and his ascetic philosophy is unclear. It is evident, however, that the women were not prepared to share Gandhi's views on *brahmachari,* sexual abstinence, and they resolved to challenge him on this point directly. Ma, the story goes, invited the Mahatma for an audience during his passage through the region in early 1930. This can only have taken place, as far as I can figure, during Gandhi's famous march to the shore at Dandi to gather salt in violation of the British prohibition against the manufacture of salt in India. Gandhi came to meet the Kamdar ladies. He found himself confronted by an angry mother-in-law and a young bride seated cross-legged before him, *saris* pulled over heads, Motiba's countenance demurely downcast. "Why are you doing this?" asked my great-grandmother getting right to the point, referring to the celibacy vow he'd imposed on his disciples. "Madam, I am doing this for freedom, for our liberty," he replied. "I don't know what freedom is," answered the old woman, "but I do know that you are ruining this girl's life. She is nothing better than a widow!" This was a serious accusation. Anyone who knows anything about India knows that there is no fate worse than that of a widow. A widow is worse than dead, in fact the best thing she can do for herself and her family is to die. If she must live, then she must live as if she were dead: shave her head, break her ornaments, dress in rags, work as a domestic slave for the favor of continuing to be fed. No wonder some widows have preferred *sati,* self-immolation, to life. Upon hearing the women's complaint, Gandhi recognized that the celibacy vow must, indeed, be causing hardship for his married followers' wives. He rescinded it. My grandfather performed his marital duty and my father was conceived, the first of six children. Five survived.

Family legend has it that Motiba, the seemingly demure bride, is the one who put her mother-in-law up to admonishing the Mahatma. Modest appearances concealed a will of iron. It is one of the many paradoxes of Indian life that women can be formally rendered powerless by the official patriarchy yet dominate behind the scenes. Mothers, particularly of grown sons, are, in fact, allowed a great deal of freedom and accorded genuine respect and authority. A mother can act openly where a young bride does better to hide her true motives. In any case, this fantastic story of my father's coming into the world is the story of a confrontation between the world of women and the world of men, between the world of the home and the world of politics; a story in which the masculine spheres of the secular and the civic are vanquished by the feminine realms of seduction and practical home management.

* * *

In time, my grandmother came to occupy the center of her own household. She was the wife of a respected son, and once she had sons of her own, her status was assured. Motiba became the heart and soul of the family. She was the one who took charge of preparations for the many religious and family holidays and made sure that her home was one in which guests were always welcome and comfortable.

In India, even today, family bonds are extremely strong, and relatives as distant as second or third cousins feel the need for frequent and long visits. It is not unusual for guests to stay for weeks or even months at a time. Motiba made sure there were plenty of extra mattresses and _rajaais,_ or quilts, in the house for the constant stream of guests whose sleeping forms covered the bedroom floors at night. A woman whose specialized trade was the assembly of these mattresses would bring her tools and reinforced thread with her and move into the house for a period of several days or weeks until the _almaris—_ armoires—were filled with new folded bedding. To encourage the _rajaaiwali_ to produce the thickest, softest quilts and mattresses possible, Motiba prepared special food for her: extra big and thick _bajari rotlo_ (earthy gray millet griddlecakes) dripping with fresh butter and served with a side of fiery homemade pickles made from green mangoes, lots of salt, oil, and red chilies; pots of hearty vegetable curry—a different kind every meal; clay saucers of creamy, sweet curd. "No one feeds me the way you do," the _rajaaiwali_ would say to Motiba, before returning to her quilting.

* * *

Diwali is one of most important Hindu festivals of the year. It just happens to coincide with the anniversary of the tirthankara Mahavir's achievement of moksha, and my Jain family celebrated it with gusto. Held during the second week of the Hindu month of

Ashvin, which falls in October or November, Diwali celebrates the return of Rama from the years of exile recounted in the epic *Ramayana*. On this occasion, literally millions of tiny clay lamps burn on window and balcony ledges all over India to light the god's way home. Diwali also marks the beginning of the new fiscal year, an important occasion for a family of merchants. Motiba made sure that in her house, Diwali was properly observed. She had the entire house cleaned from top to bottom. New clothes were made for every member of the family. Motiba prepared special foods, including *laapsi,* a dish of sweetened cracked wheat eaten to give the new year a sweet beginning; *puris; shreekhand,* a saffron-flavored pudding made from thickened yogurt; and *undhiyu,* a hearty stew of winter vegetables, green bananas, and chickpea flour dumplings. Motiba cooked all this food on a *sagadi,* a contraption made from a tin bucket set upon ropes of clay with a hole for inserting hot coals. Three lumps of clay were pressed at equal intervals around the rim of the bucket, and the cooking pot was balanced on top of these. Any burnable fuel could be used for coals, but by far the most readily available and the cheapest was dried patties of cow dung mixed with straw.

Before dawn each Diwali morning, Motiba would have the servants sweep the threshold of the house clean. Then she would sit down before her front door and focus her creative powers. Using tinted rice flour, Motiba traced abstract patterns of *rangoli*—curving, crisscrossing lines similar to antique Celtic designs—at the entrance to her home. To form the colored patterns upon the floor, she sat on her haunches and let the powder fall in a steady stream

through the fingers of her moving hand. *Rangoli* can be quite intricate and can take over an hour to create, yet the artist knows they
will be obliterated with the passage of the first people in or out of
the house. *Rangoli* is a seasonal and ephemeral art, done at home,
for the family. It is a quintessential woman's art. Though her mas-
terpiece would last for only a few minutes, Motiba took great care
to create a different design in a different color every day. The only
legacy she earned from this effort is the one usually bestowed to
mothers: the fond memories of her children.

* * *

In the traditional Kathiawari manner, Motiba returned often to her
piyar, her father's home, after her marriage. A married daughter's
visit to her parents' house is a welcome vacation from the unrelenting household work of life at her in-laws. In her own father's
house, she is spoiled, fussed over, fed her favorite foods, allowed to
sleep late. When possible, a woman will return to her parents'
house to give birth and will remain there for at least two months
on a sort of maternity leave before returning to her regular job at
her husband's family's house. Motiba and her children spent many
summers at her father's house.

The Kharas had left Gokhlana in 1913, just five years after
Motiba was born. They moved to the nearby town of Amreli. Each
brother built a big *haveli,* or mansion, for his respective family. The
two younger brothers built their houses next door to one another.
The eldest brother built his across the street. Motiba never forgot
her first country-bumpkin impressions of town life. "The streets

were so vast, I felt certain I would get lost. Everything was big and new." The Kharas lived in Amreli for many years, spending months at a time there even after they had established extensive business networks abroad or alternating, with one brother staying in Amreli while the others were off tending business.

For Motiba's own children, summer vacations in Amreli presented a chance to bond with cousins and to be spoiled by a different set of grandparents. This was especially true for my father, Motiba's firstborn. A daughter's eldest son has a very special status among her relatives. He is the *bhanej,* and nothing should be withheld from him; no sweet, no toy, no tyranny over other children. Every story of my father's childhood indicates that he was in many ways a perfectly spoiled brat. My Shashimama ("mama" meaning "mother's brother" and Shashimama being Motiba's younger brother) still likes to show the teeth marks inflicted on his arm by my father when they were small boys. Vacations at Motiba's father's house in Amreli were carefree, coddled moments that my grandmother's children remember fondly.

On our way back from the epic trip to Gokhlana, my father, Dhirajmami, and I stopped in Amreli to visit the old Khara *havelis.* Eventually, the Kharas outgrew Amreli just as they had Gokhlana, and the family moved on to bigger towns and cities, but the houses the Khara brothers built in the 1920s are still there. We stopped at Muljibhai Khara's house, stepping through the small door of a large carriage gate into an interior courtyard of perhaps twenty by thirty feet. Around the paved floor rose three full stories of elaborately balustraded floors. The courtyard was completely open to the sky above, whereas around the periphery of the house stained-glass windows with carved wooden shutters let in a bit of light while shielding the interior from the outside world. My father sighed. In a corner stood a great copper vessel on a stand. "All our bath water used to be heated in that whenever we'd come to Muljidada's house." He turned to Dhirajmami. "Remember how Ba used to call you when you first came to this house as a young bride?" They chimed in together, smiling: "Dhiraaaj?" the second syllable rising in a questioning pitch over a long diphthong. "She used to call from upstairs, and Dhirajmami would run right up to see what she wanted."

The most memorable event that took place in the Khara _havelis_ in Amreli was the marriage of Motiba's first cousin Pushpa. Push-pamasi ("masi": mother's sister) is one of the most elegant Indian women I have ever met. She dresses simply in the traditional uni-form of elderly Gujarati ladies, a plain white cotton _sari,_ but the last time I saw her, the _sari,_ of a white with the most subtle hint of cream, was of the finest muslin with a discreet design woven into the border. She wore the requisite pair of gold bangles, but these were inset, in a perfectly understated way, with diamonds. Her simple solitaire earrings flashed with the brilliance only very good diamonds can produce.

Pushpamasi was married on December 8, 1940, when the Khara brothers were at the zenith of their business success. As she was being married to a high-ranking government official, her wed-ding could be nothing less than grand. Special foods were brought in from all over the country. The sweets, notably, were sent by the

best purveyor of Bengali sweets in Calcutta. As a bride, Pushpamasi
was by all accounts exquisitely beautiful. Her trousseau was com-
posed of *saris* of the finest silks from Japan and China, as well as
heavy, deeply dyed *kanjivaram* silks from South India with wide
borders of gold *jari* thread in complex weaves, and a nearly price-
less intricate double-ikat woven silk *sari* from Patan. In addition to
eighteen *tolas* of gold, her jewelry boasted the best Burmese rubies
and sapphires, emeralds from Venezuela, diamonds from South
Africa, and pearls from the South Seas.

The entire Khara clan was invited to Amreli to participate in a
series of ceremonies and celebrations taking place over several
days. Though Motiba was heavily pregnant, she wouldn't have
missed this event for the world and had brought her two little sons

Premchandbhai Khara's haveli in Amreli, where Dipukaka
was born during Pushpamasi's wedding.

with her, my father Prabhakar and my uncle Vinayak. On the final
of five full days of wedding celebration, an uncle sought out my
father and said, "*Bhai aavyo chhe,*" literally, "Your brother has
arrived." My father had met innumerable cousins at this huge family gathering, all of whom were referred to in the cozy way of
Indian family relations as *bhai,* "brother." He understood this uncle
to be telling him that yet another obscure cousin had arrived at the
wedding. In fact, Motiba had just given birth in a back room of the
house to her third child, a little boy they named Dilip. My father's
brother had indeed arrived, smack in the middle of the grandest
wedding in Khara family history.

* * *

No matter how rich they got or how many decades they lived in
town, the Kharas were always known to the people of Amreli as
gokhlanawalas, which could be loosely translated as "hayseeds from
Gokhlana." They never entirely shook their village origins. Why did
they leave the village? It was serendipity, precipitated by a teenage
boy in the family who, at an impressionable age, made a rash decision. Sometime right around 1900, no one alive knows exactly
when, Jakalben Khara, Motiba's paternal grandmother, wanted to
have her *kaambis,* or heavy silver ankle bracelets, repaired. In those
days, Jakalben dressed in the distinctly regional clothing of village
Kathiawar. She wore an open-backed blouse called a *kamkha,* tied by
a string at the back of the neck and the waist, tightly fitted in front
with gathered pouches to contain the breasts, and nearly completely covered with embroidered motifs. She wore a gathered,

full-length skirt, or *chaniyo,* into which was tucked a *kapdu,* or half-sari, that was brought around the back and pulled up over the head and the right shoulder to drape in front before being drawn around and tucked into the left side of the skirt. The *kapdu* could be pulled down to completely cover the face in *laaj* in the presence of males or for going out in public where one might be seen by males. Finally, she was covered with jewelry. From her earlobes hung heavy gold earrings. More earrings adorned the outer edge of each ear, going all the way up the side. She wore heavy chains of gold around her neck, multiple bangles of gold and colored glass on each arm, heavy sculpted silver *kaambis* around her ankles, and silver rings on several toes. On the left side of her nose, she wore a nose ring. A married woman should be so ornamented. To be bereft of any of these ornaments was akin to being naked—or poor—in any case, not attired in a manner consistent with one's station in life.

Jakalben's *kaambis* needed to be repaired, so she sent her seventeen-year-old son, Motiba's uncle Premchand, to Amreli (the nearest town), to have them fixed by a jeweler known to the family. Premchandbhai left by bullock cart, hitching a ride with someone going into town. He was to deliver the broken *kaambis,* stay the night at a relative's house, and return with the repaired *kaambis* the next day. Not a difficult mission for a seventeen-year-old. But Premchandbhai didn't return the next day. In fact, it would be over a year before they heard from him again, and several years after that before he returned to Gokhlana.

On the way to Amreli, Premchandbhai Khara made an encounter of the sort that one is likely to make when traveling alone for the first time. He met a man who had recently returned from Burma. During the hours they traveled together, bouncing along the dirt track behind a team of plodding bullocks, this stranger told Premchandbhai the most amazing things. Burma was a land of unimaginable opportunity, a place of easy living where great riches were just waiting to be made. Young Premchandbhai drank all of this in: the exoticism, the temptation of wealth, the boundless opportunity. By the time they reached Amreli, he made a shocking and fateful decision. He would sell his mother's *kaambis*. So what if Jakalmaben had to walk about with naked ankles like the poorest of beggar women, this was the chance of a lifetime. He would sell the *kaambis* and use the money to get himself to Burma.

Premchandbhai had never been on a train before in his life. He had as yet had no contact with the world outside his village, a world of empire crisscrossed and connected by the steel rails of the British Indian Railway. But fearless in the way only a teenager can be, he sold Jakalben's *kaambis* and bought a train ticket for Calcutta, the nearest to Burma the railway could take him. When Premchandbhai Khara stepped onto the train, he stepped into the world of nineteenth-century British imperial India. It was a fateful step, one that would eventually take him and his entire family into the twentieth century and the wide world.

Motiba's Undhiyu

The name of this dish means "upside down" in Gujarati. At the height of the winter vegetable season, before the searing heat of summer ends the harvest, tender fresh produce was collected and placed in a terra-cotta pot that was sealed with a terra-cotta lid using a layer of wet clay around the rim. The pot was then placed upside down in a pit in which a fire had been made and allowed to burn down to hot coals. More coals were heaped around the pot and the vegetables inside were allowed to slowly steam their way to doneness. This is a Jain version of the famous dish, which otherwise usually includes eggplant and may include potatoes. Jains believe that eggplants and cauliflower contain high levels of microscopic organisms (i.e., many lives) and are therefore to be avoided. Orthodox Jains also consider all root vegetables, which grow in dirt, to be unclean and do not consume them.

INGREDIENTS FOR THE UNDHIYU

2 green bananas
1 medium-size *dudhi* (a kind of squash)
2 c. *tindola* (a vegetable not unlike mini zucchinis)
4 Tbsp. vegetable oil
2–4 green chilies, depending on taste, minced
pinch asafoetida
1/2 tsp. turmeric
1 c. fresh peas, podded
2 tsp. fresh fenugreek leaves, coarsely chopped
2 c. whole broad beans (papdi)
1 1/2 c. green *tuver* (pigeon peas)
salt
1/4 c. fresh or frozen grated coconut
1/4 c. coriander leaves, finely chopped
water

Methi Moothia (Chickpea flour dumplings)

1 c. *chana* flour

pinch baking soda

1/4 c. methi leaves, coarsely chopped

1 green chili, minced

1 Tbsp. lime juice

1/4 tsp. sugar

water

4 Tbsp plus 1 tsp. vegetable oil

For the *methi moothia*: Combine *chana* flour, baking soda, and methi leaves in a bowl. With a mortar and pestle, make a paste of minced green chilies, salt, lime juice, sugar, and oil. Add paste to the chunna flour and methi leaves. Add just enough water to bind the ingredients. Heat 4 tablespoons oil in a small frying pan or heavy-bottomed casserole. Form dough into little dumplings and deep fry in hot oil until golden brown. Drain on paper towels. Set aside.

For the *undhiyu*: Cut green bananas (with peel), *dudhi*, and *tindola* into large (approximately 2-inch) chunks. Heat the leftover oil from frying the *methi moothia* in a large, lidded casserole. Add bananas, *dudhi*, *tindola*, minced green chilies, asafoetida, and turmeric and fry until just fragrant and warm. Add remaining vegetables (peas, fenugreek leaves, *papri*, *tuver*) and salt. Stir and cover. Reduce heat to minimum and cook for up to two hours, stirring vegetables every once in a while so they cook evenly. About 1/2 hour before serving, add the *methi moothia*. Just before serving, add half the fresh grated coconut and chopped coriander and a little water. Cover and steam for about 3 minutes. Garnish with remaining fresh grated coconut and chopped coriander. Serve with *bajari rotlo*, a dark, earthy, millet flatbread.

Motiba's Bajari Rotlo

INGREDIENTS

1 c. *bajari* flour (Indian millet flour)
water

Add enough water to millet flour to form a dough. Knead well, then pat into flat cakes about 6 inches across and 1/2 inch thick. Dry cook on a *tavadi* (a terra-cotta *tawa*) until done. Drizzle with *ghee* or spread with fresh homemade butter. Serve with *undhiyu* and mango pickle (see recipe).

Motiba's Mango Pickle

In the old days, from January through March during the pickle-making season when the mango tree boughs hung thick with little green, unripe mangoes, Rabari tribeswomen went house-to-house in the villages and small towns of Kathiawar offering to grind each family's pickle spices (*masala*). Lugging the tools of their trade along with them, these women would take turns lifting and dropping a baseball-sized wooden pestle (*sambelu*) into a heavy stone mortar until the family's *masala* were ground to the desired consistency. In the kitchen, everything was at the ready for pickle making, so that the freshly ground spices could be used immediately before they lost any of their newly released aroma and flavor. Motiba used to prepare her pickle mixture in great brass pots, and store the finished pickles in terra-cotta urns with cloth covers and strips of cloth tightly coiled around the necks of the jars. The terra-cotta jars were cleaned thoroughly by scrubbing them with white clay and rinsing them with boiling hot water. This was done at least twice before the jars were set out to dry in the sun, ready to be filled with a new year's supply of mouth-watering pickles.

Ingredients

1 dozen green (unripe) mangoes*
2 c. coarsely ground fenugreek seeds (*methi kuria*)
2 c. hulled mustard seeds (*rai kuria*)
1 1/2 c. red chili powder
1 Tbsp. ground turmeric
1/2 tsp. asafoetida (*hing*)
salt
2 c. vegetable oil (peanut or sesame)
sterilized canning or jam jars with lids

Wash mangoes. Cut each mango in half, and remove inner part of seed. Chop into 1-inch pieces. Place mango pieces in a large, stainless steel bowl. Sprinkle with 1/2 tsp. ground turmeric. Salt lightly. Mix well and let set overnight. The next morning drain off liquid from mango mixture. Spread mixture out on dry, clean cloths in morning sun to dry for 3–4 hours.

Bring oil to a boil in a stainless steel or enameled saucepan. Remove pan from heat and allow oil to cool to lukewarm.

Put asafoetida in the center of a large rimmed *thali*. Make concentric circles around the asafoetida, beginning with deep yellow turmeric, then the crimson ground chilis, then the pale yellow mustard seed powder, next the ground fenugreek. Make a final circle of salt. Heat 2 Tbsp. of the oil and pour onto the asafoetida at the center, being careful not to get oil onto the other spices. Cover oil-soaked asafoetida with a small overturned bowl. Let sit for one hour. Remove the small bowl over the asafoetida, and mix all the spices together. Pour dry mangoes onto the spices. Mix well.

Sprinkle a tablespoon of salt to cover the bottom of each jar. Fill each jar approximately 3/4 full and pack mango mixture into the jar to press out as much air as possible. Repeat until jars are to within one inch of top. Pour oil, now room temperature, over mixture in jars until completely covered. Seal jars tightly with lids. Store in a cool, dry place. The pickle should keep well for one year.

NOTE: In season, green mangoes are readily available in Indian grocery stores in most major North American cities. However, very tart, cored Granny Smith apples may be substituted with surprising success when mangoes cannot be found. The hulled mustard seeds, *rai kuria*, are sometimes sold in Indian grocery stores under the general heading "Pickle Masala." One has to be careful, however, because complete ready-made pickle masala mixtures are also packaged as "Pickle Masala."

2

Rangoon

It was the most beautiful city in the world.
The way we lived there, we will never live anywhere again.

During their trip to Rangoon in 1956, my aunts Bharati and Usha were treated like princesses. Bapuji made sure their stay included lots of shopping and taking in the sights, an excursion up to the mountain resort of Maymyo, a visit to Mandalay. One afternoon, Bapuji summoned the family's Rangoon jeweler to the house. In the middle of the drawing room floor, the jeweler unfurled a large piece of velvet. My aunts were seated opposite him, my grandfather off to the side. One after another, the jeweler produced little silk pouches containing rubies, sapphires, pearls, and diamonds, which he scattered upon the cloth's lush surface. The rubies smoldered, the sapphires sparkled coolly, the diamonds flashed, and the pearls lay luminescent in the afternoon light. "Which ones do you like best?" asked Bapuji. The little girls didn't really know the value of what they were seeing, especially Usha, the youngest. For them, it was like choosing between bits of prettily colored glass or marbles. "I like the red ones," chirped Usha. "Five sets with rubies," commanded Bapuji. Reconciled to married life and family responsibilities, Bapuji had become a successful businessman. While he had taken a hard line against conspicuous consumption as a youthful idealist, he wanted only the best for his children. He had five children, so he wanted five sets of jewelry, one for each daughter when she became a bride and one to present to the future bride of each son, each set to include earrings, a necklace, a ring, and two bangles. "I like the clear ones best," countered Bharati. "Five sets with diamonds," ordered Bapuji. When the girls had finished choosing, the jeweler was sent away to fill the order. He made up five complete sets with rubies, five with sapphires, five with diamonds, and five with pearls, all in twenty-two-carat gold. Bapuji put the jewelry in a bank vault in Rangoon for safekeeping while he waited for his children to grow up and find marriage partners, never suspecting that in a few short years all his assets in Burma would be confiscated by the Burmese government, including the jewelry he'd put aside for his children. The daughters never got to add the Rangoon jewels to their wedding finery. The sons never presented the rubies or diamonds to their brides. The pretty stones my aunts picked out one sunny afternoon in Rangoon exist now only in their minds' eyes: the flash of the diamonds, the fire of the Burmese "pigeon's blood" rubies, forever lost, burning only in their memories of Rangoon and the magical sojourn they spent there as little girls.

* * *

I have heard stories like this about Burma all my life. It is the paradise my family found, and then, like so many other Indian families, lost— suddenly, brutally, irretrievably. Beginning in the mid-nineteenth century, the British colonial masters offered up Burma as a land of opportunity for enterprising Indians. They needed the Indians to build the infrastructure of empire and colonial extraction: railroads, ports, roads. They needed them to run the rice mills, load the ships, handle all the administrative minutiae of daily governance. They also needed Indian capital to underwrite the great enterprise of getting the rice, the teak, and the oil out of the country. Moreover, the British saw Burma, like neighboring Malaya, as a safety valve for a burgeoning Indian population. Burma was rich in natural resources, overflowing with rice, the Asian staff of life, yet empty of people compared to India with its teeming millions. And it was nearby, mere hours by steamer from Calcutta to Akyab on the Arakan coast.

After the annexation of Rangoon and the Irrawaddy delta region to British India in 1852, Burma became an official extension of the British Indian colony. Indians could travel there freely, return home when they liked, go back and forth whenever and as often as they pleased. Indians were far freer to set up their own businesses in Burma than in India. Whether Chettiars, Bengalis, Marwaris, or Gujaratis, they quickly became the principal land-owners; moneylenders; merchants; rice millers; and, eventually, cinema owners and purveyors of every conceivable good and service in the land. At the other end of the economic spectrum, tens of thousands of workers were brought in from the poorer classes of India to perform the hard, menial labor in the mills, in the timber yards, and on the docks. In this respect, the British strategy of importing Indian labor was no different in Burma than it was in Fiji, Malaya, the Caribbean, or East Africa. Indians, whether rich, endowed with a English education, or desperately poor, were suited to the varied needs of the British imperial project. By the time the British empire was dismantled after World War II, it had dispersed by a process of deliberate migration policy over 6.5 mil-

lion Indians to British territories outside India. A little over 1 million of these ended up in Burma, among them, my family.[1]

* * *

The first ticket Premchandbhai Khara bought with the money from
the sale of his mother's *kaambi* was from Amreli to Rajkot, a journey
of three hours by steam locomotive. From Rajkot to Ahmedabad,
Premchandbhai traveled for eight more hours. From Ahmedabad, he
had a choice of itineraries. He could go down to Victoria Terminus in
Bombay via overnight train and from there take a "through carriage"
to Calcutta via Allahabad and Mogul Serai (near Benares). Or he
could make his way north to Delhi on the meter-gauge railway, and
from Delhi take a "through carriage" directly to Calcutta.[2] Either
way, Premchandbhai's journey from Amreli to Calcutta by train took
at least three days, covering as many as 3,000 miles. Traveling alone
and on limited means, Premchandbhai went third class, sitting and
sleeping on the hard wooden seats, wiping the coal dust from the
train's steam engine out of his eyes and off his sweating brow, as he
gazed between the iron bars of the railcar's window at the ever-
changing landscape of India. He bought peanuts, bananas, oranges,
and fried snacks from the itinerant vendors who moved up and down
the aisles, balancing woven baskets on their heads. At each stop along
the way, he purchased tea in little hand-turned clay cups that he
dashed down upon the rails when he'd drained their steaming con-
tents. To young Premchandbhai, a village boy wholly innocent of the
modern age, the three days between Amreli and Calcutta went by in
a flash. Giddy with the sheer gumption of his grand adventure, he felt

as if he was whizzing across the vast Indian subcontinent. One day he was sitting on a bullock cart on a dirt path out of Gokhlana. A mere seventy-two hours later, he was standing on the banks of the mighty Houghly in the British imperial capital of Calcutta. There, with the last of his money, he bought a one-way, steerage-class ticket for steamship passage to Akyab, on the Arakan coast of Burma.

When he reached Akyab, he hadn't a single rupee left to his name. He headed for the local Jain boarding house, where he was granted free room and board until such time as he could find a job and get himself on his feet. By the time Premchandbhai arrived in Akyab in 1900, Indians had been pouring into Burma in search of economic opportunity for fifty years. Each community—the Chettiar moneylenders from South India, the Gujarati traders, the Bengalis—took care of its own. At the Jain boarding house, Premchandbhai found home-style vegetarian cooking and people who spoke his language, who shared his religious beliefs, and who were full of advice on starting a new life in Burma.

Within a few days, he found a job. It was a modest one. He was to help out in the shop of a fellow Kathiawari who sold kitchen utensils imported from India. The shopkeeper was a Muslim and therefore a nonvegetarian, so Premchandbhai continued on at the Jain boarding house. Then, within the year, the shopkeeper died. This was a tragedy for his wife and children but a stroke of good fortune for Premchandbhai. The Muslim merchant's wife had never been involved in the business and since she respected the requirements of *purda,* couldn't consider taking up work that would expose her to the public gaze. She begged Premchandbhai to take over the shop. He accepted. For the first time since leaving Gokhlana, he wrote home, informing his family—to everyone's astonishment—that he was alive and well and in possession of a profitable business in Burma. Couldn't they send over his brother Muljibhai? He could use the help, and there was money to be made. They sent Muljibhai, Motiba's father, my great-grandfather.

I heard this fantastic story of her family's start on the road to riches directly from Motiba. Khara family members have confirmed it, though there are some who are vague about the details or even totally unaware of how the dots between Gokhlana and Burma were ever connected. There are others in my immediate family, however, especially those with more affinity for the Kamdar side, who view this whole story as Khara self-aggrandizement. They point out that many Indians, including Kathiawaris, went to Burma in those days in search of fortune. They recall that there was a severe drought followed by a massive famine in Kathiawar in 1899[3] that might have been just the thing to push a desperate family, whose herd of cows had likely been decimated, to sell some of the women's jewelry in order to send one of the sons, just one, to Burma with the hope of finding a better life there. But then, selling the family jewels because you are in danger of starving does not make for the stuff of family legend the way my grandmother's story does. In any case, a different truth, if there is one, has long vanished. All that remains is memory, myth, and legend. And even if another, truer story could be discovered, it is by telling its very own rags-to-riches tale that the Khara family created an identity and gave the inchoate flow of its members' collective experience

meaning and history. After all, the Rajput kings boast of a genealogy tracing their origin to the sun. If kings can be spawned by the
sun, then merchants can be enriched by daring young men taking
the bit of history in their teeth. Whether or not it is true, Motiba's
version of the Khara family's ascent to riches is a great story.

What is indisputable is that within a few short years, the Khara
brothers turned a shop selling kitchen utensils into a highly profitable import-export business. Burma produced little or no manufactured goods. Joining the many Indian merchants who came to
dominate trade in Burma, the Kharas undertook to provide the
local populace with anything it might desire that was not made
locally, which is to say almost everything. The only thing the Kharas would not sell were goods deriving from the slaughter of animals, such as leather items. At various points in time, the brothers
dealt in such diverse products as steel machine tools and Swiss
chocolates, though textiles were always the mainstay of their business. The Kharas were very successful. They acquired enough capital to build rice mills and made a handsome profit on Burma's
number one export crop.

By 1920, Motiba's father, Muljibhai Khara, was able to gather
his prosperous family on the roof of the family's grand villa in
Akyab for a group portrait. In the photograph, one can make out
some tropical foliage and the neoclassical balustrade that encir-
cled the rooftop terrace. There are actually two photographs, evi-
dently taken the same day, with exactly the same cast of characters
except that my great-grandfather himself only appears in one of
the pictures. Curiously, my grandmother, age twelve years, and

her new stepmother, Samrathben, who was all of sixteen, swapped outfits so that each is wearing the other's clothes in the second photograph. As this exchange of outfits indicates, the two young women had become very close, so close that none of Motiba's children learned until very late in life that Samrathben, the woman they knew as "Motiba," grandmother, was not their mother's real mother.

It is obvious that the family has dressed in its finest for the occasion, and the clothing, together with the crystal vases and the carved teak tables, convey my grandfather's success as a merchant. The women wear exquisitely embroidered *cholis,* or

Muljibhai Khara's family on the roof of the family
villa in Akyab, Burma, 1920.

blouses, with gold fringe sewn onto the hems of the sleeves. Their heavy silk *saris,* drawn demurely over their heads, have wide borders of gold. My grandfather's second wife holds a plump infant on her lap who would grow up to be my kindly great-uncle Manumama, Dhirajmami's now-deceased husband. The older sons stand behind. They wear jackets and shoes. Seated in the center are the adults, with the younger children at their feet, including a sister who died in early childhood. Strangely, her image is the only one that is blurred, as if her death were foreshadowed somehow in that uncanny way photographs can have of capturing things we do not "see" at the time.

The Khara family sans père. *Note that everyone has changed outfits for this second photograph.*

Everyone looks very, very serious. Certainly, one gets the impression that dignity counted more in that bygone era than in our own,
where one must smile toothfully so as to give the eternal impression of having fun. Maybe it was only having to stay still for so long
while the image developed on the old glass negatives, but still, my
grandmother looks more than serious. She looks intensely sad.
And beautiful. And very young, yet strong. She has high cheekbones; full lips; buttery skin; and luminous, haunting eyes. I have
stared into these eyes for hours, trying to imagine the girl looking
out from them. I don't know what was happening on that day in
1920. I do know that Motiba had lost her mother a few years earlier and that she missed her very much. Her younger sister, my
Jayamasi, the one who later lived in Singapore and London, was so
traumatized by this disappearance that she refused to be near anyone but my grandmother and would scream inconsolably if left
with anyone else. So, Motiba was made to drop out of school in the
fourth grade so she could keep her little sister company during the
long days the sheltered girls spent at home.

The villa in Akyab where Motiba grew up was utterly de-
stroyed by the Japanese during World War II, which is a shame
because it looks as if it was a beautiful house. Motiba's childhood
in Akyab, if confined, was a pampered one. There were scores of
servants to cater to her every need. If she was hungry, she had
only to convey an order to the kitchen via one of her maids. When
she shed her clothing, she simply dropped it on the floor, where
it was picked up and whisked away to be washed and pressed and
put away by the next morning. There were maids to brush and

plait her hair, maids to oil her skin and massage her legs, maids to keep her company. A hierarchy of servants placed those brought over from Kathiawar at the top; those from elsewhere in India next; and the Burmese, who did the hardest work, last. The head cook was a Kathiawari Jain woman whose competent hands could be entrusted with the feeding of a large and devout vegetarian family. Young Motiba's social circle in Akyab was firmly limited to young ladies from similar backgrounds. Indeed, family members were preferred above all other acquaintances, and Motiba grew up, as was typical in her day, in the company of legions of cousins: first, second, once- and even twice-removed. Samrathben and the children took regular and lengthy trips to Amreli, where they stayed in the family's *haveli*. Important Jain festivals and weddings were the most common reasons for a trip "home." More often than not, Motiba's father stayed in Burma to run the business while his wife and children were away in India, often for months at a time. After the family moved to Rangoon, they made regular trips to the hill station of Maymyo to escape the debilitating heat and humidity of the capital. There, Motiba and her cousins shivered deliciously under their shawls, savoring the cool mists and mild days of the hills. Whether traversing India by train or meandering up the Irrawaddy River to Mandalay, Motiba always traveled with a large group of Khara family members: aunts and uncles, brothers and her sister, and an always-expandable number of cousins. The long hours and days of the journey were passed gossiping, playing Parcheesi, snacking, and napping on the lap or shoulder of a close relative.

Of Burma, Motiba remembered most the luxurious life she enjoyed there as a child; the beautiful pagodas; and, with some envy, I think, the independent, cheroot-smoking Burmese women. When asked about the country, Motiba would inevitably make a comment along the lines of, "In Burma, the women are very strong, very smart. They handle all the money and run all the businesses. They work very hard, while the men just take it easy." I always interpreted this less as a fully accurate commentary on gender relations in Burma than as a glimpse into Motiba's perspective on sexual politics outside her own protected sphere.

The Khara brothers moved their business headquarters from Akyab to Rangoon soon after Muljibhai Khara had his family's portrait taken on the terrace of its villa. From Rangoon, they branched out, opening a network of outlets all over Burma. The Kharas' move to Rangoon was a typical one for successful Indian merchant families. Rangoon was the business capital of the country and by the time the Kharas got there, fundamentally an Indian city. In fact, by 1931, the year my father was born in Burma, fully half the population of Rangoon was Indian. Most of the buildings were owned by Indian landlords, most of the shops were run by Indians, most of the money was exchanged through Indian hands. The lingua franca of the city was Hindustani, liberally peppered with Burmese, Tamil, Chinese, and English words.

The Khara brothers, like most other Indian merchants, set up their offices in the Surati Bazaar area in the heart of the Indian section of town. Variously scribed by the British as "Surtee," "Soorti," or "Soortee," the bazaar is named after the Indian Muslim merchants from Surat, the ancient port city and trading capital of coastal Gujarat, who settled there before the British built colonial Rangoon. When the British began to build up their colony in Burma, they found a population of Muslim Surati merchants already established there. In 1858, following the failure of the Sepoy Rebellion and the transfer of official administration over India from the East India Company to the Crown, the British added to the Indian Muslim population of Burma by there exiling the last Mughal emperor of India, Bahadur Shah Zafar. A considerable entourage of Bahadur Shah's family and courtiers accompanied the emperor into exile in Burma. The descendants of this last remnant of high Mughal culture intermarried with Surati, Chinese, and Malay Muslims, creating a vibrant community that came to represent nearly half the population of Buddhist Burma's capital city.

In the early decades of the twentieth century, Rangoon's Surati Bazaar was a kaleidoscope of people from every region of India. There were Marwaris, Tamils, Bengalis, Gujaratis. There were Muslims, Hindus, Sikhs, Jains. On one corner, wrapped around an ancient banyan tree, was a sort of all-purpose Hindu shrine, with niches for the worship of Lakshmi, Hanuman, and Ganesh. This island of Hinduism was surrounded by a sea of Buddhist pagodas and Muslim mosques. Further on was a larger temple to Shiva, with a massive carving of the temperamental god tenderly cradling in his protective arm his voluptuous consort Parvati. In the narrow lanes, brilliant silk and cotton *saris* hung in long banners of fuchsia and emerald over the balconies to dry. There were sweet shops selling *barfis,* grain merchants sitting among piles of rice and wheat, spice merchants surrounded by little golden and scarlet piles of ground turmeric and dried chilies. *Paanwalas* set up their supplies and tools on small wooden trays outside the temples, near the tea stalls, on the street corners. People squatted along the sidewalks near vats of hot oil where *bhajiyas* and *pakoras* fried temptingly. All year long, it was hot and densely humid. The air smelled like fermenting fruit, with occasional whiffs of cumin, coriander, ginger, and raw sewage.

Yet this richness of religious and ethnic diversity, of color and smell, existed within the rational grid of a British colonial city par excellence. With its broad avenues; parks full of flowers; lakes fringed by great trees; and graceful colonial architecture of high ceilings, balconies, and colonnaded galleries, Rangoon was regarded as one of the most beautiful cities in Asia. Along the Rangoon River ran the Strand with the Post and Telegraph Office; the Court House; the Customs House; and, of course, the celebrated Strand Hotel, rivaled only by the Raffles in Singapore as the epitome of colonial elegance in the East. The next several blocks backing up from the riverfront were laid out in neat rows of broad parallel avenues: Merchant Street; Dalhousie; then Canal, which at a certain point became Fraser; followed by Commissioner's Road, on which stood the Central Jail, just opposite the Jail Garden, followed by Rangoon College on one side, the Phayre Museum on the other. Commissioner's Road turned into Montgomerie just before it reached the railway station, followed by the "native burying grounds" and, finally, the separate Protestant and Catholic cemeteries. These avenues were neatly bisected at regular intervals by absolutely straight, perpendicular streets: Keighly, Morton, Phongyi, Godwin, Latter, then China Street in the heart of the city's Chinatown, followed by Mogul Street in the center of the Indian section.

In this wonderful specimen of British colonial urban planning, the smaller parallel lanes in-between the named streets were numbered progressively, so that it was quite easy to find one's way about the city. The resident or visitor to Rangoon in the 1930s could stroll in any number of parks and gardens: Victoria Park, of course; Fytche Square; the Garden of the Agricultural and Horticultural Society; Dufferin Garden; and, in the shadow of the great Shwedagon Pagoda, the Cantonment Garden directly across from the European Infantry Barracks. To the west of the city, along the banks of the Rangoon River, was the Government Timber Depot and the sawmills; to the east of the city, the banks of Pazundaung Creek were lined with rice mills. Further east, along the Pegu River, were the Petroleum Godowns: the riverine boundaries of colonial Rangoon were explicitly defined by the three main export products that were the reason for the British presence there in the first place: teak, rice, and oil.[4]

After the Kharas moved to Rangoon in the 1920s, and later when Motiba returned with Bapuji as a married woman with her own household in the early 1930s, Rangoon was a boomtown. New buildings were going up everywhere, their unmistakable Art Deco curves and clean lines replacing the fussiness of an earlier sensibility. All the buildings in the Surati Bazaar area, from Mogul Street to Fortieth Street, from Merchant Street to Montgomerie Street, were built on the same basic plan, and the interior spaces, whether serving as businesses or residences, were nearly identical. None of the buildings exceeded five floors, a limit primarily imposed by a lack of elevators. Peculiarly, most buildings boasted a single stair-case rising straight up the center, dividing each floor neatly into two equally sized spaces. This single, central staircase extended from the street all the way to the top floor at a single angled pitch, with no double-backs or landings, and was extremely steep. The stairs were so narrow, it was difficult for two people to pass or to climb the steps together. The Kharas bought flats in these new, modern build-ings, so appealing in the wilting heat with their fresh coats of pastel yellow, green, and blue paint neatly covering the new plaster. They set up their offices in similar buildings nearby, and life wove itself between trips up and down the stairs of home and business.

* * *

Once Bapuji reluctantly reconciled himself to the duties of mar-ried life, he knew he had to make a living for his growing family. His in-laws were only too happy to help him make a start in busi-ness in Burma. After working for the Kharas for a time, Bapuji opened his own office in Surati Bazaar. P. B. Kamdar & Company, like Khara Brothers & Company at one point, was located at 30 Mogul Street, in the heart of Rangoon's Indian section. At the time, it was a choice location, directly across the street from what was then the imposing State Bank of India building. Number 30 was located upstairs on the second floor of the building numbered "28–32." Bapuji used to sit there at his massive teak desk covered with neat piles of papers, his books lined up in rows on shelves behind him, some tea things on a nearby tray.

Bapuji was still, naturally, an ardent supporter of India's independence movement. He was part of the group of prosperous Indian merchants in Rangoon who welcomed Nehru and his young daughter Indira to Burma when they visited in 1937. My father was only six years old, but he remembers with pride that he and a classmate at the Anglo-Vernacular Gujarati School were chosen to present the great leader of India's independence movement with garlands of flowers. He recalls Nehru telling the school assembly that it was insulting for them to refer to their school as "Anglo-Vernacular." They should be proud to be Indians. The Indian merchant community's support for Gandhi, Nehru, the Congress Party, and the cause of Indian independence was unwavering. They never doubted that an independent India would protect their interests as Indian citizens abroad. If fact, they looked forward to the day when they would be allowed to conduct business free from the yoke of British imperialism. It came as quite a shock when they discovered, after the war, that the government of independent India was far more interested in cementing a relationship with its counterpart in a newly independent Burma than in the welfare of the Indians who had made Burma their home.

Members of the Indian commercial class, such as my family, were the middlemen of the British imperial apparatus in Burma. As such, Indian merchants were both envied and loathed by the Burmese, and after Burma's independence, these Indians were systematically dispossessed and expelled. Only those whose livelihoods could not be extricated from Burma stayed on. For the Burmese, the Indians fell into two categories: capitalists or the lowest of laborers, exploiters or pariahs. When the Indians replied to early Burmese nationalist criticism that they, like the Burmese, were slaves of the British, the Burmese replied, "Then we are the slaves of slaves." Terrible riots broke out in Rangoon in the 1920s and again in the 1930s, when hundreds of Indians were killed by resentful Burmese mobs. By the late 1930s, tensions between Burmese and Indians had grown acute.[5] Bapuji moved his family to the quieter environs of suburban Bauktaw, commuting to his office in Surati Bazaar by train. Telephone service was nonexistent. Many were the nights that Bapuji failed to come home, and Motiba never knew if it was because he'd decided

Portrait of my father as a baby in Rangoon, Burma, 1931.

to sleep at the office rather than risk traveling through troubled neighborhoods or because he'd met with foul play. Sometimes Bapuji was away for days. No one in the family dared take the train into Rangoon to find out what was going on.

* * *

Motiba kept herself busy managing her household. The villa Bapuji bought in Bauktaw was large, with airy rooms and great verandas. High concrete walls surrounded the garden where the children played among a riot of flowering shrubs. All around were grand villas built by other prosperous Indian merchants, many Gujaratis but also Punjabis and Bengalis. Bapuji's best friend, Shamjibhai Parekh, had a villa nearby, where his wife and five children lived. My father and Shamjibhai's son Rasik were great boyhood pals, running in and out of each others homes, eating indifferently in one or the other, attending the Anglo-Vernacular Gujarati School together. Once, when Shamjibhai had to return to India on some business, young Rasik stayed with Bapuji and Motiba for several months. In turn, Bapuji stayed with the Parekhs whenever Motiba and the children went to India on one of their extended holidays. In the afternoons, Motiba got together with the other Gujarati women in Bauktaw for tea and ruthless games of Parcheesi. The Jain ladies in the community were particularly close, sharing preparations for religious holidays, visits to the temple in town, details of gossip from the community back in Kathiawar.

When the Burmese government expelled what was left of the Indian community in Burma in 1964, it gave every villa in Bauktaw belonging to an Indian family, including the Kamdar and the Parekh homes, to a Burmese family. The Anglo-Vernacular Gujarati School where my father studied has been converted into administrative offices for the Burmese military. The State Bank of India building on Mogul Street no longer houses that bank, though its name remains emblazoned across the stately exterior. A Burmese family now lives in the room that was Bapuji's office across the street. They've artfully divided the long narrow flat into a sleeping loft and a living area, giving pride of place to a new Mitsubishi twenty-seven-inch television. Outside the entry door, one can just make out from behind the rows of electrical wire casings snaking up the wall in the stairwell the tantalizing words ". . . Bros. & Co.," the only trace of the Khara brothers' once-thriving business. The apartment where Motiba's younger brothers Manubhai and Shashibhai lived in some grandeur until well into the 1970s has literally fallen apart, the chandeliers ripped out leaving bare patches in the plaster ceiling, strips of wood missing from the walls, partitions half gone, the floor tiles broken.

Before World War II, there were 5,000 Jain families in Rangoon—a number large enough to need a temple but small enough to settle for the top floor of a largish building in the heart of Surati Bazaar. Motiba climbed the stairs up to the temple hall hundreds if not thousands of times, steadying herself on the beautifully carved and deeply lacquered heavy teak banisters. The Rangoon Jain temple was founded in September 1899. In its heyday, the crush of people on religious holidays was so great that children clung to their mothers' hands in terror lest they become separated in the crowd. My father was one of those children. In those days, the statue of Mahavir Tirthankara seated in eternal meditation in the central altar area was richly gilded. Now, one century later, the Jain temple in Rangoon is empty. There are only five families left. They do their best but have limited means to keep the place up. Motiba never visited the temple after the family's flight from Burma in 1942. Yet, she would have resisted feelings of attachment for this place that once meant so much to her. She would have found the fleeting history of Rangoon's Jain temple ironic proof of one of the central tenets of her Jain beliefs: the transitory nature of existence.

* * *

The beginning of the end of it all for Indians in Burma came quite abruptly in Rangoon on the morning of December 23, 1941,[6] when, out of an azure sky, a perfectly symmetrical formation of Japanese warplanes let rain a hail of bombs onto a totally unprepared civilian population. No one had any idea what was happening. People came out of their homes and shops to ogle and point at the glittering aircraft high in the sky. With their faces still gazing upward in wonder, they were blasted to smithereens.

The bombing was directed at the commercial center of the city, in other words, at the heart of Surati Bazaar. Most of the casualties were ethnic Indians. Though the British command viewed Burma as an administrative backwater of little importance, and therefore an unlikely target for the Japanese, they had, as a precaution, sent many of their women and children up to the mountain retreat of Maymyo. They did not warn the other residents of Rangoon of any danger, not wishing to alarm the local population. It was important that Indian civilians remain at their desks and on the docks as long as possible: without them, the city would cease to function. As a result, there were no bomb shelters, no procedure for clearing away the dead or ministering to the thousands of wounded, no rational plan for evacuating the city or repatriating to India over a million people potentially stranded in enemy territory. After the Japanese warplanes departed on that fateful day, mangled bodies and severed limbs lay pell-mell on the streets, the blood of the victims shimmering under the bright sun. By nightfall, dogs were feasting on the corpses left uncollected on the deserted city streets. A cemetery worker named Maung Pu Gale reported to the local newspaper that he buried 5,000 bodies in the days after the bombing of Rangoon.[7]

People began leaving immediately. Many of the Burmese in Rangoon simply returned to their native towns and villages. The Indians had much farther to go. And no easy way to get there.

Before the bombing, Bapuji's plan had been to wait out the war in Rangoon. He had set about stocking the villa in Bauktaw with provisions to last at least a year, filling huge tin containers with cooking oil, rice, wheat flour, dried beans and lentils, sugar, salt, and spices. The war in Europe seemed to him, as it did to many others, a very distant affair. Of course, many were aware that there was fighting between the British and Japanese navies in the waters of nearby Malaysia and Singapore, but they had great faith in the ability of the British army to protect them. Moreover, they believed the Japanese army to be some distance away, laboriously making its way to Rangoon over land. My grandparents were so sure of their security that Motiba and the children, including the new baby Dilip, born at Pushpamasi's wedding in Amreli in December 1940, returned to Rangoon from Kathiawar in the summer of 1941. But everything changed on December 23. After the bombing of Rangoon, there could be little doubt of the danger they were in. By February 1942, Motiba and the children were on their way back to India. They were among the lucky few to evacuate Burma by sea, a means of escape reserved for people who had the money to pay their passage. No steerage passengers were allowed. Of the over 500,000 Indians who fled Burma in the first half of 1942, only 70,000 got out that way. Four thousand were evacuated by plane. The rest walked. Even for privileged Indians, the sudden departure from Burma was a traumatic one. It haunts them to this day. Many never got over how unexpectedly they had to leave, how little they were allowed to take with them, how impossible it became ever to return. Most of them lost everything they owned. Children had to abandon their playthings, families their homes and all their possessions. "They only allowed us to take one suitcase per family onto the boat," remembers my aunt Ramaben Parekh.

People were absolutely crammed together on vessels that pitched and rolled. Who knew when a Japanese naval ship might appear to torpedo the lot into the sea? With a fourteen-month-old baby, a three-year-old, and a ten-year-old, it was a harrowing journey for Motiba, whose husband, like many other men, had decided to stay behind for as long as he could, hoping to save something of his business and his property. Motiba had no milk for her children. Thanks to the kindness of other passengers, she was able to procure some rice flour to dissolve in water and give to baby Dilip to keep him quiet. After they arrived in Calcutta, they had to make their way over the entire width of the Indian subcontinent by trains filled to bursting with refugees. My father, who remembers some of the journey, says that despite the climate of fear and the crush of crowds, people acted generously toward his young mother, helping Motiba hoist herself and the three children up into the crowded train compartments, squeezing themselves improbably to create enough space for a small suitcase, three little kids, and one tired woman.

Few realized that their hasty departure would be a permanent one. The less well off, some of whom had lived in Burma for several generations, really knew no other home. Most were acutely aware of where they came from in India, but having never seen the village or the town their ancestor had left, had to set off for a "home" they'd never known. Naturally, they assumed that as soon as the war was over, they would return to Burma. The business class was used to traveling to and fro between Burma and India, used to locking up their houses or leaving them in the care of a relative or the household help while they went off for a couple of months' holiday in India. Surely, as soon as the war was over, they'd move back, dust off the furniture, clean and polish the *thalis*. But life for Indians in Burma would never again be as it had been.

Bapuji stayed on in Rangoon for several weeks after Motiba fled with the children. Finally, he realized that he too had to escape. He left on one of the last boats to make it from Rangoon to Calcutta. There was no time to get any of his assets out of Burma to safety in India. When he arrived in India, he discovered that his business partner and dear friend, Shamjibhai Parekh, was in the same situation. He too had left everything he owned behind. Shamjibhai was keen to go back to Burma and try to salvage whatever he could. Without any of his Burmese assets, he'd have to start over from scratch, and his family would be at risk of considerable hardship. Ignoring the pleadings of his wife, Shamjibhai set off on a return journey, traveling by train and then by road transport as far as Chittagong. At that point, the determination that had brought him all the way across India failed him. He decided that, come what may, he could not risk anything happening to him in war-torn Burma: his wife would become a widow, his five children destitute orphans. He went back to Bombay. When my grandfather heard the story, he told Shamjibhai, "I will go for you, and get out what I can." So it was that Bapuji, himself the father of three sons, having only just safely escaped the bombardment of Rangoon, returned to Burma. Legend has it that he was the only paying passenger on the boat he took from Calcutta to Akyab. The person who sold him his ticket tried to talk him out of going. During the crossing, the captain of the steamer quipped, "I hope you have some warm clothes." "Why?" asked Bapuji, "The warm season is just beginning and it is never cold in Rangoon." "No, but it can get mighty cold in Tokyo!" replied the captain. Bapuji was determined to help his friend, but once in Burma he realized that he would never make it into Rangoon, and if he did, had little chance of making it back out alive. He was able to get his hands on some inventory Shamjibhai had in Akyab and had it shipped safely back to Calcutta.

In another stroke of luck, some of the Parekhs' cash had made it out of the country thanks to the acumen of their bank, the First

National City Bank of New York, now known as Citibank. The Parekhs had outlets for their imported goods all over Burma. They sold textiles, chocolates, clocks, small tools, anything they could bring into the country. Farmers in the rural areas paid for their merchandise in gold, usually in the form of jewelry. The Parekhs collected the gold and brought it to Rangoon, where they deposited it with their bank. When Citibank pulled out of Burma in the early days of the war, it brought 3,000 *tolas* of the Parekhs' gold out of Burma and deposited it into its Calcutta branch. On the basis of what my grandfather and Citibank were able to get out of Burma for them, the Parekhs' fortune was saved. They eventually built their business into a multiarmed family empire in Bombay, becoming one of the more prosperous families in that great city.

Every family has its own archive of dramatic tales from World War II. These stories are from ours. They are stories of an exodus from a promised land, and none is more painfully difficult to imagine than that of Motiba's father Muljibhai's harrowing journey out of Burma by foot. Perhaps because the Kharas' business interests in Burma were so substantial by 1942, Muljibhai Khara was the last family member to leave. By this time, he and his two brothers owned villas, apartments, business offices, and storefronts all over Burma, from Akyab, where they had started out; to Rangoon, where they'd shifted their headquarters; to outlets in many outlying areas. It couldn't have been easy to leave all this to the kind mercies of the Japanese and the desperation of the Burmese and Indians left behind.

Muljibhai Khara left Rangoon in April 1942 on a boat to Mandalay, traveling up the Irrawaddy River. The boat was packed with refugees fleeing the capital and rode low in the great muddy currents. From Mandalay, Muljibhai walked all the way to Manipur, India. It took him ten days. He traveled with a group of people of all ages. Men, women, the elderly, children, and babies. Some had managed to drag a trunkful of belongings with them as far as Mandalay. This was possible when traveling by boat, but from Mandalay everyone had to walk. The trunks and all the treasures they contained were quickly discarded along the way. People continued with just what they could carry, and what they could carry diminished with each passing mile. They trudged forward on dirt roads that were at some points no more than vague tracks through the infinite jungle. For days at a time, they could not be sure if they were even going in the right direction. April is one of the hottest months of the year. During the daytime, it is over ninety degrees, the humidity near 100 percent. They traveled through dense jungle, full of venomous snakes, poisonous spiders, voracious mosquitoes. An old lady collapsed. She was still alive, but they left her where she fell. They had to keep walking; to lose the group was a potential death sentence for any who tarried. They marched on, crossing the Irrawaddy valley first, then the Chindwin River, then the Khankhadaung and finally the Mowdok Taung mountains, traversing the land of the Chin people. The Indians making the trek were urban people, unused to physical exertion, unskilled at surviving in the jungle. All they had to keep them going was terror behind them and the hope of home ahead. As they wound upward into the hills, reaching elevations in the passes of 5,000 and even 8,000 feet, the sweltering heat of the day gave way to frigid temperatures at night for which the refugees were totally unprepared: they had no shawls, no blankets, no shelter. Their meager supply of food ran out. There was no clean drinking water, sometimes no water at all. The children began to sicken.

Along the way, the flood of refugees pooled in exhausted, improvised camps. With no adequate sanitation, these tropical waysides became fetid fields of muck, breeding grounds for cholera, smallpox, malaria, and dysentery. At the first sign of diarrhea, children were abandoned so the contagion wouldn't spread. They were thrown into the rivers to drown so their death would be fast and they wouldn't linger, frightened and alone, the prey of animals that emerged from the dense jungle at night to feed on the dead and dying. For Indians, family is everything, filial duty a sacrament, devotion to children a consuming joy. The headlong flight out of Burma wore people down to a point where they did the unimaginable—abandon along the trail the mother who'd so tenderly raised them, toss the small child clinging to its weary parents in terror into the river—in order to survive.

During the last weeks of the exodus, at the final refugee camp in Tamu, on the Burmese-Indian border and just a few miles from Imphal, India, and safety, the pace of evacuation, rather tardily organized by the British, became frantic. Families were separated, the weakest left behind in the chaos of shouting truck drivers and the mass of desperate humanity madly scrambling for a place on one of the last vehicles out. By this time, 70 to 80 percent of the refugees were ill. They were hungry, their possessions reduced to the clothes on their backs—and some had even lost these. "A mob without discipline of any sort, with a complete absence of morale,"[8] according to a Brigadier Short, a senior British medical officer on the border. "Complete exhaustion, physical and mental, with disease superimposed, is the usual picture . . . all social sense is lost . . . they suffer from bad nightmares and their delirium is a babble of rivers and crossings, of mud and corpses."[9]

Muljibhai Khara, my great-grandfather, was there. He saw all this, survived it, and told the story of what he saw to his children, who told it to their descendants, who told it to me. In all, approximately 450,000 Indian men, women, and children made the trek from Burma overland to India. Between 50,000 and 100,000 perished in the attempt. Fewer than half the refugees who made it to India ever returned to Burma. Those who did return were soon forced to leave again, whatever properties they had recovered after the war stripped from them one final time.

* * *

After the exodus from Burma, one of Motiba's brothers, Mangalji, ended up in Delhi. He had a friend who got him a contract there to repair the Lal Quila, the great imperial Mughal Red Fort. As soon as he'd gotten himself and his family settled in the pleasant neighborhood of Karol Bagh, he sent a postcard to the British viceroy at his headquarters in Simla, telling him that he'd just come overland from Burma and had information on the location of Japanese bases there. His friends thought he was mad. The viceroy was much too exalted a personage to acknowledge correspondence from a minor Indian businessman who'd just lost his entire fortune in Burma. His friends were wrong. He received a visit a week later from a general who'd been sent personally by the viceroy to fetch him. Mangalji-mama was promptly flown to Simla, where he met the viceroy and shared with him all he knew. In return, he received a businessman's dream: a certificate from the viceroy of India entitling Mr. M. M. Khara first preference for military contracts. Needless to say, he was able to parlay this certificate into a nice fortune during the last years of the war.

Mangaljimama returned to Burma in 1947. One of his old school chums, a Burmese named U Nu, had become the head of the government that took over independent Burma after the assassination of Bogyoke Aung San in July 1947. U Nu made Mangaljimama Burma's commercial representative in Australia: "You are a Burmese, born and raised here. Now do something for Burma." Alas, the early days of Burma's independence when a Burmese leader could tell an ethnic Indian, "You are a Burmese" were short-lived.

Throughout the 1950s, Burma struggled to define a new national and economic identity. The Indian merchants who had returned after the war and started up their businesses again lived their lives much as they had before the war. They kept a low profile, stuck to business, kept out of politics. Bapuji was one of these. He returned to Rangoon after the war, salvaging what he could and doggedly carrying on his business. The family did not join him this time, however. The children were older and were settled in school back in India. Bapuji had managed to build a big house in Jetpur just before the war with some of the money he'd made in Burma, furnishing it with solid teak furniture custom-made to his specifications in Rangoon and then shipped to Kathiawar. So, the family stayed in Jetpur, the children coming for visits, such as my young aunts' fairy-tale Burmese sojourn in 1956. I have the Western Union telegrams Bapuji sent from Rangoon "via RCA" to my parents in Seattle, Washington, in the late 1950s, one on the occasion of my birth on November 8, 1957 ("WISHING MANY HAPPY RETURNS ANXIOUS UMAS HEALTH HOPE BOTH PROGRESSING REGARDS PRABHUDAS"), and one a year later for my first birthday ("GREETINGS WISHING NANIMIRA VERY MANY GAY HAPPY BIRTHDAY RETURNS AND JOYOUS DIPAVALI AND HAPPY NEW YEAR TO YOU ALL PRABHUDAS"). He sent these from the Post and Telegraph Office on the Strand, just a couple of blocks away from his office on Mogul Street.

Year by year, however, things became more and more difficult. Restrictions on business practices were piled on all non-Burmese persons. It became illegal for Indians to conduct almost any business at all. For one thing, they could not legally hold business licenses. The usual practice was to find a Burmese "partner" in whose name the license could be procured.

Bapuji himself suffered a terrible blow when an acquaintance of his, a Ratilal Manji, who was known in Rangoon in those days as the "King of Cotton," was charged by the government with doing some illegal business. In the course of searching his office, government agents found Bapuji's name in one of Manji's date books. Manji was already cooling his heels in a Rangoon jail, and Bapuji was in imminent danger of suffering the same fate. One day as he was taking his morning constitutional along the Rangoon River, Bapuji paused near the jetties and, looking up, "heard" the name of a Bengali lawyer. He believed it was a message from God. He immediately got in touch with the lawyer, who agreed to take on his case, little suspecting at the time that he was embarking on a legal battle that would last for years.

In the end, many years and many rupees later, Bapuji was convicted of illegal business practices, including smuggling. Then a miracle occurred. In the middle of Bapuji's lawyer's speech proclaiming his client's innocence and stating his intention to appeal the case to a higher court, the presiding judge suddenly interrupted. With no explanation, the judge announced that he was dismissing the charges. But Bapuji was still in real danger. His friends entreated him to leave the country immediately. Reluctantly, Bapuji left that very night, taking nothing more than a couple of thousand rupees and the clothes on his back. He made his way to the house in Jetpur. It was the summer of 1959. Bapuji fully intended to return to Burma, as he had done twice before, once in the early months of the war and once more when the war was over, but he never was able to go back. In 1962, General Ne Win seized power in a military coup that marked the definitive end for those Indians still in Burma.

Ne Win announced a new plan for the nation dubbed "the Burmese Path to Socialism." A massive campaign of nationalization down to the level of small retail shops ensued. Non-Burmese, mostly Indians and Chinese, were systematically dispossessed of everything they owned. The Burmese government did not pay compensation for expropriated businesses and properties. Almost no Indian businessman escaped, and Bapuji was no exception.

Though he and his family were safely out of Burma, all of his properties, inventory, deposits in Rangoon banks of cash and jewelry, and other assets were seized in his absence. My Bharatiphaiba, the same aunt who remembers picking out twinkling gems on a long-ago Rangoon afternoon, recalls that Bapuji was helping her with her math homework at their home in India when a man came to the door with a telegram. Bapuji got up, read the telegram, then very calmly came back to the table where they were sitting and said, "Now I will be able to spend a lot more time with you." That's all. That was the only sign he gave that he'd just lost everything he owned in Burma.

By May 1964, the government of India had identified over 300,000 recent refugees from Burma. With their homes and businesses taken from them, most Indians had no option but to leave. On departure, the humiliation continued. All valuables were confiscated: jewelry, of course; watches; cameras; radios; banknotes of more than fifty rupees. Women and men alike were thoroughly searched. There are stories that the determination of the Burmese authorities was so great that no valuables should leave Burma in the possession of Indians that gold teeth were extracted at dockside before people were allowed to board.

Later Bapuji did try to get his assets back, even appealing to India's prime minister, Jawaharlal Nehru, directly. After all, Bapuji had been a stalwart supporter of India's freedom struggle, first as a young Gandhian and later by giving money to the Congress Party. He had been part of the circle of successful businessmen who hosted Nehru and his daughter Indira when they visited Rangoon in 1937. He reminded Nehru of these things. But the pandit turned prime minister had other matters on his mind. Nehru said that the government of India would be willing to help Bapuji recover his assets in Burma, but only on the condition that it keep 80 percent of whatever was recovered. Bapuji is reported to have told Nehru to go to hell, or words to that effect, saying, "I earned that money with my own sweat, and I would rather give it to the people of Burma, where I made it, then pay it all in taxes to the government of India, which did nothing to help me in Burma."

For many years, Bapuji pursued every avenue he could think of to recover his Burmese assets. He had a great sense of having been betrayed by the very Indian leaders he'd supported all his life. Quite futilely, he published letters of grievance against the government in Indian newspapers. He never took up business again, and the family lived off of remittances sent to India by my father, who by this time was in America, and, eventually, by my father's younger brother Vinayak, always called by his nickname, Vinoo.

* * *

For more than thirty years, from 1962 to the mid-1990s, Indians were personae non grata in Burma. Now Burma's cash-strapped dictatorship is prepared to offer former Indian residents of Burma hassle-free entry into the country. The military junta has even offered to return ownership of certain nationalized industries and properties to their former Indian owners. But most Indians who were settled in Burma before World War II are afraid to go back, even for a visit. The manner of their exit from Burma was too bru-

tal, their memories too awful for them to contemplate even a fort-
night's return. Besides, in thirty-odd years, many of them have
become too rich and too free—in America, in Australia, in Europe,
or back in India—to think about returning to a land where they
would be stripped upon entry of every human right they've come
to take for granted in their new homes.

But they have never forgotten Burma. Nearly sixty years after
he left as a youth of seventeen, my uncle Himmat Khara was able
to recall the rational grid of colonial Rangoon vividly, sketching a
map of the entire central city from memory. He remembered the
different locations of the Khara brothers' offices and the places
where the family had lived. On the neat grid of his map, Himmatmama carefully marked each address in the blue ink of a fountain
pen taken from his breast pocket.

Himmatmama's map is accurate.

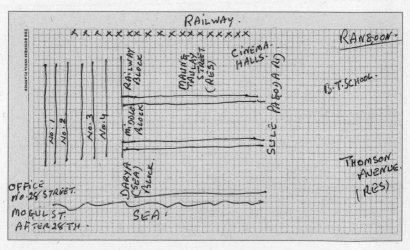

Himmatmama's map of Rangoon.

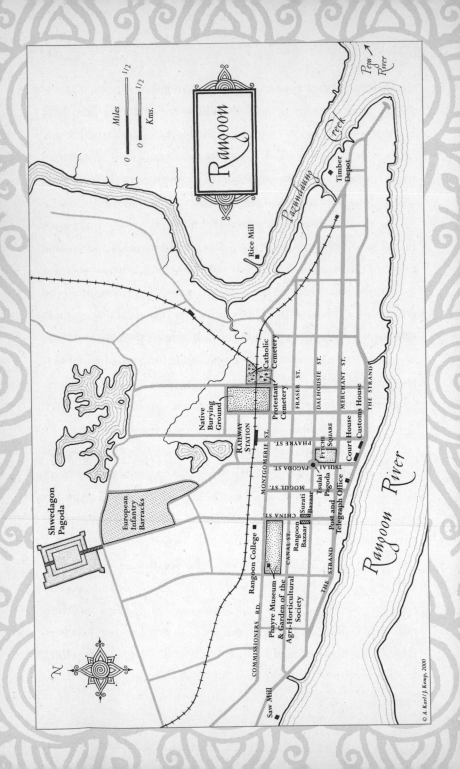

The layout of Rangoon has not changed in sixty years. But the names of all the streets have: Dalhousie Street is now Mahabandoola Street. Phayre Street is now Pansodan Street. Sparks Street has become Bo Aung Kyaw Street. The city itself has been renamed Yangon, the Burmese name for Rangoon, meaning—ironically given the oppressive political situation—"end of strife." These changes are symbolically important to Burma's nationalist project but seem superficial to the life of the capital: the neat grid of the colonial city, the many parks, the graceful architecture are all as they were in the 1930s. Economic and political isolation have given Rangoon/Yangon the uncanny air of a city that time forgot. Only the Japanese billboards (Fujitsu, Honda, Konica, Fuji, Toyota), the recent-model Japanese cars, and the illegal but ubiquitous television satellite dishes beaming Hindi soap operas from ZeeTV are there to remind one that more than half a century has passed since the heyday of colonial Rangoon.

Old habits die hard, and many people who grew up in Rangoon before the war continue to call the streets by their original British names. Though China Street has been rechristened Konzaydan Street and Mogul Street is now called Shwe Bon Tha Street, these two avenues still define the commercial center of the city. The Chinese still dominate "China City" along the old China Street, and the Indians are still concentrated in Surati Bazaar. Here the *paanwalas* set up their trays on paved sidewalks next to vendors squatting near vats of flavored agar jelly, pots of steaming noodles, bowls of river snails, and plates of fruit. There is still a sweet shop selling fresh *barfis* near one of the remaining Hindu temples, and thousands of Indian Muslims flock to the neighborhood's beautiful mosques, one on each block along the former Mogul Street.

Bauktaw remains a neighborhood of broad streets lined with huge private bungalows surrounded by walled gardens. But none of these houses are owned by the Indians who built them. A Burmese family has now lived for more than thirty years in the home that once belonged to Shamjibhai Parekh, a home my father knew well and where my grandfather used to stay for months on end whenever Motiba was in India on one of her regular home visits. The lady of the house told me, "This house belonged to the Parekhs. Shamjibhai Parekh. Very good people. They gave us everything, even the furniture. It is all here. Just look around. And the house has not changed at all. We have kept it exactly as it was. We never had any money to change anything in the house." The house stank of urine from the toilet at the back, and the air hung motionless around an empty teak settee in the living room where people near and dear to me once sat and talked. I am the only person from our community to visit the house in nearly four decades.

On the evening I visited Bauktaw, the electricity had been cut, plunging the entire neighborhood into pitch blackness. My hosts and I picked our way by flashlight along the lanes, stopping to inquire of people here and there whether they knew which house had belonged to Prabhudas Kamdar. To my great dismay, I could not discover my grandfather's house in the impenetrable darkness. Rasik Parekh believes the house may have been further out, in a suburb known as Gaushala. My grandfather always said that it was taken over during the war by the Japanese military command, and houses in Gaushala were used during the war by both the Japanese and the Indian Nationalist armies. On the other hand, my father remembers living in the same lane as the Parekhs. Memory is a slippery thing. How can I grasp it? The only people still alive who knew these places were mere children when they lived in Rangoon.

One of the last Indians now living in this once-posh enclave is a Punjabi gentleman in his seventies. A tall man of erect bearing who speaks perfect English, he was an administrative officer in the ordnance depot of the British Indian Army, and survived countless hardships and horrors during the war. He was with the first unit to come into occupied Burma and saw hand-to-hand combat with Japanese troops. He walked out of Burma with his family in the great land exodus of April 1942. They left home with eighty-four trunks and a bullock cart, and arrived in India with only the clothes on their backs. One of their family members became ill, and they fell behind the group they were traveling with. When they finally reached the refugee camp at Imphal, they found everyone there, including the people in their own group who'd gone ahead, dead: the Japanese had bombed the camp just hours before they got there. At the end of the war, he and his family thought life would return to normal, and they went home to Rangoon. When other Indians, those who, like him, had come back, began to leave again, he stayed on, blind to the irreversible changes about to take place.

"From landlords, we became tenants," he explained. "It happened overnight. All these villas you see here in Bauktaw, they all belonged to Indians. Our family owned several of them, as well as buildings full of flats in town. We were so rich, I had no memory of

ever not having as much money as I wanted, so it never occurred
to me that it was possible to lose it all. I was unprepared. And
before I realized it, it was too late. We couldn't leave, as so many
others had done, and we had to give everything away. We had to just
sign it over, just like that." This man, his wife, his son and daughter-in-law, and several grandchildren now live in a single narrow
room with a small kitchenette and toilet at the rear. The grand villas his family once owned are all around them. They must walk past
them every day. The man's attitude is, of necessity perhaps, philo-
sophical. "I am a Freemason. What we learned in the lodges, I have
seen. One must not regret what one has lost."

The Bauktaw Hindu temple is still there. It is now nearly abandoned, though a few families piously maintain it as best they can.
On the evening I visited, the building was closed and locked. A
female caretaker emerged to open the gate, her hair covered with
a hennalike paste. Her scrawny child, hair similarly plastered, ran
along behind us. They were clearly not expecting any visitors, and
had been interrupted at their evening toilet.

In the lanes around Surati Bazaar, there are still a lot of Tamils,
descendants, for the most part, of the laborers brought over by the
British to work on the docks. Many of them frequent the large
Hindu temple in the Surati Bazaar area. Originally dedicated to
Shiva, the temple boasts many images of the god with his entwined
locks of cobras, his buxom consort Parvati, their loving son Ganesh,
the faithful bull Nandi. The feel of cool, time-worn marble under
bare feet; the odor of incense; the presence of a couple of smiling
women preparing banana leaves for the distribution of *prasaad,*

everything is as it is and should be in any Hindu temple in India. But inside the temple, a whole section of wall is given over to the worship of the sage Sai Baba, and to the left of the principal image of Shiva at the temple's back wall is a huge diorama depicting Burmese Buddhist monks greeting a serenely seated Gautama Buddha.

There are also a few members of the merchant class left, people who, for one reason or another couldn't or didn't want to leave. I have a distant relative who lived on in Rangoon until the mid-1970s. Based in Bangkok, Thailand, he still comes back for short stays in a flat he has somehow managed to hang onto. In his apartment, an old, ornate teak living room set—two armchairs, a sofa, a glass-topped coffee table—is pushed against the periphery of the room so everyone can sit comfortably on the floor, and— rarity of rarities—a huge air conditioner both chills the air and protects the interior from any penetration by the outside world.

He knew Motiba's younger brothers Manu and Shashikant well. They were all best buddies throughout the difficult years of the 1960s and 1970s. "I take life easy," he tells me. An evident bachelor, he has sufficient means to move about where and when he pleases, packing up a few items of clothing and hopping on a plane or a boat or a train for any destination in Asia at a moment's notice. "My friends are always trying to get me to move to America or Europe, but I tell them, 'I am an Asian. I don't want to live outside of Asia. I don't wish to live in the White man's world.'" "I take life easy," he continues, "because we have lived through hell, and only when you have lived through hell can you realize when you are living in heaven." I press him to describe what he means by living through hell. "Well, we never knew each morning when we woke up what would happen that day. People were being denounced right and left. They could just come and take you away and take everything away from you. There was, what do you call it, 'summary justice.' That was it. No recourse. But we had a hell of a good time during that period. We would get together at each other's places and just enjoy the life, just eat, talk, laugh. Our life during that bad time was, in a way, very sweet because we had each other."

The experience of "living through hell together" has produced one of the closest communities of religiously diverse South Asians in the world. While I was in Rangoon, the task of helping me find my way around what was left of the Gujarati community there was shared by a network of friends of diverse faiths. My Muslim hosts introduced me to one of the last survivors of Rangoon's Jain community. It is wonderfully ironic, given the prejudices against Muslims that unfortunately persist among some of my relatives, that at both ends of the century, my Jain family was helped in Burma by the kindness of Muslims. Young Premchandbhai Khara was taken in and given a job by a Kathiawari Muslim merchant in Akyab. One hundred years later, I am taken in and offered all manner of assistance by a Muslim family in Rangoon. The family who helped me did so at considerable risk from a government that does not look kindly on fraternization between Burmese and foreigners, especially those holding U.S. passports. Their generosity was humbling.

The Jain gentleman told me, "Any vegetarian who may come to this city, everyone knows, they can just come to my house and they will be fed. Just give me one hour's notice, and I will accommodate anyone." He lives in the "Middle Block" of the former Mogul Street with his wife and two children in a tiny railroad flat. There is almost no furniture, just an old Art Deco–style teak desk, a glass-doored cabinet in which a modest collection of unremarkable china and glassware is as much stored as displayed, a couple of straight-backed chairs, and a Toshiba television set hooked up to the neighbor's illegal satellite receiver dish to catch Indian programming. They've built into the long rectangular space a private bedroom, just big enough for a double mattress, a dresser, a couple of wardrobes. Next to the tiny kitchen in the back is a toilet. One washes one's hands in a small sink next to the door to the toilet in the kitchen. By American standards, they are living very poorly indeed, yet these are educated people, clearly intelligent and possessing a high degree of social grace and a higher degree of generosity. They are a mixed couple: she is a Hindu. He explained that his parents were committed to the idea that he, their only son, would marry a Jain, but due to the near-total lack of eligible Jain girls in Rangoon when he came of marriageable age, a compromise was finally accepted. He and his wife appeared very happy as a couple. She is lovely, a devoted mother and a warm and welcoming hostess.

Though I'd already eaten, I couldn't refuse the meal they offered me in their home. Actually, I was comforted by the familiar Gujarati vegetarian fare: thin, tender *chapatis* and "drumstick" curry (named for a fibrous, celery-like vegetable, not severed chicken legs), fresh *lassau* (garlic pickle). They fed me at a small table in the kitchen.

My Jain host was born in Rangoon. He has never been to India, never even been out of Burma. He told me he was afraid to go to India, afraid that if he met someone who claimed to be a relative, he'd have no way of knowing whether or not the person really was a relative or was only a con man out to trick him. He was not happy that his children have to go to a nationalized school where the medium of instruction is Burmese. His older child, a daughter, receives private "tuitions" in English after school. He and his wife speak Gujarati at home, so the children will learn their "mother" tongue, though they confess that their Gujarati has become "all mixed up," shot through with Urdu and Burmese, after living in Rangoon for so many generations.

The women and paterfamilias from my Muslim host family accompanied me to dinner at the home of another of the five Jain families in Rangoon. They claimed to like the strictly vegetarian Gujarati *thali* of *puris,* vegetables, the yogurt-based soup called *khadi,* and rice. At dinner, the women talked easily in a mishmash of Gujarati, Burmese, and Hindi/Urdu. But their appearances were strikingly different. Whereas the women in my host family looked typically Burmese in their *longyi,* long glossy hair, and Southeast Asian features, the Jain women looked absolutely Indian dressed in *saris* with coordinated jewelry. On another day, I was invited for tea at the home of a pure Surati Muslim family. My first Jain host escorted me there. In deference to him, perhaps, we were served only vegetarian pastries and fresh fruit with small cups of strong, sweet tea. The members of this family have the regal features of the Mughal imperial court of Bahadur Shah Zafar. The women wear *salwaar kameez* in typical north Indian or Pakistani fashion, and always put on a head scarf and a black robe over their clothes when they go out in public.

In Rangoon, I found myself for the first time in my life—outside the rarified circles of the Westernized intellectual elite of New York, New Delhi, or Bombay—in a world in which Hindus, Jains, and Muslims mix comfortably and even affectionately in each other's homes, over meals no less. In Gujarat, this kind of easy mixing in people's homes would be quite extraordinary. Though Hindus and Jains and Muslims may be good friends in public domains, such as school or work, it would be unusual for them to get together in the private sphere of the home. Hindu and Jain proscriptions regarding food, especially food prepared by the wrong caste of person or nonvegetarian food, make it extremely difficult for the religiously observant to casually accept or extend dinner invitations. Then there is the matter of protecting the family's women, carefully sheltered at home, from exposure to people "not in our community." I found none of that in Rangoon. And as people brought out their wedding albums and photographs of important community events, it became clear these close relationships across religious lines went back many years.

Perhaps because of Burma's isolation from the rest of the world, the "identity" politics that rage in India (and elsewhere) seemed entirely absent among Indians there. There was an easy camaraderie between Gujarati Jains, Hindus, and Muslims. The Gujarati merchant community in Rangoon is tiny compared to what it once was. Everyone knows everyone else. They have lived

and struggled through the same terrible difficulties: war, threatened expulsion, expropriation of property, summary arrest, torture, and even the ever-present possibility of execution. If they
have survived, it is by trusting each other.

Yet it was extraordinary that these people welcomed me, an
American who looks White and speaks little Gujarati, as if I were a
long-lost member of this close-knit group. Purely on the basis of
my indisputably Gujarati name; my relationship to the Khara family, some members of which were known to some of the people I
met; and an appreciation of my interest in the history of the community in Burma, I was treated with the utmost generosity and
affection by one and all. I was a rare emissary of a piece of the community that had gotten away and they were what was left of the
piece left behind, and so my entire stay had the feeling of a reunion
among long-lost family members, though I was related to none of
them by even one drop of blood.

* * *

The tactics used by Burma's military regime have not become
kinder or gentler with the passing decades. The government sur-
vives only by the systematic repression of the people, and by the
exploitation of lucrative cash crops, such as opium, and the selling
off of the country's vast teak forests and valuable reserves of petroleum and natural gas. Shortly after my safe return from Burma, the
person with whose family I'd stayed, who now lives in the United
States as a political refugee, called me. He raged, in a quiet and
deeply sad sort of way, at his impotence here to do anything about

the plight of his people. I had brought him photos of his family: his sweet-natured wife, who'd personally massaged my tummy and legs when I became ill with a bout of severe gastrointestinal upset; his little son whom he hadn't seen since the child was a baby; his teenage daughter growing up fast; his eldest son, already almost a man, whose eyes glistened with tears when I presented him with the small gift his father had sent from America. The family is not allowed to leave the country. As one who has fought long and visibly for a return to democracy in Burma, their father dares not return: torture, prison, even death await him.

In contrast, the air-conditioned business offices of the last pillar of the ethnic Indian merchant community in Rangoon sits right off the Strand. Here is a man who has clearly survived—and prospered—by cozying up to Burma's military regime. In the foyer of the building, there are a lot of posters for engines and other products manufactured by the Indian company Kirloskar and a selection of personal care products from the American firm of Procter & Gamble. "Yes, yes. We are agents for both companies," he confirmed proudly. He seemed vaguely hurt that the world outside Burma doesn't understand the advantages the current regime has brought to the country. "You see," he boasted, "we have no crime in Rangoon. You, a woman alone, could walk down the streets here anytime and nothing would happen to you. The government has taken care of that problem for us. When they came to power, they had the lists of people who were troublemakers. They just went around and picked these people up. They gave their families a couple of years to cool off, then they told them these people had been disposed of. Actually, they'd been shot right away. And now we have no crime in Myanmar."

* * *

I went to Burma with a great deal of trepidation. Many of my relatives warned me not to go. Those who were born there or who'd lived there before the war were worried I'd get in trouble the moment I entered the country, for no other reason than that I bear a surname the dictatorship might recognize as belonging to an expelled Indian family. Advocates of democracy in Burma and supporters of Aung San Suu Kyi—the leader of the country's democratic opposition—objected to my going on moral grounds: Suu Kyi has said that foreigners should not visit Myanmar. It only serves to bring money and lend support to a regime that freely indulges in forced labor, forced military conscription, and a willingness to violate almost every right enumerated in the United Nations' Declaration of Human Rights. The bloody massacres of 1988, in which the Burmese military regime mowed down hundreds of unarmed civilian protesters, many of them teenagers and even children, remain fresh in everyone's mind. The United States has imposed sanctions on Myanmar and regularly makes known its disapproval of the current regime through official protests, boycotts of official meetings held there, and the extension of aid and comfort to democracy activists. Many believe that no personal motivation should be allowed to overwhelm a moral obligation to snub the country, and thereby, its evil leaders.

Despite these warnings, I decided I had to go. I had to see this mythic place where my family had lived for decades, where my father was born, where we'd made our fortune—before losing it. Burma exerted the same pull over my imagination that it must have on that of Motiba's uncle, the young Premchandbhai, when he sold his mother's *kaambis* and set off for Burma to seek his fortune. The only essential difference being that nineteen-year-old Premchandbhai set off for Burma at the dawn of a new century in search of his future, whereas I, at the close of that same century, was in search of my past. Instead of arriving by steamship from Calcutta, as my ancestor did in 1900, I came to Burma by regular jet service from Singapore. It was a short flight. One of the world's pariah states is only a couple of hours away from the material splendor of Singapore's Changi Airport-cum-shopping mall.

What a paradise Burma must have seemed to my ancestors, a land of limitless opportunity and easy living. Burma was my family's first America. *Suvarnabhumi,* in Sanskrit; *Sonapranta,* in Pali; Burma: the golden land. A veritable horn of plenty stretching out into the warm waters of the South China Sea, the country was once the world's leading exporter of rice. It is wound through with rivers teeming with fish. Rich paddy fields give way to vast mountains covered with teak, bulging with the finest rubies and sapphires in the world. The plains cover underground fields of petroleum waiting to be pumped to the surface and reserves of natural gas waiting to be piped to ships at the Rangoon docks. All across the land are a handsome people, smooth skinned and lithe limbed, gentle and generous. And everywhere the flash and spark of countless pagodas great and small, as if the sole purpose of any wealth is to gild layer upon layer of bright gold upon the spires reaching heavenward into the cerulean sky.

*   *   *

When I flew into Burma, it was January and the temperature was ninety-seven degrees. As I looked down, the silt-laden sea near the Burmese coast looked like melted chocolate. Along the shoreline, thousands of rivulets, like the undulating locks of a giant Medusa, disgorged a continuous load of mud from wide, wet mouths. Then, within yards of the limply lapping waves, an infinite mosaic of paddies began, their facets so exactly fitted that only the land needed to form the dikes between them was spared from cultivation. Every inch of the mirrored plain was given over to the cultivation of rice. Here and there, a flash of wondrous gold: each village had its pagoda, the gilded spires set off from the rest by an architectural base washed in purest white or palest blue. Just outside Rangoon/Yangon, paved roads appeared with a few small lorries ferrying goods in and out of the capital, a car or two, but mostly people walking. A few rode bicycles. All of them, men and women, were clad in *longyis,* the saronglike skirt worn by both sexes. Right up to the edge of the airport tarmac, water buffalos were happily immersed up to their dusty backs in deep green ponds.

At the Yangon airport, an Asian businessman was waived past the obligatory exchange of hard currency: "Oh, you have business visa, Sir. Please, you business visa don't have to pay." Wordlessly, the businessman picked up his leather bag of golf clubs and exited the immigration area. The regime has constructed many golf courses around the capital. They are convenient for entertaining the businessmen who come to visit Myanmar, most of whom are Japanese these days, what with the U.S.-led embargo, and most of whom love to golf. To make the game more interesting for his genial hosts, the businessman-golfer might propose that they set a little penalty of, say, $10,000 for each hole lost. It's funny how a businessman who usually plays a very good game can have such a run of bad luck, sometimes losing every hole in an afternoon's round of golf. His host, a high-ranking general in Myanmar's army and ruling party, feels badly taking so much of his guest's money. The least he can do is make sure that the desired contract with the desired terms is put through as quickly as possible. Or such are the tales I hear about what goes on on Myanmar's golf courses.

* * *

The last Mughal emperor, Bahadur Shah Zafar was exiled to Burma by the British. He was never allowed to return to his beloved India and died in 1896 in Rangoon. His tomb is a monument to the ache of exile, and a focus for the Indian Muslim community of Rangoon, many of the members of which trace their lineage to the emperor's exiled entourage. Bahadur Shah was an accomplished poet in that most poetic of languages, Urdu. On the wall next to his crypt, inscribed in magnificent Persian script, is a poem that laments that though once he was the ruler of all of India, now he cannot get ahold of even six feet of Indian soil in which to take his final rest.

The Suratis of Rangoon are conscious that like the last Mughal emperor of India, they too are exiles in Burma. But though they feel a genuine attachment to the Indian subcontinent and a longing for the lost grandeur of Mughal culture, most cannot or would not leave. They are too deeply rooted in Burmese soil, the land where they were born, the land where they have their businesses, their homes, and their families.

To be an exile is to endure the unstoppable pain of separation from a land to which one is forbidden to return. To be the descendant of exiles is to be even more completely severed from "home." With the passing of generations, the homeland becomes a mythic place outside real time or place, the abode of unknown ancestors, longed for, yet fundamentally unknowable. Nothing remains of the ancestors' world or, worse, faint traces, tantalizing hints, uninterpretable signs that point in vague directions as tracks half effaced in the sand that double back on themselves. The children of exiles are the trustees of a home they can never know.

The thing my family regrets about Burma is the personal loss of home and property and not the greater dispossession of the entire country from its people at the hands of a military junta. I know that however much the Indian merchant community suffered in Burma, however unfair their dispossession, almost none of them would have willingly sacrificed much to save Burma. "We are *banias,* businessmen, we don't get involved in politics. I don't think we'll have any problems." This comment came from an uncle of mine who was thinking of visiting Burma and wondered if it would be safe for him to do so. His attitude is evidence of the "rootless cosmopolitanism" of which Indians were accused in the first years of Burma's independence. It is the reason thousands of Indians were brutally expelled from Uganda during the 1970s. Yet this devotion to family, community, and moneymaking over place is what has given the Gujarati *bania* community—and other diaspora communities—its ability to survive. An ancient nomadic tribe, the Kathiawars who spawned my family were always, in the words of my father, "people from someplace else." Certainly, in the century just ended that is who we became more than at any other time in our history: people from someplace else. The wanderings my family has undertaken in the past one hundred years in pursuit of more tempting opportunities have added layers of lost homelands to our past. Kathiawar remains the land of origin, but the decades-long sojourn in Burma is layered on top of it, a second lost homeland.

A people from someplace else are ever outsiders. They can easily be resented. At the same time, their rootlessness breeds a kind of tribal loyalty. In the absence of a continuum of place, we cling to a continuum of religion, custom, language, cuisine and the recognition and sharing of these with people like us no matter where they live in the world. It is a cultural continuum that is portable. It can be moved as easily as a suitcase from Singapore to London, taken down and brought along to New York or Chicago, found in the home of a relative or community member in Nairobi or Tokyo.

The women from my host family see me off at the Yangon airport. After each good-bye, one of them reappears with yet another parting gift: a small plastic "harp of Burma"; a wooden plaque with tiny dolls in traditional costumes glued onto a map of Myanmar.

With a final wave and a heavy heart, I go through immigration. When I arrive at Singapore's sumptuous Changi Airport, I dump my things in the business-class lounge; survey the selection of finger sandwiches, fresh fruit, petit fours, chilled Evian, freshly brewed coffee, orange juice, and sodas; and collapse into a comfortable chair. Near me is a group of American businessmen from the Midwest and Texas, shaking hands, exchanging bits of information to identify themselves as bona fide members of the transnational ruling class. One has just come in from Bangkok, another from Beijing. One is headed for Frankfurt. Business is good. The golfing was great. The ultimate *banias*, I think, are these Americans. With the exception of a few truly unsavory spots—Burma, Iraq, Libya, or Sudan—the world is pretty much their oyster.

When my family was kicked out of Burma, it returned to India. Some members stayed there, but many left for a place an Indian peasant once identified for me as "London, America," the first world, the transnational world of global capital. They left to be highly trained in portable skills, to toil in the knowledge industries, to launch multinational businesses or work for multinational corporations. The international business-class lounge of any airport is as much home to me as to the captains of American business I observed in Singapore. You can plug in your laptop, turn on your cell phone, and—just like that—you're connected, but only, in fact, with people who move in the same disconnected world you do. The roots have been cut. The plant must live on air.

3

Bombay

Cala mana mumbai nagari
("Let us go my love to Bombay")

—Niranjan Bhagat, Gujarati poet

Bombay has been called a whore, a temptress, a slut. The city is a woman, enticing, betraying, extracting great sacrifice, sucking one dry. Indian speakers of Marathi, Gujarati, and Hindi call the city "Mumbai" after a local female deity, Mumbadevi, whose distinguishing characteristic is the lack of a mouth. Mumbai is now Bombay's official name. But the real propitiatory deity of the city is Lakshmi, the goddess of wealth. Bedecked in silk and jewels, standing on a lotus flower, a smile on her lips, gold coins spilling from her outstretched hand, pretty Lakshmi beckons her devotees. Glittering and glamorous, she holds out the promise of fortune but exacts cruel sacrifices from her worshipers even as she entices them. Smuggling, extortion, bribery, prostitution, bonded labor, shoot-'em-up crime bosses, and corrupt political power brokers: Bombay has welcomed them all to her moist bosom for more than 300 years.

As every British and Indian schoolchild knows, Bombay was a dowry gift. The territory around what was then a loose collection of malarial islands came to the British crown with the Portuguese Infanta Catharine of Braganza upon her marriage to Charles II in 1661. Poor Catharine never produced an heir, but her dowry eventually proved the marriage a damned good arrangement for England. The British built the city of Bombay for the sole purpose of making money, and they made a lot of it. In the process, a few Indians got rich too. By the mid-nineteenth century, Bombay had become the commercial and industrial capital of India, home to the great business houses of the Tatas and the Wadias, Bombay's Carnegies and Vanderbilts.

Two classes of Indians came to Bombay: merchants and laborers. The first merchants came from Gujarat when the East India Company began moving its operations down from Surat in the late seventeenth century. Gujarati *banias*, Parsis, and Muslims acquired great wealth and formed a business elite that persists in Bombay to this day. Sindhi traders came to Bombay. Baghdadi Jews came, among them the Sassoons, one of the most illustrious names in the history of the city. The laborers came from neighboring Maharashtra. Later they came from South India, from Bihar, from as far away as Bangladesh, from anywhere poor to seek a better life in the great city, enticed by Lakshmi's tempting promise of beauty and wealth.

Today there is still money in Bombay, and glamour. Bombay is New York plus Hollywood, home to the biggest stock exchange in South Asia and to a film industry with a distribution range that stretches from the Gulf of Arabia all the way through Southeast Asia. The city is like a magnet pulling in the dispossessed and the ambitious, the desperate and the starstruck from the entire subcontinent. But Lakshmi gives of herself grudgingly, and those who've been blessed by her favor are not eager to share their good fortune. The big money in the city is, for the most part, in the same hands it has been in since the seventeenth century: with the Parsis; the Gujaratis; the Sindhis; and, of course, the foreigners. For the rest, living pell-mell in decrepit buildings or packed into illegal slums on patches of squatted land or simply laid out to sleep on a spare stretch of sidewalk at night, Bombay offers the consolation of dreams, spinning out hundreds of films a year where the decent but poor young man gets the beautiful rich girl for his bride; where the bad guys are (eventually) beaten by the good guys; where for a couple of hours a person can live in a vicarious world of big mansions, fast cars, fancy clothes, and pristine mountain vistas fresh from the foothills of the cool Himalayas against which young men can cavort with pretty, buxom girls unencumbered by parental restrictions. Bombay's best known sobriquet is "City of Gold," but it is also Mayapuri, the City of Illusion.[1]

What better to attract people than gold and dreams? Greed is a great social leveler. In Bombay, as in most of the world these days, money is not only its own reward, it is all that is required for social success. Old money can be more respectable, but new money is more plentiful and, therefore, more powerful. In a country hidebound by several thousand years of social history in which most individuals are born into a distinct caste with equally distinct limitations on career aspirations, Bombay has long been a beacon of opportunity for people of every kind. For centuries, it never mattered in Bombay where one came from, what religion one professed, what food one ate, what language one spoke, what was one's caste or class: one made one's reputation in Bombay on achievement alone.

* * *

Bapuji moved the family to Bombay in 1965. At that point, he knew Burma was lost forever. The Gujarati-speaking Kamdars found a natural home in Bombay, which generations of Gujarati residents had made quite their own metropolis. Bombay had become not only the cultural and political capital of Gujarat but also its administrative capital. Under the British, the "Bombay Presidency" encompassed a vast region that—a smattering of "independent" native states excepted—included much of modern-day Maharashtra and the eastern portion of Gujarat. After India's independence in 1947, the region was called "Bombay State," divided in 1955 into two separate linguistic areas dubbed Gujarat and Maharashtra. It was only in 1960 that these were formally separated, creating the modern states of Gujarat and Maharashtra. By the 1960s, when Bapuji arrived with the family, Bombay's well-established Gujarati population and cosmopolitan, business-oriented environment made it a comfortable place to settle down. The Parekhs and other friends, relatives, and business associates from Burma had decided to move to Bombay as well, making the prospect of life in the city all the more appealing.

Bapuji chose the seaside suburban enclave of Juhu for the family's new home. In those days, Juhu was an open, uncrowded area well to the north of Bombay proper with a beautiful beach. Bapuji selected an apartment block across from a park and a cricket field, which were protected from future development. The building was owned by a Gujarati family and the tenants were all Gujarati Jains or Hindus. The family paid a monthly rent of 250 rupees, a sum that would remain unchanged for more than thirty years. There was a Jain temple only a couple of blocks away and several other relatives, Kamdars and Kharas, had already moved into the area. With its open spaces and Gujarati residents, Juhu was removed from the hustle and bustle—and the temptations—of Bombay proper.

Bapuji remained a strict follower of Gandhian ideals forty years after his youthful enthusiasm for *Satyagraha*. It was natural that he be attracted to a place where Mahatma Gandhi once stayed. In 1924, Gandhi had gone to Juhu to recuperate from an appendectomy in the seaside villa of a wealthy industrialist. Motilal Nehru, Jawaharlal's father, spent time with Gandhi there, charting strategy and eventually launching the Swaraj, or "Home-Rule" party. The beach house in Juhu was, for a time, a gathering point for a slew of Gandhi's supporters. Once he had recovered his health, Gandhi moved on. Some forty years after Gandhi's departure, Bapuji arrived in Juhu and established his own enclave of Gandhian life and ideals.

* * *

Bapuji had always been proud of his intellectual bent. From his earliest days as a star pupil at the then-new English-medium Kamribai High School in Jetpur, he spent most of his time reading, listening to news on the radio, or discussing serious subjects such as politics and philosophy with his friends and a select number of family members. He called himself a "library Jain." He never went with Motiba to the temple or participated in any of the religious gatherings or rituals that were so important to her. He had no use for even the most important Jain religious holidays, such as Paryushan, a ten-day period of fasting after the monsoon during which, at a minimum, no green vegetables and no dairy products are to be consumed. While Motiba would cook for the rest of the family according to the dietary requirements of Paryushan, Bapuji insisted on eating normally. As far as he was concerned, Gandhian that he was, the most important gesture of religious observance was to live correctly every single day. The social pleasures of belonging to a community bound by common religious practice and belief were lost on Bapuji, as were the charms of performing certain rituals, eating special foods, or wearing special clothes on holiday occasions. Bapuji believed these acts were trivial. In this respect, he and Motiba could not have been more different.

Yet, Bapuji's highly disciplined life gave a stability to the days that everyone could count on and around which other family members could organize their comings and goings. He also doted on his grandchildren, believing, like his mentor Mahatma Gandhi, that all children were fresh emissaries from God, possessed of a saintly innocence. In a child's company, the otherwise austere man became affectionate, even playful. When his grandsons were young, he took them along on his daily trips to the market in Ville Parle to the *pastiwalas,* sellers of used newspapers and magazines, to pick up the latest issues of *Newsweek* and *Time*.

Bapuji's one sensual weakness was fruit. He loved fruit of all kinds, but none more so than Alphonsos, the kings of the mango family and a Bombay specialty. No other mango can compare with the Alphonsos' silky flesh, firm yet pliant and rich with a pungently sweet golden juice. Every year from late April through early June, during the peak of the mango season, Bapuji made it his personal mission to go to the market and select cratefuls of the best Alphonsos, being careful to choose candidates at various stages of ripeness.

He'd hire a boy to help him get them home in a rickshaw. Under Bapuji's vigilant eye, the boy had to get the mangoes up the stairs and into the apartment without bumping the crate against a door-jamb or, God forbid, letting it slip from his skinny grasp. With tender concern, Bapuji would then prepare a soft bed of straw for the mangoes under the iron bedsteads in the back bedroom. The straw cradled and insulated the mangoes while at the same time allowing air to circulate around their plump green and rose skins. Every day, Bapuji tended his Alphonsos, gently turning them so that they would ripen evenly, taking every bit as much care with them as a mother hen with a clutch of eggs. The moment one of the mangoes reached its peak, Bapuji would allow a grandchild to carry the precious fruit to the women in the kitchen. During mango season, the entire family feasted on the saffron-colored fruit. Bapuji himself ate mangoes morning, noon, and night, indulging in a pleasure whose end would inevitably come with the arrival of the monsoon.

If Bapuji revered the life of the mind, Motiba loved all that was social. Not that she wasn't sharp. In fact, Motiba had quite a reputation in the family and the community for her wit and her perceptiveness. She read every day, usually in the afternoon during the siesta period after lunch. Motiba read the *Mumbai Samachar,* the Gujarati newspaper founded in 1822 by Fardumji Marzbanji when Bombay was the capital of Gujarati intellectual life. She also read *Akhand Anand,* "Endless Joy," a digest of excerpts from the classics of Gujarati literature as well as current articles, and *Dashashrimani,* a Jain magazine. Motiba also made regular visits to the Jain temple in Ville Parle near the Juhu flat, and when she had a chance, to the

larger Jain temple at Dadar. She was a devoted follower of the Jain
sage Sri Kanji-Swami Gurudev. When Gurudev visited Bombay to
conduct *pravachan,* performing exegesis of the sacred texts of the
Jain *tirthankaras,* huge white tents were set up on the *maidan*, an
open area that usually served as the neighborhood cricket field,
just opposite the Juhu apartment. The faithful would gather for
days at a time and listen to his teachings. Many of Motiba's relatives
and close friends attended these meetings. They would come up to
the apartment for *cha,* tea, and refreshments. Some inevitably
stayed the night, and an occasion for a spiritual gathering became a
social and family event.

Motiba was the center around which family and community
life revolved. She spent the larger part of her day mothering the
household, including the steady stream of visitors who came for a
night or two, or a week, or a month, or even several months. The
apartment in Juhu was modest, to be sure: an 800-square-foot,
two-bedroom, one-bath apartment shared by eight members of
an Indian joint family. There was no air-conditioning and no ele-
vator. There was a refrigerator, eventually a Sony television, in
time a telephone, and the electric ceiling fans that made Bombay's
sultry climate bearable—when the electricity wasn't cut. People
didn't come to the Juhu flat for luxury accommodations. They
came for Motiba and Bapuji, who despite their reduced circumstances after the loss of their properties in Burma, retained a very
high standing in the community of Kathiawari Jains to which they
belonged. They were still people of *khaandaan* and *amiraat,* of
noble birth and character.

We all remember Bombay in the 1960s as a beautiful city where life was easy. We children went to Juhu Beach every day. The soft, white sand was covered with colorful little shells that sparkled along the tide lines. In addition to swimming and beachcombing, there were camels and ponies to ride, and vendors offering all kinds of tempting snacks. Most of these were strictly off limits, due to quite sensible fears that we American Kamdars, with our delicately susceptible constitutions, might catch a roaring case of "Delhi belly." But we were always allowed to pick our very own fresh coconut from the green pyramids next to the *nariyalpani* stand. We watched in awe as a boy of about our age whacked off the top of the coconut with a few quick strokes of his razor-sharp machete. Then we'd suck up the sweet coconut water through a straw, using a shard of coconut shell the boy had carved for us to spoon out the tender coconut cream. At least a few times, we went into Bombay proper and visited Hanging Gardens, where we played hide-and-seek around the elaborately carved animal topiary. We also visited the Taraporewala Aquarium. My cousin Raja had caught, with his bare hands, a small shark off Chowpatty Beach that was subsequently taken to live at the aquarium. We children tried to pick out which shark was Raja's. In the evening, we ate *bhel puri* on the beach as we watched the incandescent orange sun sink into the Arabian Sea, wondering at the thought that the same sun leaving us was just coming up in Los Angeles, where we lived most of the time.

One of the most amusing things we did as children in Bombay was play kite war. We were not generally allowed to go out into the park and play, but we could go up and play on the rooftop terrace of the building. There, Vittal, a boy about the same age as myself who came to the apartment every day to do the washing up, mop the floors, and hang up the clothes, showed us how to dip the kite string into a pail of watery glue and then run it through a plate of crushed glass. We'd send the brightly colored diamonds of tissue paper aloft to vie against those soaring from every rooftop in the neighborhood, trying to sever their kite strings before they did ours!

My mother bought a countertop electric oven and introduced the household to the art of baking. She could never use eggs in Motiba's strictly vegetarian Jain kitchen, but she became fairly adept at turning out eggless cakes, biscuits, and breads. On my tenth birthday, however, she decided I should have a proper cake from a bakery. We all trekked out to a famous Western-style pastry shop downtown where I terrified the baker by announcing I wanted a "devil's food" cake. The poor man had no idea what I was asking him to conjure out of his kitchen and was clearly taken aback. We settled on chocolate. Motiba and Bapuji were tolerant enough to allow the cake, which was made with eggs, into the house, though naturally they did not eat any of it.

The hardest part about life in Bombay for me was school. My Americanness was both an asset and a handicap. My mother decided to enroll me in a local English-medium Catholic school rather than try to send me every day all the way down to the American school. My English was, of course, much better than that of any of the other students; much better, in fact, than the teachers' English. Moreover, I spoke American English, and the teachers and other students had trouble understanding my broad diphthongs and odd vocabulary. In math, on the other hand, I tested several grades below my "standard," but it was determined I should be put in a class with children my age. I only lasted a week. The staff and children taunted me terribly because I didn't yet have a uniform, and my teacher resented my fluent English and, I felt, my Americanness. My first morning, I was perplexed to see the other children jump up from their seats and shout, "Good morning, sister," to the teacher. This was not the way we started our day at Woodlake Avenue Elementary School in the San Fernando Valley. As she replied with a "Good morning, children," she strode huffily over to where I sat frozen with surprise, grabbed my forearms with a claw-

My sister Devyani, age six, and I, age nine, dressed up as brides on the balcony of the Juhu apartment.

like grip, and lifted me up until my feet no longer touched the ground and my face was level with hers. "You will stand and greet me when I enter the room," she hissed. Then she dropped me onto the floor. I had enormous bruises on my arms for several weeks after. This experience, and the trauma of being the only "White kid" at school, convinced my mother that it might not do me too much harm to skip school for a few months while we were in India.

* * *

A delightful period of leisure began. From time to time, probably when the grownups had had enough of us children careering around the apartment, Vittal was charged with taking us across the street to the grounds of Bhailal K. Patel Maidan and keeping an eye on us while we played. I liked Vittal very much. He was a nice boy with a ready smile, wide eyes, and strong limbs. But one day, I caused an uproar in the household because of an act of social cruelty I inflicted on him. My meanness upset everybody, especially Motiba. For some reason, Vittal had made me angry. I don't have any recollection of what he could have done. He was never, ever anything but delightful company. But I did resent the freedom he had to come and go as he pleased and his distinct air of worldliness that seemed unfair in a child exactly my age. Anyway, something happened, and I wanted to hurt Vittal, to get back at him. I went to Motiba and I asked her how to say "servant" in Gujarati. "Why?" she asked. "I just want to know," I lied. Then I found Vittal and told him, "*Tu khali nokar chhe*." "You are only a servant." Vittal's cheeks turned crimson. His eyes filled with tears. He turned and fled the room. My feeling of triumph at having succeeded with my plan was immediately shot through with regret and shame. Red-faced, I retired to the back bedroom where I distractedly pretended to read a copy of *Reader's Digest*. An hour or so passed. Vittal was missed. Soon a full-fledged search was on. His parents, who themselves worked for the family, came to the apartment. High-pitched discussions in rapid-fire vernacular ensued. Apparently, Vittal wasn't at his family's hut either. A party was sent out to search for him. Motiba came to talk to me. Did I know of any reason Vittal would have run away? "No," I lied again. I lied with the simple panic of a child who knows she's done wrong and desperately wants not to get into trouble. "Why did you ask me how to say 'servant' in Gujarati?" Motiba queried. She was on to me and, of course, I was forced to confess.

Then the worst happened. Bapuji was informed about what had gone on, and I was summoned to speak with him. In a state of sheer terror, I went alone to meet my grandfather. Contrary to what I expected, he didn't seem angry, only extremely sad. With moist eyes, he told me that Vittal was a child like myself, but that unlike me, he didn't have the good fortune to go to school. He had to work, it was true, but no one thought of him as "only" a servant. Vittal was like a member of the family. Now he'd run away. It was all my fault. To bear the knowledge of my wrongdoing against such a kind person as Vittal was my true punishment. I left the room in tears. Vittal went missing for four full days. When he turned up again, I was immensely relieved. I thought maybe he'd died of hurt.

In a way, he had. Though we continued as before, Vittal and I were no longer friends. He punished me by being "only a servant" from then on.

The family servant, the old tailor, the cook, the faithful retainer, the beloved ayah: in Bombay, these people are more than stock characters in a picaresque novel, they are figures of daily life for the upper and even the middle classes. Any serious observation of the relationship between the served and the servant in Bombay can make one a believer in the Hegelian master–slave dialectic, for in many ways it is the master who is dependent on the slave and the slave who runs the master's life. As an American who is part Indian and who has lived in India at various times in my life, I am constantly shifting between points of view on these and myriad other social matters. I do and do not understand. I do and do not accept. I do and do not condemn. The hard economic realities of a society deeply divided by class and caste, into haves and have-nots, are evident and cold. Yet the human relationships across these divides are often genuinely warm, sometimes lasting entire lifetimes, even continuing over several generations.

For several decades, Bapuji had a devoted manservant named Jagmurrath. Hailing originally from a village near Gorakhpur in Uttar Pradesh, Jagmurrath was hired at the age of twelve to work as a peon in Bapuji's Rangoon office. Everyone called him "Durwan." Durwan practically raised my father and joked affectionately about the time Dad, then a rather spoiled child, had bit him. Whenever he came into the presence of my grandfather, he would greet him by performing *saashtaang dandwat pranaam,* a form of deep reverence expressed by lying down prostrate on the floor with the hands extended and joined as in prayer. He stayed with Bapuji through thick and thin, war and exile, until well into the 1960s, traveling with him back and forth between India and Burma. When Durwan became too old to work, Bapuji supported him with a small pension and hired his son. When Bapuji lost his business in Burma and had to reduce his expenditure, he got Durwan's son a job working for Motiba's cousin Kantumama. Bapuji was as devoted to Durwan as Durwan to him. Whenever Durwan was ill, Bapuji personally nursed him. With his own hands he would prepare *sheera,* a special food made from *ghee, gol,* and wheat flour thought to boost the immune system, and chide Durwan for not taking care of himself. In later years, when he was quite an old man, Durwan would visit the family in Bombay and reminisce with Motiba about times past. The entire extended Kamdar-Khara clan considered Durwan to be very much a member of the family and though they expected him to uphold his end of the social contract through loyal service, remained steadfast in their regard and affection until the end of the man's life.

The genuine and reciprocal affection that characterized many of these relationships could hardly compensate for the disparity in living circumstances between the servant and the served. Vittal lived in a slum just a few buildings away from our apartment. We could see the shacks from our balcony. The living conditions in Vittal's slum were scarcely imaginable, and so painful to view that even as a child, one learned not to "see" the poor. In fact, there was mind-numbing poverty all around. To cure us of this kind of complacency, my mother decided that we should once make the train trip from Juhu into downtown Bombay in a regular second-class car. She wanted us to understand that not everyone traveled first class. It was the first—and last—time we attempted this experiment. A few minutes into our journey, a little girl of perhaps three was thrust into the car by a pair of adolescent boys. The child made her way through the compartment, dancing so as to make the bells around her ankles tinkle, her palm extended for coins. She had been blinded, her eyelids sinking down unevenly into useless sockets. Her arms had been broken and reset at odd angles, several of her fingers had been cut off, all to incite more pity in her spectators. These boys either owned her outright or were agents charged with working her through the trains. In any case, I will never in my life forget the look of rapacious greed in their eyes as they pushed her into the compartment, watched her make her halting way down the aisle, and collected her at the end. Most people gave her coins. My mother indicated to me that we were not to do so. She showed me with her eyes the boys supervising their charge's progress through the car and later explained to me that they were going to take away any money the poor child collected. We would be supporting this ugly enterprise if we were to give the little girl anything. Still, I felt badly for her. I was deeply shocked by what I was seeing and by the profound human and economic implications I sensed but barely understood. I was, after all, only ten years old.

* * *

Amid the extremes of Bombay's wealth and poverty, and as a conscious antidote for both, Bapuji followed the strict daily regimen of a *pukka* Gandhian. This was one of the reasons that we called my grandfather "Bapuji." After all, the man known to millions as the Mahatma was called "Bapuji" by those closest to him. Even Jawaharlal Nehru, independent India's first prime minister, called Gandhi "Bapuji," "respected father," a term of affection and high regard. My own Bapuji emulated Gandhi in many of his actions. During a great famine in Bihar in 1966, for example, he was so moved by the tales of suffering he was reading in the newspaper reports that he decided to go to Bihar to do whatever he could to help. He stayed there for several months, distributing food and giving what comfort he could to the starving. Senior family members thought him a little mad and warned him that he could do little or nothing of use and might well be putting himself in danger of falling seriously ill. My aunt Bharati remembers the stories Bapuji told when he did come home about how utterly destitute the people were, how they had absolutely nothing, not even, in many cases, a scrap of cloth to wear. Taking pity on one poor old woman who had been reduced to utter nakedness, Bapuji had removed his *dhoti,* a length of muslin wrapped around the waist and legs by Indian men in lieu of Western trousers, and ripped it apart then and there. He gave the woman half of the garment so that she might recover a bit of her dignity, keeping the other half to clothe himself.

Bapuji rose every morning at four o'clock, meditated for an hour, then went for a brisk walk. Upon his return, he bathed, washed his handwoven plain white *dhoti* and *kurta* with his own hands while he was in the bathroom, put on a second identical set of clothes, and emerged damp and clean to hang the set he'd just washed to dry on the line that stretched the length of the kitchen balcony. (The other members of the family, less Spartan in their habits, had their laundry done by a servant.) Only then did Bapuji sit and have a simple breakfast of fruit and fresh *bhakhari*, *thepla*, or *rotlo*. With unbending discipline, my grandfather maintained the same morning regimen for decades. The rhythm of his morning was so exact and so dependable that the rest of the family members timed their own waking, ablutions, and meal preparations according to it. During Bapuji's morning walk, the others had a full hour to bathe and wander about in their pajamas. The women could move about the apartment freely with their heads uncovered and their hair down. In fact, without this hour, it would have been difficult for everyone to do what he or she had to do every morning.

Bapuji nearly always took his morning walk alone. Once in a while, he let one of his grandsons accompany him. Once, I went with him. I was the eldest grandchild. An American, I spoke English, the language of *Voice of America* and the *BBC*, my grandfather's favorite radio programs, and a language traditionally reserved, in my own and many other Indian families, for educated males. My walk with Bapuji occurred during a period when I was a young adult and had not yet married, a time when Bapuji seemed to accord me something I can only interpret as "honorary male" status. He would call me in to sit with him and talk politics, history, world affairs, and even philosophy and religion. I was not expected to cover my head or act in any of the ways required of the other females in the household. Just a few years later, after I married, this abruptly changed. Invitations to serious talk in the

back bedroom ceased. I was suddenly expected to dress mod-
estly. I had, in my grandfather's eyes, become a woman.

At five o'clock in the morning, Motiba gently shook me awake.
"*Mira, Bapuji jaay chhe.*" "Bapuji is going out." It was still quite dark,
but another day in Bombay was on its way. Soon, the sparrows
massed in the tree outside the window would begin their frantic
chattering, a sound that would in turn be eclipsed by a cacophony
of shrill Hindi film songs; whining rickshaw engines; honking
horns; and a concert of clanging pots and pans as housewives
upstairs, downstairs, next door, and across the way began a solid
morning of cooking.

In the last of the predawn silence, Bapuji sat cross-legged, meditating on top of the cot on which he'd slept, his eyes closed, one
hand resting softly on each knee. The mosquito netting drawn back
behind him formed a diaphanous backdrop in the fuzzy light of the
nascent dawn, giving my grandfather a saintly aura. Without moving, Bapuji opened his eyes, looked at me steadily, and said, "So,
you've decided to join me. Be warned, I walk fast." With that, he
rose. We slipped our *chappals*, sandals, on at the door. On the stair-
case, we passed the *dudhwala*, the milkman, hauling his copper jugs
of fresh milk up the stairs, his cow and her calf tethered at the base
of the stairs. Behind us, Motiba opened the apartment door for the
dudhwala to fill a stainless steel pot with milk that had to be boiled
before she could prepare everyone's morning tea.

There was now enough light filtering through the haze of morning cook fires and the lifting mist to see clearly, though the landscape still had a muted quality. With purposeful, even strides

Bapuji passed Kala Niketan, a posh silk *sari* boutique where an old man wearing a smartly matching, if somewhat faded, safari jacket over a pair of baggy shorts was washing off the marble steps. The rickshaw drivers were still asleep in their three-wheelers; the taxi drivers dozed in the back seats of their open cars, a woolen scarf around their face the only protection against noise, damp, and the eyes of passersby.

To our left, clinging precariously to the edge of the road on the lip of a great, reeking swamp, stretched an immense slum. To our right, directly opposite the slum, the road was lined with the private compounds and bougainvillea-draped villas of some of India's most famous movie stars. Juhu is Bombay's equivalent of Malibu Beach, and Bapuji's morning walk took him through the heart of it. The slum was still cloaked in darkness, but on the other side of the street, the mansions of the stars were lit up here and there with the garish fluorescence of hundreds of high-voltage projector lights illuminating the last of a nightlong marathon of shooting. "Bollywood" movie stars are rich people in a poor country. Their real-life homes provide ready-made backdrops for the improbable lives of the wealthy heroes, heroines, and villains they play in their films. We children would often go up to the rooftop terrace of our Juhu apartment building after dark and pick out the homes of the stars where scenes were being filmed. "Look! Over there. Tonight they are shooting at Amitabh Baachan's house over on Tenth Road. You know who is starring? Hema Malini." Starstruck teenagers in the neighborhood waited patiently outside the gates of these villas for hours, hoping to capture a glimpse of a favorite actor. When shooting was going on late into the night at Meena Cottage, directly behind our apartment, it was hard to sleep. The bright lights and the knowledge that just yards away from where we slumbered, one famous star or another was breathing, walking, sitting, or drinking tea was simply too enervating.

All of this was anathema to Bapuji, who couldn't have cared less about the activities of inferior people engaged in a morally and intellectually "polluting" medium. Bapuji strode resolutely down the road, looking neither left toward the slum nor right toward the shuttered mansions of the stars, his simple Gandhian garb cutting a white swath between Bombay's extremes of wealth and poverty. We reached the beach. The wood-framed booths of the *rekadiwalas*—snack huts selling roasted peanuts; *kulfi;* fresh coconut milk; and that inimitable Bombay snack mixture of puffed rice, potatoes, onions, sauces, chilies and, coriander known as *bhel*—stood deserted and forlorn. Lit up like Christmas trees at night, their peeling paint and slapdash construction were sadly visible in the early morning light, like ladies of the evening exposed to the unforgiving light of day. Bapuji kept up his unrelenting pace, taking no notice of whether or not I was still with him. He forged ahead, a man with a schedule to keep and a mission to accomplish. The gulls reeled over the halfhearted waves of the Arabian Sea. They had plenty of flotsam to pick over in search of a meal: soggy sandalwood garlands, frayed brown coconut husks, and necklaces of battered flowers that had washed back up upon the shore after being tossed into the sea for an offering or a spe-

cial prayer the night before. Stretching to the horizon along the
tide line were solitary *chappals;* plastic bottles; and soaked newspaper cornets tossed down by happy beachgoers after consuming
last night's portion of hot, salted peanuts. Along the far side of the
beach, the villas of the richest movie stars and industrialists sat
behind high walls lined with towering coconut palms that arched
over the perfect lawns.

A Koli fisherwoman holding a jute fishing net appeared like
Venus on the half shell out of the waves. Her skin was a lustrous,
deep mahogany. Her slim body was completely revealed by her wet
sari, which clung transparently over her full breasts and supple,
well-muscled limbs. In a country where a life of indolence, result-
ing as much from extreme class and caste consciousness as from
the wilting nature of the climate, often leads the more privileged
down a rapid descent into flabbiness, plumpness, and even obesity,
this was a magnificent specimen of womanhood. Bapuji did not
give the slightest sign of having seen her. Even if she had walked
directly in front of his eyes, he would not have noticed her beauty.
She was of a class of people not worthy of notice in "our" community, and her sexuality was a troublesome distraction from man's
higher purpose. Bapuji, the former teenage *brahmachari,* immune
to the charms of his own beautiful young wife, was certainly not
going to pay attention to a passing fisherwoman as common on the
shores of Bombay as the gulls and the discarded coconut shells.

At the creek at Versova, Bapuji turned back. By the time we
reached the road, the sound of bicycle bells and rickshaw buzzers
filled the air. It was about to become very hot. The slum had begun to

stink under the mounting sun. In the colony's open garbage dump, slime-bellied, black-haired pigs and mange-eaten bitches with great dangling teats hanging from their skeletal bodies rooted in the waste.

Most of the people who lived in this slum were from South India. They were viewed by the "real" Bombaywallahs—the native Koli fisherfolk, the local Maharashtrians, and the Gujarati and Parsi merchants—as foreign to the city, unwelcome interlopers, with a reputation for drinking too much cheap liquor and beating their wives. Yet all the servants in our household and in those around us came from this slum. Of course, the ones who worked for us were "different"—hard-working, honest, loyal, dependable, and pleasant. They earned a tiny salary together with one free meal a day and occasionally received cast-off clothing. After washing up pots and pans, doing the laundry, and mopping the floors, they returned to dwellings of the tiniest proportions, cobbled together out of cast-off burlap grain sacks and bits of tarpaulin. Many of the children were visibly wracked with malnutrition, their black hair faded to a rusty red, their bellies swollen out like those of pregnant women over their bony legs, naked but for a smudge of black kohl around their eyes and an amulet tied around their necks with a black cotton thread.

On our return, as on our way out, Bapuji paid no attention to the slum, its people, or its garbage heap. We turned onto Sixth Road, entered our building's driveway, and climbed the stairs to the apartment. The pleasant smell of tea and fresh breads greeted us from the kitchen. Bapuji's cot had been transformed into a sofa. The pallets in the women and children's room had been folded and

put away. The mosquito nets had been stored and the table set.
Bapuji said nothing to me or to anyone else and headed straight for
his bath. I went into the kitchen where Motiba and my aunts looked
at me expectantly over their teacups. "He walks fast," I said. They
smiled and sipped their tea.

* * *

My father arrived in Bombay in 1947, the very year of India's formal
independence from British rule. He was sixteen, and had been sent
to Bombay from Jetpur to complete his secondary school studies. As
he was the eldest son, Bapuji wanted him to have the best education
possible. My grandfather, Gandhian patriot that he was, was also
determined that his son learn to appreciate "indigenous" as opposed
to Western values. Bapuji himself was busy trying to resurrect the
family's business interests in Burma in the aftermath of the war. The
rest of the family was settled in the big house he'd built in Jetpur with
some of his Burma money. But my father had outgrown Jetpur's English-medium Kamribai High School. So, Bapuji sent him off to
boarding school at Bharatiya Vidya Bhavan in Bombay. Bharatiya
Vidya Bhavan, "House of Indian Knowledge," was a school and cultural center founded by no less a towering figure in Gujarati cultural
life than the novelist and playwright Kanaiyalal Munshi. In the
immediate postwar years and the early years of India's independence, Munshi's Bharatiya Vidya Bhavan was the catalyst for a renais-
sance in Gujarati music, theater, and dance in Bombay.[2]

Though my father's education took place in English, the language of the best-educated elite, he was also quite involved in the

Gujarati cultural side of Munshi's project, appearing regularly in plays produced by Munshi's wife, Lilavati. Bombay was—and still is—home to a thriving Gujarati theater. This was a perfect environment for my father, whose thespian career had been launched a few years earlier at Kamribai High School in Jetpur. There, he had played the role of Prithviraj, the Hindu prince who, to win the

My father, Prabhakar Kamdar, age fifteen,
dressed up as Prithviraj.

hand of his beloved, defeated the Muslim invader Mohammad
Ghauri in 1206. A studio portrait of my fifteen-year-old father
dressed up for his starring role as Prithviraj shows him as a slim
youth with high cheekbones, a gallant mustache painted on his still
smooth face, looking every bit as handsome and noble as the legendary thirteenth-century Rajput prince.

Bombay was also the capital of India's film industry. The first
Indian moving picture was made in 1896 by Harishchandra Sak-
haram Bhatwadekar when he recorded a wrestling match in Bombay's Hanging Gardens. On July 14 of the same year, the Lumière
Brothers' pictures were screened at the city's Novelty Theatre. In
1913, Dada Saheb Phalke made India's first feature film, _Raja Har-
ishchandra_. Motion pictures quickly became the defining industry of
Bombay and the city's most popular pastime.[3] By the time my father
arrived in Bombay in the late 1940s, the film industry was well
established, and literally scores of cinema houses had been constructed to cater to the public's insatiable appetite for both Indian
and foreign films. When he wasn't studying his high school subjects
in English or acting in Gujarati plays at Bharatiya Vidya Bhavan, my
father went to the movies. He went to lots of movies. He saw Hindi
movies, Gujarati movies, British movies, but mostly lots and lots of
American movies. He went to the Eros, the Regal, the Strand, the
New Empire, the Broadway, and the Metro—all grand cinema
houses in the best Art Deco style. Bombay had embarked on a major
project of modernization in the 1930s. The clean curves of Art Deco
architecture rapidly vied with the ornate Edwardian and Victorian
administrative and commercial buildings erected by the British to

define Bombay's urban space. Along Marine Drive, Bombay's version of Nice's Promenade des Anglais, an entire string of Art Deco apartment houses were constructed, giving a new, modern look to the old British colonial outpost.[4] Art Deco, with its clean, curving lines, was evocative of aluminum and airplanes—and of the movies of Fred Astaire and Ginger Rogers.

My father particularly loved the Metro cinema, where he saw the films of John Ford. A veritable outpost of American cultural imperialism, the Metro was built by Metro-Goldwyn-Mayer on land acquired in 1936 for a symbolic rent of one rupee per year on a 99-year lease. My father thinks he saw *Gone With the Wind* there, since "the Metro was grand. It was a place for the more spectacular films." But he isn't sure. When I quizzed him closely on which films he might have seen in Bombay during those years and in which theaters, he admitted that he'd seen so many American films in Bombay in 1947, 1948, and 1949, and continued to see so many films after he arrived in America in 1949, that he could no longer remember exactly which ones he saw in India and which ones he saw in America. Such is the cultural continuum of the experience of watching Hollywood films: for an hour and a half, one is stateless, existing in the vicarious realm of the moving image.

There are two exceptions to my father's cinematic amnesia regarding which films he watched where during the late 1940s. Both are light comedies starring Clifton Webb: *Sitting Pretty* and *Cheaper by the Dozen*. The reason my father did not forget these films was that he was forced to watch them as many as thirty times apiece, until he could faithfully reproduce the entire dialogue and recount every detail of American life depicted on the screen. It was 1949. My father, having completed his studies at Bharatiya Vidya Bhavan, was admitted to Elphinstone College. He would have preferred Wilson College, but his admission to one of the most venerable of Bombay's institutions of higher education was nothing to sneeze at. Then someone suggested that he should go to America instead. What an idea! To

My father poses with his high school friends in Jetpur just prior to his departure for America.

go to England to study was a time-honored privilege of the cream of the Indian elite. Oxford or Cambridge—that was what a father wanted for his son. But America? My grandfather was skeptical at first. Then an uncle who'd actually been to America intervened. Why not? America was the land of the future. England was washed up. An American education was just the thing for the intelligent son of a successful businessman and anti-British freedom fighter such as my grandfather. Inquiries were made. Applications were sent. My father was granted admission to Chauncy Hall, a preparatory school for boys in Boston, Massachusetts. The idea was that venerable Chauncy Hall, founded in 1828, would protect and prepare my young father for admission to the Massachusetts Institute of Technology. A passport was acquired. But what was truly necessary before my father's departure, according to his pal and uncle, Shashi Khara, was an education in American manners and customs. The only way to accomplish this: glue my father to the raspberry-colored velvet seat cushion of the Strand cinema, where a Hollywood double feature was playing, and keep him there until he'd learned enough not to embarrass India, himself, or—heaven forbid—the Khara clan.

And so it was that my father's American education began in a Bombay cinema house. Shashimama forcibly escorted him to the Strand where, for days on end, he was made to watch the Clifton Webb comedies. As a member of the wealthy Khara family living in a vast new Art Deco flat on Nepean Sea Road, Shashimama was confident in his superior knowledge of matters relating to American dress and social comportment. He was also a strict taskmaster. My father's "exam," as Shashimama called it and on the successful passage of which the trip to America depended, was to demonstrate his ability to recite every line of the movies' dialogue, to understand every mannerism, to be sure of every rule of etiquette inferred from the behavior of the characters. In these films, life is a comfortable, lighthearted affair. In *Sitting Pretty,* the handsome husband in his well-cut tweed suit and felt fedora cruises off to the office in his enormous American automobile, leaving the beautiful Maureen O'Hara, his wife, at home in stockings and high-heeled pumps, a little apron tied over her very becoming dress, to tend to their suburban bungalow, where a shiny new refrigerator sits prominently in the kitchen. A life of plenty, of ease, of modern simplicity. When they go to another couple's house for dinner, they dress up: he in a white dinner jacket and black tie, she in a simple black dress with gloves and pearls.

It was supremely important to get the sartorial details right. Not content with keeping my poor father locked up in the Strand cinema for hours at a time, Shashimama conscripted the family's old tailor to join the educational experience. The poor old man was made to sit through dozens of screenings of these films until he could swear himself capable of reproducing exactly every item of male clothing on view. I asked my father how they knew which color fabric to use, since the films were all in black and white. He replied, "Oh, Maureen O'Hara would say something about a 'brown tweed suit' and we'd jab the tailor in the arm and say, 'Brown, you have to make it brown.'"

So it was that my father arrived in Cambridge, Massachusetts, for a pre-college year of prep school with a suitcase full of clothes stitched by an Indian tailor in Bombay to the specifications of a Hollywood movie wardrobe. I wish these clothes had survived! I'd love to see the dinner jacket with the white satin lapels, the brown tweed suit. Of course, the rest of the students were wearing deeply cuffed blue jeans, plaid flannel shirts, argyle socks, and saddle shoes. Too late, my father learned that Hollywood's America and the America of Cambridge, Massachusetts, were two very different countries.

As my father remembers it, when he went in September 1949 to the American consulate in Bombay to get his visa, he was only the third applicant that year. Since the consulate had the authority to grant, as he recalls, fifty visas, he had no trouble getting his. Today, of course, the long line of hopeful visa seekers snakes all the way down the road in front of the American consulate in Breach Candy. People wait years for their visas to come through. Tense moments, such as the dreaded interview where every effort is made to trip up the applicant who may secretly wish to emigrate to the United States, are the stuff of legend among Indians in Bombay today. Even solidly middle-class people with family members who are American citizens can have a difficult time procuring the magical stamp that will allow them into the United States. Incredible as it now seems, in 1949 the United States was not the destination of choice for Indians. In that respect, Bapuji's decision to send his eldest son to America was indeed prescient.

Motiba was not at all pleased with the idea of her firstborn traveling to America. It just seemed much too far away. And what about his religious beliefs? How was he supposed to remain a vegetarian over there, where everyone ate meat? What about drinking alcohol? And most alarming, what about those American women he was sure to meet? Of course, every one of Motiba's objections could be countered by the well-known experiences of Gandhi in

England over a half century earlier. But no one could give her any precise assurances about America. One simply didn't know enough. America was a brand-new destination. Appropriately, my father left for America by airplane and not, as privileged England-bound Indian sons had done for decades, by ship. My father's passport reveals the details of his itinerary: he left Bombay's Santa Cruz Airport on September 27, 1949. On September 28, he was stamped in and out of Cairo's Farouk Airport on a "Direct Transit" basis. Another stamp indicates that he arrived in London later on September 28, with "Foreign Currency Imported: U.S. dollars 30." Luckily for my father, this was not the only money on his person. A separate page indicates that he left India with a total of 15 British pounds and 200 U.S. dollars, taken out of the country

My father's 1949 Indian passport photo.

under the authority of Permit ECBY/799/33–49S. On September 29, he left London and was admitted to the United States in Boston on the same day, 1949.

It took my father two days by air to make the trip, about twice as long as it takes today. During every minute of those two days, if family legend is to be believed, Motiba cried her heart out. How could she stand to see her first baby go so far away? When would she ever see him again? Her precious son did return three years later, in 1952, but he left almost as soon as he arrived. He didn't want to go back to America. He missed India terribly. He missed his family. He missed his mother. He was only twenty-one years old. He wanted to stay home for good. But Bapuji would have none of it. My father was to return to America, finish his studies, and make something of himself there. The situation in Burma was extremely unstable. Who knew what was going to happen? It was best that the eldest son assume his family duty and establish a beachhead in America. So, reluctantly, my father went back to the States. I'm sure Motiba cried again. She was busy, of course, with her four other children. The youngest, my Ushaphaiba, was still a little girl. Bapuji had not yet moved the family to Bombay, and Motiba's life in the Jetpur house was a comfortable one. Much of her family, the Kharas, was living nearby in Amreli. Yet she missed her boy. It seemed to be the fate of Khara women to have their sons go off to the far corners of the earth in search of opportunity. Her own grandmother had experienced it with her son running off to Burma at the turn of the century. Now Motiba's firstborn was doing the same thing to her. Only the destination had changed. And all because of the movies.

* * *

The family's move to Bombay brought its members into far greater contact with the world beyond the close-knit community of Kathi-awari Jains than they had ever before experienced. Even in Burma, most of their lives were spent within the predictable spheres of the Gujarati merchant community of Rangoon. Bombay was the global capital of Gujarati-owned business, but it was also "the gateway to India" and a portal to the wide world beyond. From its docks, ships left daily for the Middle East, East Asia, Africa, Europe, and America. And the world came to Bombay, via the ships that steamed in from the Suez Canal, but also, by the time Bapuji moved the family there, via airplanes, foreign films, and newsreels.

Despite his best efforts, once the family was settled in Bombay, Bapuji could not protect his children from the seductions of the city or from the temptations of worldly life. My father was not the only child he was not able to save from the movies and the inevitable trip to America that followed. Once they were settled in Juhu, going out to the movies became one of the now-grown Kam-dar children's favorite pastimes. Bapuji disapproved of these out-ings, seeing nothing good in such a frivolous and spiritually corrupting form of wasting time. Trips to the cinema had to be made very surreptitiously. For my father's younger sister, my Bharatiphaiba, going out to the movies during her college years became a passion. I remember clearly her and her younger sister's strategies for getting around my grandfather's unrealistically aus-tere expectations of their comportment. He forbade them to read women's magazines, which he viewed as silly and immoral. But the moment Bapuji left for his late afternoon walk, my aunts Bharati and Usha would whisk out from under the mattresses copies of *Femina* and *Stardust,* the notorious Bollywood gossip rag with all the dirt on the film stars. Motiba, fully aware of what they were up to, raised no objections.

* * *

But then, Motiba had a very down-to-earth approach to life. Years later, when her cousin Himmat's son Raja—the one who as a ten-year-old had caught a shark at Chowpatty Beach—had a very public affair with the Indian film star Rekha, Motiba was the one who could be counted upon to have the latest gossip on the matter. The affair was quite sensational news in the family, as it was, briefly, in the movie gossip rags of Bombay. Rekha, the eventual star of Mira Nair's film *Kama Sutra,* was, after all, famous for her never-ending string of lovers. Her most celebrated dalliance had been with the Indian film megastar Amitabh Baachan. So, when Motiba began to tell us the latest about Raja and Rekha, we listened with rapt attention. According to Motiba, the scions of the Khara family did not approve of the relationship, both because it involved an actress, and therefore automatically a woman of ill repute in their view, but also because they didn't appreciate seeing the family name dragged across the pages of Bombay's gossip magazines. Motiba told us that Raja's mother, my Padmamami, a woman who was never one to flinch from tackling conservative family members head-on, summoned some of these dowagers and old uncles to her apartment on

Marine Drive. "Come over and meet her. You'll see for yourself that she's really very nice." Plump matrons in simple white cotton *saris,* rosettes of diamonds at their ears and flashes of disapproval in their eyes, made their way over to the apartment, husbands in tow. They were escorted to the posh living room of my aunt and uncle's flat, served a cold drink, and engaged in small talk as they waited for Raja and Rekha to make their appearance. According to Motiba, it was nearly five hours before the happy couple emerged from the bedroom! (When I told Padmamami this story, she flatly denied that anything of the sort had ever taken place. She couldn't imagine where Motiba had come up with such a tale.) I asked my grandmother, married by her father at the age of fifteen to a man she'd never seen who then refused to sleep with her for several years, what she thought about it all. She replied smartly, eyes smiling, "Oh, things have changed since I was a girl."

For all that, Motiba never suspected the extent to which her own daughter Bharati had developed a passion, if not for a movie star, for the movies themselves. And perhaps not even so much for the movies as for the opportunity the cinemas provided to spend several hours in air-conditioned bliss whiling away time that was supposed to be spent at school. Bharatiphaiba had to go to the movies during school hours because that was the only time she was allowed out of the house on her own. Though a college student, she lived, as proper young ladies were expected to do, at home. There was no way Bapuji would have given her permission to go out at night on any pretext, much less to see a movie. Moreover, most of the big cinemas were in Bombay proper, far from suburban Juhu. Bharatiphaiba found the perfect solution to her problem: as a student, she had a special first-class commuter train pass to travel from Juhu to her college in downtown Bombay. She loved the train trip. At that time, she says, the first-class compartments were uncrowded and clean. The trains were efficient, and in no time, they'd let her off at Churchgate Station. Bharatiphaiba was so seduced by the movies and the pleasantly cool, air-conditioned interiors of the sumptuous theaters, that she hardly attended any of her lectures at Bombay University. She spent much of her time at the Eros, where *My Fair Lady* had a long run. As the year wore on, she knew she was in ever-greater danger of failing her exams and that her father would not be pleased. But she didn't know what to do or how to stop. The whole experience of escaping the heat of Bombay for a couple of hours of pure fantasy was too irresistible. Then a marriage proposal came from a young man who was just finishing his medical training in America and needed to find a bride, marry, and get back to the States in short order. From my aunt's point of view, this news was too good to be true. The young doctor from America was a knight in shining armor, and Bharatiphaiba leapt at the chance to be carried away to a new life. She accepted the proposal, married, and left for New York just days before her final exams were scheduled. Her secret life at the Eros cinema was never discovered.

* * *

As more of Motiba's children emigrated to America, the relationship between the family's life in Juhu and the family's life in America became more porous. My father's younger brother Vinayak, whom the family calls "Vinoo" and I know as Vinukaka, joined my father in the mid-1950s. Bharatiphaiba was carried off by her white knight of a husband in 1968. In all, three of Motiba's five children left her to live in America. Only her youngest son and daughter remained in the Juhu apartment with her to the end.

In the early days, communication between India and America was rare. The first decade my father was in the States, the primary form of communication was letters, and Motiba wrote her son regularly. (My mother says she never knew what Motiba said in these letters, penned in Gujarati, but that my father would grind his teeth all night long in his sleep after receiving one.) Until 1965, when the family moved to Bombay, urgent communication was via telegraph. Later, at least through the end of the seventies, my parents would call only on very special occasions or if there was something terribly important to say. It was extremely expensive in those days to call India. I remember that before making one of these calls, my parents would write down everything they needed to say so they could fit it into the three-minute minimum set by the telephone company. The calls had to be arranged operator to operator, and the American operator would say nothing less portentous than, "This is the United States calling." Her Indian counterpart would reply, "Go ahead, United States," and we would be connected. In those days of presatellite communications, you could hear the distance, the tens of thousands of miles of cables between us and Bombay. There was the Trans-Atlantic Cable, the Trans-Pacific Cable, and then God—and Ma Bell, of course—only knew. Some seconds after speaking, you could hear, finally, your own words echoing at the other end. Then, through a sound as of distant wind blowing, the voice on the other end of the line would come back. You felt an entire planet away, and, indeed, you were. By the 1980s, there was direct dial service from the United States to India, though from India you still had to book a "trunk call" and wait your turn. Now, in the age of satellite communications, calling India is as simple—and almost as cheap—as calling across town, and sometimes the connection is better. There is only the twelve-hour time difference to remind you that the two countries are an entire world apart.

As Motiba's children in America became more settled and prosperous, they visited Bombay more frequently. No trip to India was made without packing one or two huge suitcases full of all the things one couldn't get there that were so easy to pick up in the States: Tylenol; blue jeans; sneakers; even, for a blessedly brief period, Tang, of all things. Motiba's home began to be filled with these items. Her three Indian grandsons growing up in the family apartment in Juhu dressed just like their cousins in West Virginia. Imported American clothes carried considerable status. They hinted at a level of wealth that permitted frequent trips abroad and the existence of stashes of foreign currency to pay for all the shopping, a status enjoyed by a very few. Middle-class Indians who had family overseas—and their numbers were considerably more limited in the 1960s and 70s than they have now become—were able to flaunt clothing and possessions otherwise available to only the extremely wealthy and to pretend to a social class to which, in fact, they did not belong.

Of all the changes the family experienced in Bombay, surely the most potent was the arrival of television. Color television was not broadcast in India until 1982, the year New Delhi hosted the Asian Games. Even this was limited to the programming on the state-controlled Doordarshan (literally "seeing from afar") channel, but it was a huge step up in home family entertainment. That year, my Bharatiphaiba, whose doctor husband had done extremely well for himself in America, brought the family a Sony Trinitron color television. Life at home in Juhu was transformed. In those days, before India opened itself to satellite broadcasts by the international cable networks, there were few viewing options: the news, read from Delhi in a Hindi so Sanskritized that almost no one outside of the capital's governing elite could understand a word of it; the immensely popular Sunday afternoon broadcast of the Hindu epic *Ramayana*; old movies (mostly Indian, some foreign); and the never-ending "cultural programmes" of traditional Indian music and dance. Soon enough, however, there were popular soap opera serials, the nightly broadcast of which was not to be missed. Of these, Motiba liked to watch *Hum Log* and *Buniyaad* and, in anticipation of the arrival of MTV India, a program called *Chhaya Geet* that offered half-hour selections of Hindi film songs with the corresponding footage.

Then, in 1991, in the wake of a balance of payments crisis that forced India to liberalize its economy, international satellite television arrived to capture a vast Indian market. Local cable operators mushroomed on every block, stringing loops of cable through building windows, over rooftops, even into the huts in Vittal's slum. Soon everyone was watching *Baywatch; The Bold and the Beautiful;* and old reruns of *Bewitched,* in which blond Elizabeth Montgomery cast her spells in Hindi. For the first time since India's independence in 1947, American life and mass culture were on view all over the city, every day and every night.

* * *

Bombay has since become a postmodern city par excellence, where past, present, and future collide and fragment, where the local and the global and everything in-between mix together in a heady *masala* all the city's own. In turn-of-the-twentieth-century Bombay, the paradigm that determines who is in and who is out, who is rich and who is poor, is the global consumer culture flowing out of and back into the image industries. There are clubs where the entry charge is 2,000 rupees or more, and where by the time you've had one drink and gotten out, you've spent just as much as you might in a similar establishment in New York or London. The clubs are packed with the golden youth of the city, dressed in Armani Exchange, dripping with diamonds, their chauffeur-driven cars waiting outside. These young people happily point to the new Benetton, the Tiffany's, the Ford automobile dealership, the availability of Coca-Cola, and myriad American television serials freshly beamed in on Star TV as tangible signs of the city's improvement. There is even a new shopping mall complete with shiny escalators and brand names recognizable the world over. In a world where you are what you consume, where the medium is the message and image is everything, Bombay's privileged young people are surrounded with sure proof that they are card-carrying citizens of the happening now of global culture.

But in the same city where kids sip Pepsis as they chat with chums on their "mobiles," the vast majority possess nothing, not even themselves. The only contact millions of people in Bombay have with the global consumer culture is with its garbage. I recently had a chance to observe a family of ragpickers as they went about their morning ablutions in front of a shack built against the inside of the retaining wall along the railroad track. There were bundles of discarded plastic bags piled high around the hut, which they had collected to sell to recyclers. The mother walked down to the ditch right next to the track and collected some water into a small bucket, which she then took up to her naked six- or seven-year-old son. She proceeded to wash him with the greatest tenderness imaginable, making sure, as I do with my son, to get behind the ears and under the arms. She used her wetted finger to clean his teeth. She washed down his legs and feet as he stood patiently in the dust. Her daughter had apparently just undergone the same treatment and was busy pulling on a grayed dress, obviously washed and air-dried overnight. I turned my eyes away from this scene into which I felt I had no right to intrude. Against what odds and in what destitution, under the gaze of passengers in hundreds of passing trains, did this family preserve its full dignity and humanity, eking out a living by collecting the plastic refuse of the consuming classes?

Only the poor, who have no choice, or the superrich, who possess an apartment in Dubai and/or London and a condominium in New Jersey or California, can contemplate staying in Bombay. Of the people most connected to our family, only the Parekhs, with whom Bapuji had such close personal and business ties in Burma, and some of the Kharas fall into this category. They alone have the resources to keep the decline in the quality of life at bay, turning on their private generators when the power goes out, using their cellular phones when the telephone lines won't work, moving from air-conditioned flats to air-conditioned cars to air-conditioned offices through streets they barely notice through tinted windows.

These friends and relatives have penetrated the Bombay of the old elites, the Bombay of the Willingdon Club and the Gymkhana, the Bombay of Malabar Hill and Cuffe Parade, the Bombay of wives who own art galleries and of parties where all the talk—and the dress—is of New York, and where the sons and daughters of Bollywood movie stars chat up America-returned investment bankers and info-tech millionaires late into the night.

This Bombay of the wealthy and teeny-tiny minority of the city's population is a comfortable place for me to bring my own young children. It is a city where they can watch *Cartoon Network* and Pokemon videos, eat pizza, and exchange Beanie Babies with their little Indian friends who have the same tastes and speak the same language. The rest of Bombay, where an embattled middle class and the teeming poor struggle to survive, has become completely foreign to me, though that is where I lived and where I went to school as a child, and where my grandparents, aunts, uncles, and cousins lived for decades.

* * *

In 1987, Bapuji suffered a sudden brain hemorrhage. He was taken to Nanavati Hospital in nearby Ville Parle, where three of his grandchildren had been born. He didn't linger long. He was eighty-three years old. My father rushed to India, but Bapuji had already been cremated when he got there. According to Hindu rituals our Jain family also observes, it is the eldest son who performs the main gestures of the cremation ceremony. This was a duty my father had dreaded, and one his being at the crucial moment far away in America saved him from performing in the end. Dipukaka, the youngest son, did the necessary.

For several years after Bapuji's death, Motiba's America-settled children encouraged her to move to the United States. They found Bombay, the city that took my family in when it was kicked out of Burma, to no longer be liveable. Many family members still in Bombay were planning their escape. They couldn't take the pollution, the commutes that had lengthened from one hour to two hours or more, the precipitous rise in crime. In the early 1990s, Bombay ceased to be a cosmopolitan city welcoming to Gujaratis. With the ascendancy of a protofascist Maharashtrian political party with close links to organized crime, it became a fiefdom marked by corruption and violence. Dipukaka, who had lived in Bombay most of his life, said that as a Gujarati, he felt the city had become a hostile place. With a heavy heart, he left the apartment in Juhu and moved to New Delhi. When he retires, his plan is to divide his time between Gujarat, where, he says, "at least I will be among own people," and Seattle, where his eldest son is now settled.

Despite the family's entreaties, Motiba remained stubbornly uninterested in leaving Bombay. She made several trips to America, staying for months at a time. My Bharatiphaiba, in particular, took extra care of Motiba during these visits, treating her like a queen at her comfortable and spacious home in Illinois. Motiba was able to experience once again something of the luxury she'd known as a young girl in prewar Burma. Life was easier in America, no doubt, but Motiba missed her extensive network of friends and relatives in Bombay. She missed her temple. There was no way she could continue her mode of life—a spiritual life at the center of a community rich with ritual and the rhythm of seasonal Jain and Hindu holidays—in America. America was too cold, both literally and socially. People lived closed off from one another in their huge private houses, moving from place to place only by car.

By choice, Motiba never moved to America. She died in the apartment in Juhu where she had lived for thirty years. With her, died the home she'd created there out of the sheer force of her maternal presence. Bombay is no longer a city we can go home to. With Motiba gone, we're stuck with America.

Motiba's Mohanthal

Visitors to Motiba's home were always offered tea. If the guests were especially important, Motiba would whip up a batch of fresh mohanthal *to serve along with the tea and other assorted snacks, such as* ghatia, sev, *small* puris, *and* bhajia.

INGREDIENTS

2 c. *chana* flour
3/4 c. plus 2 Tbsp. ghee
2 Tbsp. milk
1/2 c. *mawa* (boiled down crumbly milk solids)*
1 c. sugar
1/2 tsp. cardamon seeds, minced or ground
1/2 tsp. ground saffron
pistachios
sliced almonds

Mix *chana* flour, 2 Tbsp. ghee and milk. Mixture will be very crumbly. Let sit for about 1/2 hour. Put the sugar into a heavy-bottomed casserole and add just enough water to cover. Cook over a low heat until thickened. Heat 3/4 c. ghee in a pot over low flame. Add the *chana* mixture, passing it through a sieve to remove any lumps. Heat, stirring constantly until the mixture turns a pinkish, light brown color. Add sugar syrup. Combine. Spread the whole mixture out in a small *thali* and cut into diamonds. Garnish with minced cardamon seeds, pistachios and thinly sliced almonds. Serve warm or room temperature.

NOTE: *Mawa* is available in the frozen food section of Indian grocery stores.

Motiba's Chai

Motiba was particular about her tea—chai in Hindi, cha in Gujarati—which she flavored in the Indian style with her own mixture of ground spices. Motiba liked her tea very hot and and very sweet and, in the village way, preferred to sip it from a saucer rather than a cup. Indian-style chai has become a popular coffee-house drink all over North America, but Motiba would have considered today's prepackaged concoctions in Tetrapaks poor imitations of the real thing.

Chai masala INGREDIENTS

1 *wati** pieces of dried ginger root
1/4 *wati* podded whole cardamon seeds
15 whole black peppercorns
4–5 cinnamon sticks
4–5 whole cloves

Grind spices together into a fine powder using a mortar and pestle. Store *masala* in an airtight container away from direct light.

NOTE: A *wati* is a traditional Indian measure equivalent to approximately 1/2 cup.

Chai INGREDIENTS

chai masala (see above)
1 tsp. tea leaves
3 tsp. sugar
1/4c. whole milk

Place a pinch of chai masala into 1 cup cold water in a suitable pot. Bring to a boil. Add the tea leaves. Stir. Add the sugar. Boil for 2 minutes. Add the milk, remove from heat and serve.

(NOTE: There is no correct way to make *chai*. Motiba always used 3 tsp. of sugar. Most people, however, make the tea milkier and less sweet, using only 2 tsp. of sugar and preparing the tea in a mixture of 1 equal part water to 1 equal part milk. Others use only milk.)

4

America

Foreigners kept coming in, of course, and Seattle kept growing.
But by this time, it was Boeing that was bringing them
in and many of them wore white collars, smelled nice,
spoke well, and weren't at all the sort one would be
afraid to have living next door.

—GERALD B. NELSON, Seattle

"I would like to eat ve-ge-tables. Do you serve ve-ge-tables?" asked my father. (He pronounced the second half of the word like the word "table" with a long "a".)

"Huh?"

"Ve-ge-tables."

"Oh, ya wan vegebles? Why'n ya say so? We don got no vegebles. Ya wanna sanwich?"

"Cheese sandwich? Do you have a cheese sandwich?"

"Ya don wanannie meat?"

"I don't eat meat. I am a vegetarian. I only eat ve-ge-tables."

"Okay, kid, I'll make ya a cheese sandwich."

My father had just landed in postwar America, a place where the corner grocery did not yet stock Garden Burgers, yogurt, or tofu. Restaurants did not serve vegetarian food or offer kindly to have the chef "create something special" for vegetarian diners. Nineteen forty-nine America was solid meat-and-potatoes country. It was a time of culinary innocence so profound that a new dish called "pizza" had to be explained to the general public. It was also a time when the definition of an American was as straightforward as a plain-talking Yankee. Identities were clearly drawn, especially along racial lines. In the South, Blacks ate, traveled, went to school, worshiped, and used bathrooms strictly segregated from where Whites did the same. Jews were unwelcome in many neighborhoods, country clubs, even universities. Asians were regarded as so impenetrably foreign as to be understood only as an inchoate mass, a "yellow horde" that might overwhelm the country on its western flank if ever it was given a chance. Miscegenation laws protected the citizens of several states from the dangers of "mixed marriages." Immigration quotas ensured that the vast majority of new people coming into the country came from Europe, lest the character of the nation be corrupted by peoples too dark, too Asiatic, or simply too foreign to the American way of life.

But like an airplane revving its engines for takeoff, all this was about to change precipitously. America's postwar embrace of technology by a triumphant military-industrial complex propelled the nation forward with greater and greater speed, until, by the century's end, the United States became the driving force of the global economy and the world's sole "superpower." Egged on by its Cold War struggle against the Soviet Union and the forces of communism, America was hungry for the best minds it could get, no matter what their provenance. Immigration quotas restricting non-Europeans from becoming U.S. citizens eventually gave way before the sheer force of industry's increasing appetite for a highly educated labor force. To win the Cold War, the United States firmly believed it had to achieve and maintain technological superiority over the enemy. It was an irresistible opportunity for engineers and scientists the world over, especially those who hailed from poorer countries where, though their skills were sorely needed, jobs demanding state-of-the-art technical skills either did not yet exist or offered salaries that were a pitiful fraction of the going rate in the States. The complexion of the country began to mottle. Just as many Anglo-Americans had feared for decades, what began as a trickle of immigrants from Asia, Latin America, and other hitherto "undesirable" areas turned into a steady stream. Inevitably, the very identity of the country, what it meant to be an "American," became complicated, even contested. The great assimilationist "melting pot" turned into a "salad bowl" of diversity. My father, arriving just as these changes were about to begin, was able to hitch a ride on America's magnificent technological momentum. The kid from Kathiawar threw his lot in with that of the United States, eventually working directly on what was to become the defining moment of the American century: the televised image of a man planting the Stars and Stripes on the moon broadcast to an audience of millions.

* * *

When my father arrived in America, immigration from Asia was strictly controlled. The Barred Zone Act of 1917 and the Asian Exclusion Act of 1924 specifically prohibited Asian Indians from immigrating to the United States. Finally, under heavy lobbying by a small group of Asian Indians in New York, Public Law 483 was passed in 1946, allowing Indians to become naturalized citizens. The law limited the number of Asian Indians allowed into the United States to 100 individuals per year. Until the 1965 Immigration Act did away with these restrictions, very few Indians made their way to America. In 1940, there were the same number of Asian Indians in the United States as in 1910: just 10,000. As recently as 1960, out of a total of 265,398 immigrants to the United States, only 391 came from India.[1]

By and large, Asian Indians were not a welcome group. In 1907, a group of Sikh laborers toiling in the lumber mills of Bellingham, Washington, were violently attacked and forced to flee north to Canada. Members of another of the early Indian communities, established by Punjabi Sikh farmers in California's San Jose Valley in the late 1800s, scraped and saved to buy their own farms only to see their lands confiscated under the terms of the California Alien Land Laws of 1913.

My father was a new type of Indian immigrant to the United States, one of the first to come after World War II to pursue higher education. Until then, England—specifically, Cambridge or Oxford—was the choice of elite Indian parents wishing to educate their sons abroad. One of the very first Indian engineering students in the United States, my father set a mold that would be filled by thousands of bright young Indians in the decades to come. The Immigration Act of 1965, which came into full effect in 1968, specifically permitted immigration to the United States by aliens under the category of "occupational immigration," those who, by "their possession of occupational skills needed in the U.S. labor market," filled a perceived national need. The great "brain drain" of highly skilled technicians, scientists, doctors, and engineers from the impoverished countries of the third world to the United States began in earnest. The number of Indian doctors, engineers, scientists, and scholars settling in America rose steadily from the late 1960s on.

My father was admitted to the United States on a student visa to attend Chauncy Hall, a preparatory school for boys founded in Boston, Massachusetts, in 1828. The idea was that he would go on from prep school to the Massachusetts Institute of Technology to study engineering. In a way, Chauncy Hall, his first stop in America, was his last stop in the world in which he'd been raised in India: a world of privilege. He did not stay long. Bapuji was facing grave uncertainties with his business in Rangoon, and when rupees were converted into dollars, Chauncy Hall seemed an unaffordable extravagance. At the age of nineteen years, in a big, powerful country where he didn't know a soul, my father was forced to do something for which no Indian son of his class had ever been prepared: make his own way in the world. There was no network of relatives in America to help him along, to give him a place to stay, provide him with home-cooked Jain vegetarian meals, subsidize his studies, or help set him up in business. He was on his own.

Abandoning Chauncy Hall, my father left Boston for Manhattan—Kansas, that is—where he enrolled in Kansas State University for the summer. Luckily for my father, new, affordable opportunities in higher education were just becoming available to foreign students such as himself. University enrollment in the United States was booming. Record numbers of young people poured into America's state universities during the immediate postwar years of the late 1940s and on into the 1950s. As the Cold

War intensified, "land grant" public universities became important training grounds for the masses of educated, technically skilled workers the country needed to preserve its competitive edge over the Soviet Union. The ideal of a liberal arts education grounded in the classics for the sons and daughters of a tiny elite—an ideal represented by the venerable Ivy League schools—gave way to practical, job-getting skills the sons and daughters of America's factory workers and farmers could use to transform themselves into a new class of well-paid technicians. Public state universities were highly democratic: all that was required was a high school diploma and a part-time job to pay the modest tuition costs. In their quest for talented students, many schools sought to recruit young people from abroad by offering them the same low tuition rates as state residents. For the first time, women also began entering universities in substantial numbers. In the spirit of the times, universities wooed women students by putting a technical spin on traditional female spheres, creating such specialized domains as "Home Science." Courses such as these would prepare women to be efficient homemakers and helpmates once they had completed their true major, "Marriage 101," and snared an educated husband. America's state universities in the 1950s were like giant magnets for ambitious young people from all walks of life. On their campuses, for the first time in the country's history, the children of America's farms, small towns, and blue-collar neighborhoods went to college, and there met, en masse, the children of the rest of the world's elite, especially students from the newly independent countries of Asia and the Middle East.

From Kansas, my father went to the only institution of higher education in America where he knew someone (a cousin from India): Oklahoma Agricultural and Mechanical College, now known as Oklahoma State University, in Stillwater, Oklahoma. He studied aeronautical engineering, paying for his tuition and living costs by working in the on-campus dairy making ice cream, a food his Jain dietary restrictions, thankfully, allowed him to eat with impunity. As soon as he completed his degree there, however, he had to think up a new academic endeavor quickly to preserve his only means of staying in America: a student visa. He had supported himself during a couple of summers working in the canneries of the Pacific Northwest: Green Giant, Libby McNeil & Libby, Stokley Van Camp, Consolidated Food Processing, and the San Juan Islands Cannery. So, from Oklahoma he headed west to the University of Washington in Seattle. His intention was to begin work toward a master's degree in engineering. He soon changed his mind. In a fit of idealism and homesickness, he decided after only one semester at the "U. of Dub" that what he really wanted to do was go back to India and do something useful for his young country. He transferred to Oregon State College in Corvallis, Oregon, where there were quite a few foreign students, including some from India, enrolled in the Soils Department, and began work on a degree in soils analysis.

He also became involved in the Cosmopolitan Club, a student organization of local and foreign students with an international theme. My father—almost criminally handsome in his twenties—was quite the social butterfly at Oregon State, always surrounded by friends and admirers. He convinced the members of the Cosmopolitan Club to take on a special project: adopt an Indian village and raise money for digging a well to provide the villagers with clean water. It was at a Cosmopolitan Club social in 1955 that my father met the vivacious Oregon farm girl who became my mother.

* * *

I have always understood my parents' marriage as a clear case of an attraction of opposites: my father, the handsome, dark young man from the exotic East, who'd grown up in privileged circumstances as the eldest son of a prosperous merchant now fallen on hard times; my mother, the fair-skinned, red-headed daughter of first-generation Danish-American farmers, who'd grown up barely scraping by in the aftermath of the Great Depression, working every summer picking beans to pay for her school clothes and books, breaking and training a wild mustang mare so that she could have a horse of her own. When they met, my father was struggling to invent a life in a new country and a new world after his family's fall from material grace after the war. My mother was trying to figure out how she could get as far as possible from the farm she grew up on and the stifling limitations of small-town America. She and her peers at Junction City High School had but one ambition: to get out of "Junktown Shitty." Oregon State College was only thirty-five miles away from the farm, but it was a portal to the rest of the wide, wide world.

* * *

*My mother, Lois Christiansen, leading the Fourth of July
parade down Main Street as a high school student in
Junction City, Oregon, in the 1940s.*

My mother joined the Cosmopolitan Club because it appealed to her
sense of adventure and curiosity about the world beyond Oregon.
She often brought her foreign "Cosmo Club" friends—who were far

from home and had nowhere to go on holidays and weekends—
home to the farm. Her parents lived in a huge white Victorian house
with gingerbreading, a wraparound porch, and a turreted tower.
Some distance in back of the house was a classic red barn that my
grandfather used for his sheet metal business, and where once my
mother had laid down as a girl among baby chicks so she could feel
their teeny-tiny feet under fluffs of down running all over her body.
There was plenty of food and plenty of room on the farm, and my
Danish grandparents were happy to welcome my mother's friends to
their home. My father came to the house a couple of times, always
one among a changing group of students from all over the world.

As it was for my father, my mother's seduction by exotic lands
and peoples began at the cinema. Just as my father had formed his
first impressions of America watching Maureen O'Hara and Clifton
Webb in the Art Deco movie houses of Bombay, my mother became
interested in India after seeing Jean Renoir's classic movie *The River*
at the Valley Cinema on Main Street in Junction City, Oregon. *The
River* is the story of a European family of many daughters and one son
who live in Calcutta on the Houghly. A handsome young European
man comes calling and catches the eye of the elder daughters in the
family, but falls instead for the pretty Indian girl who lives nearby.
The intrepid little son dies of snakebite after attempting to charm a
cobra that lives in the garden. This tragedy is followed by the birth of
a new child: another daughter. All through, there is the river flowing
ever past. It is a long, languorous, beautifully done film, and it made
a strong impression on my teenage, cowgirl mother who had never
seen any place remotely like the one portrayed in the movie.

In 1956, when my mother was asked if she would be interested in participating in a special international seminar to be held in India, how could she refuse? A trip to India? How much further away from Junction City could a girl get? In her capacity as president of the Cosmopolitan Club, my mother had contacted the Tata Foundation in India to see if it could help the club do some useful work there. She showed the letter conveying the Tata Foundation's favorable response to Bob Stripple, a professor who ran the Y Round Table from a nearby office. As my mother wrote to her parents in a breathless letter soon after, "He read half-way through the letter from Tata and literally hit the ceiling!! He had just remembered a letter he had received from the regional secretary yesterday. The World University Service is having a conference in Poona, India (Sudha's town). The secretary wanted to know if Bob had any prospects for going. People from all over the world would be there. Bob said I was the only one he would recommend from O.S.C. and he would give me a *very high recommendation* and could get other influential people to do the same!!!!!!!"

There was one, big hitch: my mother needed $1,000, an enormous sum in 1956. How would she get the money? She wrote her parents: "What would you think of my going? Are you able to help me out financially, and if so, would you? I know it is an awful, awful lot to ask, but I think it might be worth more than all the money in the world to go as it would straighten out in my mind just what I do want in life." A priceless outcome indeed! Going a bit over the top, she continued, "Then, if I decide to spend the rest of my life in India working on just the problems that we would be

studying at the conference, I would know exactly what I was getting into, as I would have been there and seen it." The rest of her
life in India? I'm sure her parents were thrilled to hear that! But
there was more: "I would also have had a chance to meet Pete's
family and visit his home in Jetpur."

Pete was my father. "Prabhakar" was too much of a mouthful for
most Americans, so he had adopted the name "Pete." Pete himself
wanted nothing more in the world than to return to India. "I talked
to Pete for about an hour last night after I found out about this. He
said it would about kill him if I were in India and he were here as
he wants to go home so badly himself." God, he was homesick, but
he was in America, and Bapuji had made it clear that his duty as eldest son required him to stay on in America and make something of
himself. As for my mother's parents, lest they worry about their
only daughter traveling halfway around the world on her own: "I
would be well taken care of on the whole trip I assure you." And the
clincher: "I would definitely be back in time for school to start."

Eventually, the Ford Foundation came to the rescue, giving
Mom a scholarship to join the World University Service Seminar
in Poona, India. "Junction City Girl to Attend Event in India," was
the headline in the local paper. My mother was realizing her dream
of seeing the wide world. She joined a small group of other American students from around the country, including a Columbia University law student, a student at the University of Chicago, a
student at Radcliffe College, and one from Randolph-Macon
Woman's College, along with students from Ohio State University, Southern Methodist University, and Southern University in

My mother (center) poses with her fellow World University Seminar delegates before their departure for India in 1956.

Louisiana. Reflecting the theme of inclusiveness in the group's mission, it was a mixed group of women and men, African Americans and Whites.

In 1956, India had been independent only nine years. It was a young nation, "Young India," heady with the possibilities of self-realization, full of the zeal of self-invention, of optimism for a great and prosperous future. Free of the yoke of British imperialism, there was no limit to what it would accomplish. In the meantime, there was so very much work to be done: eliminating poverty, spreading

literacy, improving health care, increasing crop yields. My parents,
like their peers, were inspired by the Yankee, can-do belief that these
problems could easily be solved by a judicious application of technological know-how. Students such as my father were being educated in America, after all, with the idea that they would go back to
India and put their knowledge in the service of the great project of
"developing" India. Enterprising organizations, from the Cosmopolitan Club at Oregon State College all the way up to the great
Ford Foundation itself, were putting their faith—and their money—into development projects: drilling wells, digging latrines,
building schools, immunizing children. Jersey cows were sent from
America to India to improve milk production. Leghorn chickens
were sent over to improve egg production. The seeds of the "green
revolution" were sent over to improve crop yields. Tractors would
replace bullocks. Highways would be built, dams erected, ports
enlarged. My parents wanted to be a part of it all.

Aside from the seminar itself, which took place over a month or
so, the World University Service Seminar students were treated to
a grand tour of India and received with aplomb by dignitaries,
notables, and royals wherever they went. My mother has extraordinary slides from her trip, with pictures of such Indian luminaries
of the time as Lata Mangeshkar, Vinoba Bhave, and the Maharajah
of Mysore. There are also slides of my mother, so slender, so beautiful, in her prim fifties full-skirted and wasp-waisted frocks or,
more interestingly, dressed up by her various Indian hosts in native
dress: my mother wearing a nine-yard Maharashtrian-style *sari;* my
mother in an emerald green *sari* that sets off her red hair to advan-

*Something to show the folks back home: Mom poses in India
in front of a statue of the Hindu goddess of music
and literature Saraswati.*

tage, a pair of cobras twined around her neck, their heads raised to
face the camera, framing her own smiling face on either side.

There are slides of ambitious projects of nation-building and grass-roots development: schools under construction, new wells for village women. There are also slides of my mother with my father's family in Jetpur: my aunts Bharati and Usha, young girls with their braids tied up in ribboned loops on either side of their heads; Motiba looking pained at being photographed. "We all knew she was going to marry Bhai. Otherwise, why would she come to us?" Motiba said years later. My mother points out that she visited other families of other Indian students she knew from Oregon State, but she also admits that she and my father were in love.

* * *

She was away about three months in all. My mother, who had hardly been outside the states of California and Oregon, visited New York, Paris, Cairo, and points all over India. When I asked her what her first impressions of India were, she said, "It was like I was not in a real world. We arrived in Bombay during monsoon. The air was so thick and hot. I could never dry off. I'd bathe, and I couldn't get dry. Then I'd put on clothes that were damp. Nothing was dry. Everything smelled of mold. You know, even in Oregon where it rains a lot, you can get dry after a shower. Well, in India I couldn't get dry. Then there were the sounds, the smells, the poverty. I felt like I'd been through some sort of time-warp and it was two thousand years ago. I felt like that even in the cities. Even years later, when I'd go back, it'd take me at least a month before I didn't feel as if I were in some kind of dream world."

My mother returned from India in the fall of 1956. In March of the following year, my parents were married. Printed on the cover of their marriage announcement is a verse from Walt Whitman:

> Lo, soul, seest thou not
> God's purpose from the first?
> The earth to be spann'd,
> connected by network,
> The races, neighbors, to marry
> and be given in marriage,
> The oceans to be cross'd,
> the distant brought near,
> The lands to be welded together.

Inside it reads:

MR. AND MRS. EJNER CHRISTIANSEN
announce the marriage of their daughter
LOIS ELNA
to
MR. PRABHAKAR P. KAMDAR
son of MR. AND MRS. P. B. KAMDAR
Jetpur, (Saurashtra), India
on Saturday, the twenty-third of March
nineteen hundred and fifty-seven
Seattle, Washington

Theirs was not the only "mixed marriage" that resulted from international fraternizing at the Cosmo Club: my mother's friend Nancy

*My parents at their wedding reception at my mother's parents' home,
Junction City, Oregon, 1957.*

married Hassan Assam from Egypt. Gloria, a girl from Beaverton, Oregon, married Kwaku, a young man from Africa. A Finnish girl, Kaino Ojala, married one of the American guys. My parents and their friends felt that the very act of marrying someone from a vastly different culture with a different color of skin and a different take on life was a constructive step toward the project of building a more harmonious world. They truly believed that their marriages and the mixed children they produced were a personal contribution to world peace and understanding. In a letter to my mother in the early days of their marriage, my father wrote, "Together we hold the future of the unity of mankind." What better way to ensure that the hatreds of the war years never return than to mix everyone up with one another to form one happy human family, one great global melting pot?

* * *

The Space Age began the year my parents were married and just one month before I was born on November 8, 1957. On October 5, the Soviets had successfully launched their Sputnik spacecraft, leaving a humiliated America behind at the starting gate of one of the Cold War's greatest contests: the space race. My mother stood in the backyard that night with a group of friends, straining her eyes up at the star-filled sky to catch a glimpse of Sputnik as it flashed past them. She was hugely pregnant with me, so, in a way, I too experienced that first flash of light high above the Earth made by an object sent into the heavens by humans. Spellbound as my mother was, she could not have imagined how much satellite technology would change life on Earth in just a few decades. Nor could she have known yet that the space race would be our family's ticket to a comfortable life.

At the time, my father was marginally employed, halfheartedly pursuing his degree in soils analysis. His younger brother Vinoo had come to America and joined the newlyweds at Oregon State College. My mother and Vinukaka would plan their class schedules

Vinukaka, Jasuphaiba, and me pose on the day of my mother's graduation from Oregon State College.

so that they could take turns watching me while the other attended class, arranging to meet at a halfway point, one handing over the baby carriage to the other. The four of us lived in a little old house next to the railroad tracks.

* * *

After she got her degree, my mother and father moved back up to Bothell, a suburb of Seattle where housing was more affordable and where Dad had better employment prospects. The house in Bothell, the only one my father ever built, was my first home. I remember munching on the raspberries that grew at the back of our lawn; hiding out under the huge low branches of the giant Douglas fir in the neighbor's front yard; and putting in my very own garden with my own miniature shovel, rake, and hoe set. My parents owned an old Studebaker sedan in those days. They'd bought it used, of course. I loved that car. There was a hole the size of a nickel in the floor below the backseat and I could sit and watch the street whiz by under us as we drove.

But for my mother, the situation in Bothell was far from ideal. My father was not working seriously on his degree at Oregon State, nor had he found a full-time job. Finally, she had had enough. She went home to her parents' farm, taking me with her. My father realized that if he wanted my mother back, he'd have to put together a more conventional life. Providentially, buoyed in no small part by the government's Cold War commitment to the development of the U.S. aerospace industry, the Boeing Company was about to begin design and production of the world's first commercial jetliner, the 707. Boeing needed to hire thousands of engineers. Luckily, my father had his degree in aeronautical engineering from Oklahoma A&M.

Dad wrote my mother a letter. He began with a description of his ideal of her as a wife in the Indian tradition—"My idea is that we plan to live in India and you would feel to have the contentment of an Indian wife about her husband and her marital status." Then, my father offered her a life totally on her own, American terms: "I am prepared to stay in this country and you can bring up Poopy the way you see fit" ("Poopy" was my parents' corruption of the French word for doll, *poupée*). Incredibly, to get my mother back, Dad was even prepared to erase his Indianness from me entirely: "We can change 'Mira' to 'Mary.'" We could be just another typical American family: Pete, Lois, and little Mary. My father would abandon his idealistic plan to learn about soils analysis and return to India to feed the starving masses. He would stay in America and get a real job.

My father was immediately hired as an associate engineer at Boeing on the 707 aircraft design team, my mother returned to him in Seattle, and they began a more conventional life together. In 1960, they had another child, a daughter they named Devyani, "gift from the goddess." On my birthday that year, John F. Kennedy was elected president of the United States. My parents were thrilled. They were Democrats, of course, and Kennedy, a member of their own generation, seemed to embody the youthful, purposeful spirit of the country. The forward march of America's progress, and of my parents' young lives, seemed unassailable.

In 1961, they bought a brand-new, split-level ranch house with a daylight basement in the tony Seattle suburb of Bellevue. They also acquired a brand-new white Rambler station wagon with a light-blue vinyl interior. My father's future in aerospace—which in Seattle meant Boeing—seemed secure forever. Our lives took on the contours of the ideal 1960s suburban family. Our neighborhood boasted rows of brand-new ranch houses. All the fathers went off to work in the morning. All the mothers stayed home. There were children everywhere. Across the street from our house was an empty lot where we played fort with other kids from the neighborhood, creating secret hideouts around the bough-draped trunks of the old Douglas firs and Western Red cedars. I took the bus to school in the morning, where I was president of my class at Woodridge Elementary, and walked home in the afternoon. Typically, there were schoolyard bullies who tortured the weaker kids, such as myself. One girl in particular used to taunt me all the way home. When I complained, she'd spit out, "America is a free country. I can do whatever I want, and you can't stop me!" I hated her for her smug American arrogance, but, unsure what America really was all about, I could never hit upon a suitable retort. It rained a lot. One summer afternoon when we were swimming in Lake Washington it began to rain so hard that as the drops bounced back off the surface of the water, we had the odd sensation of taking a bath and a shower at the same time. In Seattle, no one thought it strange to swim in the rain.

* * *

That year, I made my first trip to India. Even with my father's good job at Boeing, it was an expensive trip for my parents to finance. Dad stayed behind to work. My mother set off alone with three-year-old me and my ten-month-old sister. To save money, we went from Seattle to Bombay on a freighter owned by the Scindia Lines shipping

company called the *Jalgopal*. We stayed in the Scindia family's own private cabin, so we were as comfortable as anyone on the ship, and ate
in the ship's dining room with the crew. There were a couple of other
paying passengers on board, but not many. The crewmen, homesick,
missing their families, and filled with the spontaneous warmth toward children that is typical of Indians, adopted me during the trip.
This was a big help to my mother. For much of the way across the
Pacific, the *Jalgopal* was following the path of a typhoon. The seas were
very rough, and the great ship pitched and rolled terribly. I can
remember watching the plates and glasses on the dining table sliding
first to one side, then to the other, a wooden railing around the edge
of the table preventing them from crashing to the floor. My mother
was sick most of the time, and she had my little sister to look after. I
spent a lot of time with various members of the crew. They set up a
little swing for me on deck, took me all around the ship, played with
me for hours. One afternoon, however, when my mother thought I
was with some of the crew and they thought I was with her, I was, in
fact, exploring on my own. I'd made my way to the top deck, where
a crewman came upon me hanging from the side rail, happily swing-
ing out over the churning Pacific. Afraid that if he said something I
might turn toward him and let go, he sneaked up on me and grabbed
me from behind, scaring the living daylights out of me but saving my
life. The ship's captain told my mother after I'd been brought down to
her, "We would not even have turned the ship around. There would
have been no point. A grown man couldn't swim in these seas, and
besides, she would have been sucked down and spit out by the
engines. By the time we'd have gotten this ship turned around, there

would have been nothing left of her to fish out of the sea." Everyone kept a more vigilant eye on me after that incident.

After docking in Bombay, we made our way by train to Jetpur to the house Bapuji had built in his ancestral Kathiawari town with some of his Burmese fortune. He'd designed it to his specifications, with custom features such as built-in grain storage bins and toilets well away from the main living quarters. Bapuji was proud of these "modern" touches. My father's younger brother Dilip and his two sisters, Bharati and Usha, lived with Motiba and Bapuji in the Jetpur house. We stayed with them for several months.

Devi, for that is what we always called my little sister, almost immediately came down with dysentery, and my mother's hands became raw and red from constantly washing her diapers. I myself fell ill with malaria. I had so many red bumps all over my body that Bapuji thought I must have picked up some kind of skin disease and sent me to a dermatologist in nearby Rajkot. The bumps turned out to be mosquito bites, hundreds of mosquito bites. Jokes were made about the attractions of my "imported blood" for the local mosquito population, or it was kindly said that my blood was so sweet, naturally the mosquitoes couldn't resist it. But my illness was no joking matter. I was vomiting and defecating blood. My temperature hovered between 105 and 106 degrees. "I really thought we were going to lose you," remembers my mother. Somehow, a correct diagnosis was made. I was given some quinine and survived. The rest of the family understood that because we came from such a rich and strong country, America, we were, paradoxically, weaklings. We simply didn't have the resistance to disease that our Indian family had. All kinds of extra precautions had to be taken with us: our water had to be specially boiled, we had to sleep under mosquito nets, we could never eat food "from outside."

I was not allowed out of the house on my own. Even my mother was forbidden from going out unaccompanied. Her five-foot-nine-inch frame, fair skin, freckles, and red hair made her absolutely the most bizarre creature anyone in the town had ever seen, a town where the only foreigner anyone could remember was an old English *memsahib* who had worked since the dawn of time at the local laying-in hospital, never emerging from the hospital compound,

Playing at fetching water on the roof of the Jetpur house, age three.

her person swathed in a white cotton *sari* and long-sleeved blouse. Each time Mom went out, she was immediately surrounded by crowds of people eager to see the alien living in their midst. And crowds in India could get ugly. It was better to stay home. In the mornings and evenings, when it wasn't too hot, I played on the

Motiba with Devyani and me on the roof in Jetpur.

agasi, the rooftop terrace. Bapuji had a little playhouse constructed up there. I used to dress up in little-girl Indian outfits and pretend to go down to the river for water, mincing across the terrace with my copper water jug balanced just so on my head. There were always family members on the roof, sitting on cotton *dhurries* (woven cotton rugs), playing Parcheesi or just relaxing and talking.

I was only three years old, turning four, and so there are few things
I remember distinctly from my first trip to India. Two incidents
stand out, both beginning from my usual outpost at the kitchen
window, which opened onto a small dirt lane that wound its way
between the high walls of the medieval city of Jetpur. I spent a lot
of time in the kitchen. That was where Motiba was. I became very
fond of Motiba during our stay in Jetpur, and very possessive of
her. I'd sit down in her cross-legged lap, fling my arms out to the
side and proclaim, "*My* Motiba. She's *my* Motiba." Motiba let me
"help" her with her work. She would set me up with my own *chapati* board and rolling pin so that I could make *chapatis* next to her
while she did the same. She let me drink tea from her saucer and,
against my mother's express wishes, fed me as much *gol,* raw
sugar, as I wanted. One day, during the quiet hours of the afternoon while the grownups slept, I went alone to the kitchen window. A group of street urchins, poor children left to their own
devices during the day while their parents worked, came chattering down the lane. "Oh look," they cried in Gujarati, which by that
time I could understand, "the White girl is there!" They began to
taunt me, calling me names such as "little white buffalo." I was
insulted, of course, but also terribly jealous of their streetwise
freedom, and suddenly I knew what I could do to get back at
them. Telling them to wait there, I went back into the kitchen. I
got out the red-and-white waxed-paper–wrapped loaf of "Modern Bread," and extracted a slice. Then I got the little pot of butter and the jar of honey and returned to the kitchen window. I had
their attention alright. Their eyes hardened with envy, and surely

Helping Motiba make chapatis *in the kitchen of the Jetpur house.*

hunger too, as I carefully spread butter and honey on the expensive slice of foreign-style bread, then slowly ate it in front of them.

On another occasion, an old beggar woman came and stood below the window. She showed me she was hungry, bringing her pinched fingers up to gesture at her mouth as if putting tiny bites of imaginary food into it. "Bring me some food," she commanded. I ran about the kitchen collecting what I could for her, made my way down the stairs, and was just opening the front door when I felt myself lifted up high into the air. All the food I'd collected went crashing to the floor. Bapuji had seen me walking past his room and heard the door opening. In a flash, he'd come to save me—and the household. It seemed this poor old woman was a witch. If I had given her something from the house, it would have given her some power over us too, and she could have used threats of curses upon the entire family to extort God knows what out of us. As I struggled to extract myself from Bapuji's iron grip, screaming and crying, he shouted at her to go away.

Soon after we had left Seattle for India, my mother discovered that she was pregnant again. As her pregnancy advanced, she had to make a decision whether to have the baby in India or try to get back to the States in time to deliver there. After another young mother in Jetpur died in childbirth, she decided she really should go back. We flew home, reaching Seattle via Tokyo and Honolulu. On the flight, I embarrassed my mother by standing up importantly at one point and announcing to the entire aircraft with outstretched arms, "My Daddy built this whole plane, this *whole* plane."

My mother gave birth in Seattle on December 2, 1961, to a scrawny little baby boy. My parents named him Pravin, forgoing in their infinite wisdom about American elementary schoolyards the other astrologist-recommended names of "Pinakin" and "Piush." Pravin soon filled out, becoming a chubby, happy baby. The rest of us also recovered our health, putting back on the weight we'd lost in India. My parents, like all the other people we knew, bought a television set. Life was good.

Less than a year later, Boeing let my father go. Out of a job, Dad decided to make a trip back to India. He hadn't seen Motiba or the rest of his family since 1952 when he'd made a brief trip home to renew his visa. A whole decade had passed. Now he was a young man of thirty, married, with three children. It was time to go back.

The pictures of my father on his arrival at the airport in Bombay in 1962 show a mature man, dashing and prosperous looking in his nice American-tailored jacket and tie. He made a very good impression. Everyone was in awe of his success and his achievement: living in America, married to an American girl, working for the world's largest manufacturer of civil transport airplanes on the cutting edge of engineering and design in the jet age. He received a hero's welcome. Everyone had to see him, the entire extended clan. He had to have a meal at each home. As he traveled from Bombay to Jetpur and then on to Calcutta, where Bapuji was making a last-ditch effort to do business between India and Burma, and then back to Bombay, he made long visits here and there at the insistence of scattered relatives. He extended his stay in India, then extended it again, first by weeks, then by months. Motiba didn't want to let him go back to America. It could be another decade before she saw him again! Who knew if she'd even make it ten more years. Couldn't he stay just a little longer?

Meanwhile, my mother was frantic. My father had managed to leave for India just before the Cuban missile crisis. My mother, alone with three children, waited in terror with the rest of the country to see whether or not the Russians were going to launch

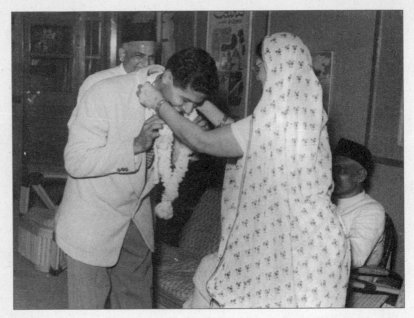

My father is garlanded upon his first return to India in 1952.

a nuclear missile attack against the United States. My father was unreachable and remained incommunicado for weeks. My mother worried whether he would ever even be able to make it back. But finally, Dad tore himself away from Motiba and India and returned to us and Seattle. The feared nuclear bombs never fell, but the crisis served, if anything, to further strengthen the resolve of the United States to win the techno-military race against the Soviet Union. My father's re-employment prospects in aerospace were excellent.

* * *

In Seattle, Boeing *was* aerospace. But in California, aerospace was everywhere: Lockheed, Douglas, North American Rockwell. There were so many companies and so many divisions of companies, and they all hummed with the millions of dollars the federal government was throwing their way so America could keep ahead of the Russians. On June 3, 1963, my father gave up his "resident alien" status and his Indian nationality for a U.S. passport and took a job with Rocketdyne, a division of what was then known as North American Aviation. President Kennedy had announced to the nation that the country's goal was to put a man on the moon by the end of the decade. It was a goal that required an all-out effort. A kind of "all hands on deck" ethos reigned, and my father, along with thousands of other engineers, was put to work. At the end of the school year, my mother and we children left Seattle to join him in Los Angeles. Douglas firs gave way to palm trees, rain to sunshine, heaters to air conditioners, tree houses to swimming pools. My parents bought a brand-new tract house with a stucco exterior and yard of hard-packed adobe in Canoga Park, minutes away from the Rocketdyne plant where Dad worked. We moved just days before my Bluebird troupe was to visit the Seattle children's television show *P. J. Patches.* I was devastated.

Shortly after we settled down in Los Angeles, however, I realized that we'd moved to the center of the television universe. For the first time in my young, increasingly television-oriented life, the real landscape in which I lived matched the landscape I saw on TV. At the time, many of the sitcoms and action dramas were filmed in Burbank, and here we were living a few miles away in the same San

Fernando Valley. Around me were rolling hills covered with brown grass and scrub oaks; on television, outdoor shots inevitably showed the same landscape. Whenever police were called upon on television to respond to some unfolding crisis, they arrived in a black-and-white L.A.P.D. car, just like the ones I saw on the streets of the valley.

One thing was different, though: the way television families lived and the way we lived. All the television families were White Americans without foreign accents. On *Leave It to Beaver,* they didn't eat weird food like *dhokla* or *kadhi,* and they didn't have a framed picture of Mahatma Gandhi with a sandalwood garland around it in the living room. I was deeply conscious that our family was different from "normal" American families. I knew we didn't fit in. I felt we weren't "real" Americans.

In those days, there was no Indian community to speak of in the United States. The only Indian people I saw when I was growing up were relatives my parents were sponsoring for green cards and a few other, miscellaneous Gujarati professionals whom we'd come to know through family connections. I had little in common with these recent immigrants, with their heavily accented English, their awkward styles of Western dress, their strictly Indian diet. Most of their children hadn't started school yet and didn't speak a word of English. Their parents spoke Gujarati at home.

We, on the other hand, only heard Gujarati when Dad talked on the telephone with his Gujarati friends and relatives, the stream of conversation regularly interrupted by American phrases and place names. The effect for us children was something like, "Gobbledy-

gobbledy-gobbledy two-for-one sale gobbledy-gobbledy-gobbledy one hell of a deal gobbledy-gobbledy-gobbledy Simi Valley gobbledy-gobbledy-gobbledy you've got to be kidding." My father told me later that he didn't want us to learn Gujarati because he wanted us to become "one hundred percent American." Dad was an immigrant in the old-fashioned, quaintly assimilationist style. There would be no bilingual, bicultural confusion for his children: he would do everything to make sure we melted into the great American pot.

From my perspective, however, the melting process was not proceeding as smoothly as my father may have wished. When my friends called, I rushed to answer the phone so that they wouldn't hear my father's accent. Otherwise, there were always a lot of questions:

"Wow, I didn't know your dad had an accent. Where's he from?"

"He's Indian."

"What tribe?"

"No, he's not an American Indian. He's from India."

"Oh, wow."

This was usually followed by an uncomfortable silence while my friend took that in and tried to remember why she'd called. Once, I was invited to spend the night at a classmate's house. When her father, who was British, found out my father was Indian, I was disinvited. My friend told me at school that her father didn't want "your kind" in his house. "But *I'm* not Indian," I protested. "My father is."

We got a lot of teasing for our Indian names. My sister Devi's name was inevitably heard as "Davy," as in Davy Crockett or Davy Jones, the too-cute singer in the Monkees. A lot of people thought

I had two brothers, one named "Davy." As for myself, the kids at school used to chant, "Mira, Mira on the wall, who's the"—fill in the blank with your choice of insult—"of them all."

Meat of any kind made a rare appearance in our house. As much as she could, my mother cooked to please my father, and that meant Gujarati vegetarian food. Motiba had taught her how to prepare a full range of Jain Kathiawari dishes during our stay in India in 1961. The odd Indian guest or relative who made it to our house was always stunned at the authentic Gujarati Jain fare my red-headed mother could whip up at a moment's notice. For us children, on the other hand, it was often difficult to answer our friends' off-hand question of, "What are you having for dinner?" When we were growing up, the only Asian cuisine recognized in the American mainstream was Chinese-American of the "chop suey" variety. Decades would pass before the average American became conversant with the *chai* and *chapatis* that can now be purchased at the local health food store. The only time I really felt our family to be in tune with culinary America was at Thanksgiving and Christmas, when Mom made turkey with all the trimmings. For those rare meals when my mother prepared nonvegetarian food, my father simply skipped the meat and ate whatever else was on the menu.

* * *

Close on the heels of the Cuban missile crisis came a tragedy that brought home, once again, the impression that all was not right in the world. John F. Kennedy was assassinated in November 1963. My parents, like my teacher and every other adult I knew, were completely devastated. It was the first time I'd seen so many grownups, including my Dad, cry. "I remember very clearly," my mother says, "that I was in the southwest back bedroom of the Canoga Park house vacuuming when it came over the radio." Everyone was stunned. We watched the funeral and the procession, glued to the television set in our living room like millions of other American families. Even to me, too young at the age of six to fully comprehend, yet old enough to know that something big and very bad had happened, it seemed that the world was ending. To be a young child in America during the 1960s was to be constantly aware of major threats, big events, horrible catastrophes that you couldn't really understand but that you knew could blow apart your whole safe-seeming, normal-seeming life. All was not right in the world beyond our California subdivision, and we children knew it.

My father applied for security clearance to work on projects at Rocketdyne that involved access to information at the level of "secret." This was at the height of the Cold War, and my father was a foreign-born individual working on technologies vital to our nation's security. He had to fill out a lengthy application, which included listing every single address where he had ever lived; every school he had ever attended; every job he'd ever had, with someone to vouch for him for every period he'd been unemployed. He also had to swear he'd never belonged to the Communist Party of America or to any other of a list of several hundred organizations deemed subversive.

My father was not allowed to talk about his work at home. It was top secret. In fact, it wasn't until much later that I figured out that he'd been working on the Apollo mission, designing the Saturn rockets that powered the Apollo space module once it was out of Earth's orbit. Years later, he referred to these as "retro rockets." "We knew how to get the astronauts out of Earth's orbit and into outer space," my father explained. "But we didn't know how to bring them back. How could we make them turn around in zero gravity? There were teams and teams of engineers working on this problem, and we just couldn't figure it out. The breakthrough came after one of the guys got back from a canoeing trip. Out on the lake, it came to him in a flash. If he wanted to turn the canoe, he had to apply force with his paddle near the rear on the side toward which he wanted to turn. The same principle should work in space, only instead of canoe paddles, we'd use rockets. See, you could fire a rocket on the back side of the spacecraft and, depending on which side you fired it, turn it in any direction you wanted. And that's what we did. That's how we got them back. We used the retro rockets."

Most of my memories of our life in Canoga Park are of evenings. It was so hot during the day. After the sun had gone down and the pavement was still warm but cool enough you could walk on it without burning the soles of your feet, all the people in the subdivision would emerge from their houses to water their lawns and chat with the neighbors watering theirs. Rocketdyne hosted family movie nights on the lawns of the company campus under towering eucalyptus trees. We brought picnic dinners. After eating, we kids would stretch out on blankets laid out over the cool grass, watching movies until we all fell asleep and our parents bundled us off to the car still wrapped in blankets. We slept so soundly that we never knew how we got from the Rocketdyne lawn back to our beds.

My little sister Anna was born on June 7, 1964, making us four children in all. I remember going to visit my mother while she was in the hospital. I was anxious for her to come home. My father had no knack for running a house full of kids. He tried to convince us that cereal with buttermilk, one of his favorite beverages because it reminded him of the *chaas* he'd grown up drinking in India, tasted exactly the same as cereal the way we were used to eating it with regular milk. We were not convinced.

In early summer 1965, Bapuji came to visit us. It was his first trip to America, and we were on pins and needles that it should be a success. My mother had to handle her difficult father-in-law on her own, because she'd gone with us children back up to Seattle to try to get rid of the house there that hadn't yet sold, leaving Dad at work in Los Angeles. Bapuji's attitude toward foreign travel was the polar opposite of the "when in Rome, do as the Romans" variety. He insisted on following his daily routine exactly as he would have done in Bombay. He rose early; expected to eat his usual foods; and spent long hours in his room meditating, reading, or listening to the news on the radio. My mother says that it always amused her to see the reaction of potential buyers touring the house when they confronted the stony visage of my *dhoti*-clad grandfather seated cross-legged upon his bed in studied meditation.

Under normal circumstances, Bapuji was not the easiest person in the world to live with. Now he'd come to America with a big chip on his shoulder against "Western imperial powers," determined that he would never be favorably impressed by anything he saw here. My mother had a terrible time of it. She would cook him a Jain vegetarian meal, and then, just as she was about to set the food in front of him, he would decide it was time for a walk. When he returned, she'd have to start all over because he did not eat "warmed over" food. He insisted that all his food be cooked with pure butter at a time when my parents were carrying two mortgages and making do with margarine. We children had to tiptoe around and make as little noise as possible so as not to disturb Bapuji, whose temper terrified us. He was not generally in a good mood. He had just lost his business in Burma for the second and last time. He was too dispirited to start all over again, and it fell to my father, the eldest son, to become the principal breadwinner for the family in India as well as for our own. This was something my mother resented, especially when she could not buy us, say, a pair of school shoes because my father had to wire a couple of thousand dollars to Bombay.

A buyer for the house finally appeared, and at the beginning of the summer my father came up to Seattle to help us move back to California. Our things were sent down to Los Angeles in a moving van while we set out to show Bapuji America. My mother's parents came along from Junction City for much of the way. We traveled from Seattle to Los Angeles via every national park we could hit: Grand Teton, Yellowstone, Bryce Canyon, Zion, the Grand Canyon. We saw snow-capped peaks, moose grazing in mountain meadows, Old Faithful with its sulfurous smells, the caramel-striped rock formations of Bryce Canyon, and the biggest attraction of all: the Grand Canyon. Bapuji was, as far as we could tell, totally unimpressed. For mile after mile, he refused even to look out the window. "We have beautiful sights in India too," he'd say whenever one of my parents would try to draw his attention to some natural wonder our car was passing. Later, we heard from relatives in India that he bragged and bragged after he got back about how beautiful, how wonderful, and how clean the United States was. While he was with us, though, Bapuji was not about to give his

With Bapuji at Grand Teton National Park.

son even a moment's satisfaction that perhaps the country he'd chosen to settle in had anything positive going for it.

While we were in Seattle with Bapuji, my father sold the Canoga Park house and bought a big ranch house in posher Woodland Hills. The new house was in an area called "Walnut Acres." The old walnut orchard, like the rest of the San Fernando Valley, had been opened up for development in the 1940s with the techniques so well documented in the film *Chinatown*. There were great, leafy walnut trees in all the backyards on our side of Woodlake Avenue. On the other side, walnut trees gave way to what was left of an old orange orchard. At the time, Woodland Hills had a semirural feeling to it. We would jump on our horses at home and within five minutes be riding up in the soft brown hills among native California oaks. Now almost all the large lots in our old neighborhood have been divided up, and the surrounding hills are covered with subdivisions sporting nearly identical "Mediterranean-style" tract homes on tiny lots.

In Woodland Hills, my mother got back to her farm roots and set up a kind of rural estate. She planted fruit trees and a huge vegetable garden and amassed a growing menagerie of animals. There was a circular drive in front of the house lined with citrus trees: lemons, limes, oranges, tangerines, even the unnatural-sounding "tangelo." There were sapote trees, guava trees, persimmon trees, apricots, and almonds. At one time, we had seven horses and ponies, three dogs, several cats, chickens, ducks, rabbits, and an aviary full of parakeets. We even had a Nubian goat that went on to a career as a working actor on the television show *Africa U.S.A.*

There was a large lawn for playing tag, hide-and-seek, and croquet. My parents couldn't afford the ne plus ultra of the Southern California lifestyle, a built-in swimming pool, but they did put in an oval above-ground pool into which we would plunge the moment we came home from school for endless games of Marco Polo with the other kids in the neighborhood.

We lived on Erwin Street. Our neighborhood was full of professional, culturally and racially mixed families. Next door lived a White American–Puerto Rican couple. The wife wore very tiny bikinis and was always stuffing her ample breasts back into the brimming cups of her bathing suit top, saying with her rich accent, "This damn bra!" Next was an Irish American married to an African American who informed the neighborhood that her father was an African prince and that she had grown up in the lap of luxury in Africa. I don't think my parents really believed this story. They thought it was sad that this woman felt she had to make up exalted origins to make herself acceptable to the neighborhood.

A lot of people in the neighborhood worked in the "entertainment industry," as the grownups called it. Right next door to us the man of the house was a writer for *The Mod Squad*. Kitty-corner in back of us were neighbors who moved in a very hip 1960s Hollywood crowd that included the Smothers brothers, Carole King, and—be still, my thirteen-year-old heart—James Taylor. The comedian Pat Paulsen lived in the house in back of ours. I went to school with kids whose fathers were set designers, sound engineers, cameramen, and screen writers. Most of the people in Woodland Hills, or such was my childhood impression, worked in television and commuted to the studios in Burbank at the other end of the Valley. I suspect the heavy Hollywood types, the *movie* people, lived elsewhere, Beverly Hills, for example, or Laurel Canyon. Living surrounded by people in television reinforced my impression that Los Angeles was the center of the universe. We'd watch an episode of *The Mod Squad* on television and the next morning say "hello" to the person who'd written it, our next-door neighbor. We'd watch police chase scenes on television, and at night we'd close our curtains to the penetrating spotlights of L.A.P.D. patrol helicopters scanning the darkened neighborhood. I don't think any television moment compared, however, with the one we saw at the Dwyers' house on July 20, 1969, when Neil Armstrong stepped onto the moon and said, "That's one small step for a man. One giant leap for mankind." We knew by then that our dad had been working on the Apollo missions. He wasn't in show business, but he'd contributed to the greatest media moment ever. He had helped make history happen.

My father was well aware that engineering jobs in aerospace lived and died as contracts flowed and ebbed. He began a series of professional moves to stay one step ahead of the next round of layoffs. From Rocketdyne, he moved briefly to Lockheed; then to Continental Airlines; and, eventually, to McDonnell Douglas, where he stayed for more than thirty years. With the space race winding down after Apollo XI, Dad shifted his focus from outer space to earthbound air travel. And with each job his commute became longer. Woodland Hills was at the northern end of the San Fernando Valley, a long way from the airport—always referred to in our family as "L.A.X."——where my father worked for Continental Airlines, and even farther from Douglas's plants in Long Beach. Dad joined the legions of L.A. commuters, and it took its toll. He was always tired. Often he would spend the entire weekend asleep on the couch in the living room.

Any little thing——such as a pair of scissors that couldn't be located——would set him off. He'd fly into rages that evolved into military-style interrogation sessions. We'd line up in a row, eldest to youngest, while he drilled us. "Can scissors walk?" "No," we'd chorus. "Can scissors fly?" "No." "Well, then, how do you think the scissors got out of the drawer?" "Someone took them out." The goal was to find who had taken them or, if that wasn't possible, because of course we'd totally forgotten how the scissors came not to be in their drawer, someone to take the fall. This was always either my brother or me. My brother got singled out, I'm sure, because he was the only boy. Me, I was the oldest and I was defiant. I can remember my father lifting me up to sit on the pink-and-brown-tiled bathroom counter so he could interrogate me at eye level, saying, "If I say the sky is purple, what color is the sky?" I was supposed to reply "purple" on the argument that his word was law, but I never would. "Blue," I'd say, "because it is blue," and his great hand, every line on his palm starkly etched, would come toward my cringing face. "If I'd replied that way to Bapuji, he would have hit me so hard I would have flown across the room!" he would yell. "That's no excuse to treat us that way!" I'd retort.

Bapuji had succeeded in asserting absolute authority over his family in another country and another time. In 1960s America,

Dad could not pull off the same feat, no matter how much he raged. "Daddy, Bapuji *garam, garam*. Hot, hot. Daddy, Bapuji, *gussawala*." Motiba explained in our mishmash private pidgin of English, Gujarati, and Hindi. Like his father's, Dad's hot temper was legendary in the family.

If Dad had to suffer a thousand insults to his authority at home, at work he got even less respect. Changing his name from Prabhakar to "Pete" wasn't enough to turn him into a "good ol' American" White boy who could bond with his peers and superiors in an industry dominated by swaggering ex–air force types. Years later, he told me about his disappointment when it had finally become clear to him that no matter how well he did or how many years he put in, he'd never be promoted into management. Money was also tight in those days. My parents really couldn't quite afford Woodland Hills. My mother wasn't working, and my father's income had to support both us and the family in India. Between the commute, the money worries, and the constant if most often subtle racism my father had to deal with at work, it's no wonder Dad felt stressed. He had to take out his frustrations on someone. We were the only available candidates. When I think back to the text of my confrontations with my father, they were always about power and authority: his power over us; his right to exercise absolute authority; his rage that even we, his own family, would not grant him that.

Dad had an Indian friend we called Purukaka who would uncannily show up at the house just when things were starting to spiral out of control. I suspect Mom would quietly call Purukaka from a phone in another room and ask him to come over. The moment the doorbell rang, we were trained to run into the bathroom and close the door, wipe away our tears, splash cold water on our faces, dry them, and then come out and pretend nothing had happened. I doubt Purukaka was fooled, but it allowed everyone to save face. If Purukaka didn't show up, my father would keep at it until he'd reduced us all to his own level of misery. Then he'd abruptly stop, in tears himself, physically and emotionally spent, tortured by guilt. After one of these sessions, he would follow us helplessly into our rooms, hugging us, kissing us, spilling hot tears onto our own wet faces. He'd go out and come back with tubs of candy, huge stuffed animals, toys we'd never dream of asking for. But it was all too extreme. We didn't want tubs of candy if we had to get beaten up to get them. Yet we forgave him. Many, many times, we forgave him.

During my entire childhood, I was convinced that my father behaved the way he did because he was Indian, that the yelling and screaming and crying that took place in our house never occurred in any other house in America. It took me years to figure out that not all Indian fathers were like Dad and that "real" American families were perfectly capable of experiencing the same, or worse.

Of course, there were happy times with Dad too. My parents bought a string of used cars. One was a huge Mercury station wagon that we kids were told had belonged to Kirk Douglas. It seemed natural living in Los Angeles that the castoffs of the stars should make their way down through the social strata to people like us living in the suburbs. My parents spread a sleeping bag over the cargo area of the wagon and filled it with pillows and blankets. When we children got tired, we'd just climb into the back, snuggle into the soft flannel of the sleeping bag, and fall asleep to the irresistible vibration of the car whizzing down the Ventura freeway. On weekends, our usual family destination was the beach. We went most often to Zuma but also to Malibu and Leo Carillo. Woodland Hills was at the inland end of Malibu Canyon, and so we'd drive straight through the hills and in a mere twenty minutes or so be on the Southern California coastline, with its mile upon mile of wide, white-sand beaches. My mother burned terribly with her fair skin. She'd keep a long-sleeved shirt on and sit under the beach umbrella with a book while Dad helped us kids build elaborate sand castles with complicated systems of dikes and moats to keep the ocean from washing our creations away. Sometimes we'd stay late, build a campfire, and have our dinner right on the beach. These evenings were magical, the waves phosphorescent in the moonlight, coming in one after another in great thunderous crashes upon the beach, the sand still warm underneath if you dug your toes under the rapidly cooling surface, and the firelight dancing on our brown faces.

We were living in paradise, but we were also living in the 1960s. When Martin Luther King Jr. made his famous "I have a dream" speech in August 1963 on the steps of the Lincoln Memorial, the men in his entourage all wore cotton *khadi* "Gandhi" caps just like Pandit Nehru and the Congress Party leaders in India. Bapuji wore a cap like that, and I thought it was cool that followers of the great civil rights leader dressed like my grandfather. My parents explained that Gandhi's philosophy of nonviolence had been inspirational for King. I was certainly conscious of the civil rights movement, which my parents, understandably, fully supported.

Then, in 1965, Watts, a predominantly Black neighborhood in Los Angeles, exploded. Woodland Hills was very far from Watts, and we were in no danger. Still, the commuting fathers were shaken. A neighbor showed us where a bullet had hit his windshield as he'd been driving down the freeway. A lot of fathers stayed home for a few days. Despite the diversity in our small, relatively prosperous neighborhood, Los Angeles was, in general, a city of racially and culturally defined enclaves, divided from each other by the endless tangle of freeways. There was a feeling out in the mostly White suburbs during the Watts riots that frustrated Blacks in the city had declared open season on the freeways. That is what had everyone terrified. The freeways were the arteries of the city, the vital bloodlines connecting places of work with the neighborhoods where professionals, such as my father, lived with their families. If the freeways became unsafe, people couldn't go to work. The whole Los Angeles lifestyle would fall to pieces.

During these years, the war in Vietnam was a constant presence on the television that sat in our living room under Gandhi's benevolent gaze. Every night on the evening news, we watched the day's statistics of U.S., Vietnamese, and Viet Cong soldiers killed. My parents' generation was too old to fight, and ours was too young. So our family participated in the war the way most of the country did: as spectators to a televised drama. By this time, my parents had acquired a color television set, and to this day, the word "Vietnam" conjures up in my mind the color of military drab green: it was the color of the soldiers' uniforms; it was the color of the tanks; it was the color of the palm trees and the swamp grass fanning out under the rotors of the helicopters as they lifted away the wounded; it was the color of the rivers through which American boys seemed always to be wading. I'm not sure what effect growing up watching all that real-life gore had on us. One thing for sure, I hated the war; hated that it took some of my friends' big brothers away; hated watching first Johnson then Nixon lie to us, "the American people," or, better yet, "my fellow Americans," about what was going on.

When Martin Luther King was assassinated, my parents were very upset. Then, one night while they were watching the Democratic National Convention, taking place just a few miles away in Los Angeles at the Ambassador Hotel, my father got up to get himself something to drink, muttering, "Watch out, Bobby, or they'll get you too." A minute later, my mother screamed and called him back to the living room: "they" had got Bobby Kennedy. I came into political consciousness during this troubled time. The way the world appeared to me during my early teens, our own government was the enemy. "They" wanted to keep up an unjust war that killed lots of Americans and lots more Vietnamese. "They" wanted to keep racial injustice alive. And a little later, "they" wanted to keep women down. I came of age at the same moment America's innocence was lost. The culture I identified with was the "counterculture."

* * *

My parents began to refer to their life in Los Angeles as a "rat race." To escape its stresses, Mom took us home to her parents' farm in Oregon for summer and Christmas holidays. Fortunately, my father got a job with Continental Airlines. One of the perks of working for Continental was cut-rate air travel for the entire family. We could fly anywhere in the United States and as long as we flew Continental, pay only the five-dollar tax the federal government charged per segment. It took some creativity to get to Oregon from Los Angeles on Continental Airlines. We had to fly from Los Angeles to Dallas, Dallas to Denver, Denver to Salt Lake City, and finally Salt Lake City to Portland, where my grandparents picked us up at the airport. It was not the most direct route, but the price was right.

We loved to visit my mother's parents. We called them "Bestemor" and "Bestefar" instead of "Grandma" and "Grandpa" because of their Danish origins. Going to Bestemor and Bestefar's farm in Oregon was like making a visit to the real America. In fact, it was a rural idyll—the self-sufficient small family farm—that was rapidly becoming extinct. But whereas at home we were always conscious that our Dad was from India and a foreigner, on the farm we got to experience what we imagined was normal American life. The farm was Mom's homeland. It was there that she had learned the skills to make sure we celebrated all the holidays the right way, where she had learned how to sew Halloween costumes, stuff and roast Thanksgiving turkeys, decorate Christmas trees, and bake Christmas cookies. Lulled by the sweet scent of Oregon summer hay, we forgot our split personalities of ethnic confusion and relaxed into a kind of easy wholeness.

When I was very young, I asked my mother, "Mommy, which way am I half?" "What do you mean?" she replied, puzzled by my question. "Which way am I half? Up and down," I said, drawing an imaginary line down my the middle of my chest, "or across?" I asked, drawing a line across my waistline. It was difficult to understand how we were different from "normal" American kids, kids who didn't have to worry about where the two halves of their identity came together.

On the farm, I didn't have to worry about which way I was half. We did simple things, such as help put up beans, tomatoes, pears, and cherries. We made quarts and quarts of applesauce. "You have to prepare for winter while the sun still shines," my grandmother would tell us. We worked between the back porch of the big white house and the "fruit room," seated around tremendous tin tubs set about in the dappled shade of the trees. One tub was for washing the fruits and vegetables; one for catching the pits, seeds, cores, and peels; and one for the freshly prepared produce. In the kitchen, rows of hot canning jars and piles of lids were arranged on clean tea towels waiting for us to fill them. My grandmother supervised the huge pressure cooker on the stove, scaring us with tales about occasions when an unattended "cooker" at a neighbor's house had exploded, splattering hot sauce and bits of fruit all over the kitchen walls and floor. We set the finished jars of fruit out to cool on the counter and then stored them in the insulated fruit room for the coming winter months. At the end of the summer, we left my grandparents' house with the back of the car full of quarts of Blue Lake green beans, Royal Anne cherries, and Granny Smith applesauce.

Summer in Oregon is glorious. On hot days, when the temperature climbs into the high eighties or even into the nineties, it is never humid or sticky. Nights are cool, and you can sleep comfortably without air-conditioning. The biggest crop grown in the Willamette Valley is grass for lawn seed. In the summer, the grass fields smell sweet, and the grass tastes sweet too if you chew on a sprig. It is cool under the forest canopies of the surrounding mountains, and the rivers career over natural rock water slides into deep, clear pools perfect for swimming. We'd take a break from canning and go to Eastern Oregon to visit Rancherie, the mountain where my mother had worked as a fire lookout when she was in college. She told us how she befriended a wild chipmunk by luring it ever closer to the tower with a trail of sunflower seeds, how she set out tin cans for target practice with her twenty-two–caliber rifle, and how she'd shot out the headlights of the local sheriff's patrol car one night when he drove up to the lookout tower unannounced.

In August, Junction City was home to the four-day Scandinavian Festival my Danish-origin grandparents helped found. The town had been settled primarily by Scandinavian farmers, and the streets had names like "Dane Lane" long before the festival was created. My grandmother sewed all of us kids elaborate nineteenth-century Danish peasant costumes. We learned which kind of lace was worn in which region of Denmark, which colors, and which style of apron and bonnet. My grandparents manned the *æbleskiver* booth while we danced Danish folk dances on a temporary wooden stage. The Scandinavian Festival is still held every August in Junction City, and the souvenir booths still stock a postcard with a picture of local children dressed in traditional costumes. I am one of the only children in the photo with dark hair and brown eyes.

Bestemor gives our Danish costumes a final check before we set off for the
Scandinavian Festival in Junction City.

The moment the Beatles took off for Rishikesh and started wearing Nehru jackets and beads, it became extremely sexy to be
Indian. I got out Dad's old black Nehru jacket, the one he'd
brought with him in 1949, and wore it with my embroidered jeans.
I wound long Indian cotton and silk scarves around my neck, and
put mirror-work vests on over my T-shirts. At home, we watched
Laugh-In, where a psychedelic colorful paisley motif was a constant. Paisley was Indian, and paisley was in. Suddenly, my friends
at school started using words like "*nirvana*" and "*maya,*" as in "It's all
maya, man, just illusion." People's parents were getting into "T.M.,"
transcendental meditation. Some of them acquired "*gurus.*"

My parents did not enter into the West's 1960s fascination with India at all. They were far too straight to have the kind of "pot parties" some of my friends' parents started to have toward the end of the sixties or to embrace the "free love" philosophy of the times. As far as my father was concerned, my appropriation of Indian hipness was just more rebellion against the moral authority of Indian culture as he knew it. This was especially true as far as the "sexual revolution" was concerned. Indian daughters did not go around braless or take the pill. Unfortunately for my Indian father, his daughter had become exactly what he had wanted her to be: a real American.

With the change in U.S. immigration law in 1965, more and more of our relatives began to come over from India. Our house in Los Angeles was the jumping-off point into American life for a whole series of family members. My father had a good job and he was already a U.S. citizen, so he was able to "sponsor" first one relative, then another. My mother cooked for everyone and taught the women how to drive and how to make *rus malai*, a dish of sweetened, cooked-down milk, out of cottage cheese from the supermarket. A trickle of arrivals turned into a stream. We stopped being the only Kamdar listed in the phone book.

When we lived on Erwin Street, my parents' Gujarati friends would come over on weekends to what they called "the farm." Most of these people were relatively recent immigrants. They were scrimping and saving to buy their own homes. In the meantime, they lived in cramped apartments. Our rural acre of lawns and fruit trees provided them with a respite from L.A.'s asphalt jungle. The women would help my mother fry mounds of *puris,* and the men would sit with my father on folding chairs under the shady boughs, happy to be able to speak their language, to reminisce about home, and to pontificate on the state of American politics and culture. If there was a "little India" in L.A. in those days, it existed in our back-yard, and probably the same thing was happening in a few hundred other backyards or city living rooms scattered across the country. India was far, far away. Airline tickets were expensive. There was no direct dial international calling, no fax machines—cum—answering machines attached to people's phones, no e-mail. We were a little island of India in a vast land of *Leave It to Beaver*.

In 1965, there were still only 20,000 immigrants from India in the whole United States. By 1980, there were almost 400,000. Since then, that number has nearly tripled. We Kamdar kids are much older than the children of the really big wave of immigration from India still under way. We not only grew up as "halfies," we grew up in a vacuum of Indian culture other than that of our own home. It took me a number of years to realize that Indian culture was much more than, and on the whole much different from, the Kathiawari Jain subculture of our own family. Our younger cousins, born in America in the late 1960s and 1970s or brought here during that time as very young children, had an entirely dif-ferent experience of being Indian in America than we did. It took a certain critical mass of people to form communities.

When we were growing up, many ingredients for traditional Indian cuisine were simply unavailable in the United States. People always brought these precious items back with them, squirreled away in their suitcases among their clothes. They also made special trips to India to purchase *saris, salwaar kameez,* and traditional jewelry. Now all these things are readily available in America: exotic groceries, traditional clothing, twenty-two-carat gold jewelry, even Hindi film sound tracks on compact disc. There are satellite television stations that beam Indian shows into American homes twenty-four hours a day and movie theaters that show nothing but Indian films. There are vibrant Indian enclaves in Queens, New Jersey, Chicago, Los Angeles, Silicon Valley, and elsewhere from coast to coast. You can get *chai* at Starbucks, order books on the art of *mehndi* from Amazon.com, and buy Taj-brand frozen Indian entrees at Safeway. I remember very clearly the day in 1985 when I saw some Indian-looking girls on the Berkeley campus. From their looks, I assumed they were foreign students or recent immigrants. Then I overheard them talking to each other in perfectly accented Valley Girl slang. Like, really, a new generation was coming up, *yaar.*

* * *

Motiba did not visit America until 1976, twenty-eight years after her son rose away from the sticky tarmac of Bombay on the silver wings of a propeller aircraft. My mother talked to her on the telephone before she left India. Did she plan to come with Bapuji? "And bring my work with me?" she'd snorted. "I want to enjoy myself! Usha will accompany me." They landed in Portland, Oregon, Motiba in her usual plain white cotton *sari,* Ushaphaiba in a pantsuit. We picked them up in a hulking blue-and-silver International Harvester Travelall and drove them down to Eugene, through the rich green of the Willamette Valley with its picture-perfect red barns and neat Victorian farmhouses. Motiba was on holiday, all twinkling eyes and warm hugs. She got along famously with Bestemor in Junction City, though neither could understand a word the other said. Her total innocence of American life made her delight in all the new things she encountered. We took her to Farrell's Ice Cream Parlor. They set a sundae in front of her so big it nearly eclipsed Motiba's diminutive face. With evident gusto, she tucked into the mountain of whipped cream and rivers of hot fudge. "*Saras. Bahu saras.*" "It's good. Very good," she pronounced.

The plan was for us to show Motiba some of the country before delivering her to Bharatiphaiba's place in Chicago. An itinerary was

Motiba peers out of a stagecoach at Universal Studios.

charted down the Pacific Coast to Los Angeles, across the Mojave
Desert to Las Vegas, then up to Colorado and the Midwest via the
Grand Canyon. Before the rest of the family left Oregon, I said my
good-byes. It was mid-August, and I had to get back to Portland for
the fall term at Reed College, where I was a sophomore.

* * *

I missed a fabulous trip. At Universal Studios, a *sari*-clad Motiba
posed on the Wild West set, taking a mock ride in a stagecoach
careering past a sagebrush-strewn landscape. A collection of
mock boulders made of Styrofoam was an excuse for her to dis-
play her superhuman strength for the family Instamatic. The high-
light of Motiba's trip, though, was Las Vegas. The ride through the
Mojave Desert, in August, had been blisteringly hot, hot even for
Motiba. The Travelall didn't have air-conditioning, and everyone
had to make do with open windows and canteens of water. Motiba
was enchanted when Las Vegas finally came into shimmering
view: an oasis of fantastic proportions, complete with palm trees
and glistening fountains. The family entered the chilled air of Caesar's Palace and was offered free drinks. Motiba ordered an orange
juice. My mother was embarrassed by all the skimpily clad young
women sauntering about. What would Motiba think? But my
grandmother was completely unfazed, happy to be sitting in air-
conditioned bliss sipping her iced juice as the slot machines
blinked and chimed around her. In fact, she didn't want to leave.
She observed later that Las Vegas had been the high point of her
whole trip to America. Like a kid at Disney World, she just loved

it, loved the neon; the posh lobbies; the chilled air; the gaudy fountains; the free drinks; who knows, maybe even the showgirls. Perhaps Motiba viewed Caesar's Palace, with its reproductions of Greek goddesses and classical pillars, as a modern version of a colorful Hindu temple, complete with *devdasis*. In any case, Las Vegas was the most dazzling place she'd seen in her entire life.

Motiba also found a neat solution to the vexing question of what to eat. Culinary choices along the interstates were slim. At the family's first stop at a roadside Denny's, Motiba asked for a vegetable sandwich. The waitress looked at her blankly. They didn't have that. After conferring with Ushaphaiba in Gujarati about the menu listings, Motiba's eyes lit up. More rapid-fire Gujarati followed, then

Motiba with her America-settled children and Ushaphaiba, from left to right: Vinoo, Bharati, Motiba, Usha, and Prabhakar.

Ushaphaiba said politely, "She'll have a bacon, lettuce, and tomato sandwich but, please, hold the bacon." The waitress thought the kitchen could handle that but warned they'd have to charge her full price even if she wasn't having the meat. Once Motiba had hit on this solution, her order never varied. All across the American West, she ate the same thing: a B.L.T with no bacon and a cup of tea with milk and two sugars, please.

Four generations: my father, Motiba, me, and my son Alexander.
Motiba's last trip to America, 1993.

* * *

Motiba made several more trips to America. She always came for months at a time: it was a long and expensive journey from India. Her last trip was to Chicago in 1992. Bharatiphaiba's husband Bipinbhai flew her over as a surprise gift to his wife on the occasion of their twenty-fifth wedding anniversary. Family members gathered from all over the United States for the party. A lavish meal of vegetarian Italian entrees and catered Indian dishes was served to a mixed crowd of Indian immigrant family and friends (mostly doctors) and non-Indian friends. All the guests had assembled and were congratulating my aunt and uncle when voices near the door began to hush and slowly everyone's attention turned toward a little old Gujarati woman making her way quietly into the room. Bharatiphaiba, who had no idea her mother was coming, nearly collapsed. Everyone was near tears. Motiba smiled softly as her daughter gathered her into her arms. Later in the evening, Motiba sat happily in a place of honor, looking on as her Indian family in America taught the use of *dandia* in traditional Gujarati folk dancing, to the non-Indians. Mirror-work skirts mixed with little black cocktail dresses, *kurtas* jostled with suits and ties, the ensemble swirling faster and faster around the parquet floor of a Sheraton banquet hall in suburban Illinois.

Two years later, cancer claimed Motiba. The woman who'd anchored those of us settled in America to the intricate old traditions of Kathiawar was no more, and we were set adrift upon the world.

Bharatiphaiba's American version of Motiba's Mango Pickle

Motiba's eldest daughter Bharati has converted Motiba's elaborate mango pickle recipe for the modern American kitchen. "All that oil," she exclaims. "We cannot eat like that now!"

Ingredients

2 green mangoes*
1/2 c. coarsely ground fenugreek seeds
1/4 c. ground hulled mustard seeds*
3 Tbsp. red chili powder
1/2 tsp. ground turmeric
1/8 tsp. asafoetida powder
salt
2 Tbsp. peanut or sesame oil

Prepare mangoes as for Motiba's Mango Pickle but let sit only 2–3 hours. Drain off liquid from mangoes and lay out to dry on clean kitchen towels. Heat the oil, and pour onto the asafoetida. Cover the asafoetida now drenched in oil with a small bowl. Let sit for 1 hour. Mix asafoetida and oil with remaining spices. Mix salted green mangoes with spices. Store in the refrigerator up 2–3 weeks in a sealed container.

NOTE: In season, green mangoes are readily available in Indian grocery stores in most major North American cities. However, very tart, cored Granny Smith apples may be substituted with surprising success when mangoes cannot be found. The hulled mustard seeds, *rai kuria*, are sometimes sold in Indian grocery stores under the general heading "Pickle Masala." One has to be careful, however, because complete ready-made pickle masala mixtures are also packaged as "Pickle Masala."

5

Kaliyuga

Property alone will confer rank; wealth will be the only source of devotion; passion will be the sole bond of union between the sexes; falsehood will be the only means of success in litigation; and women will be objects merely of sensual gratification. Earth will be venerated but for its mineral treasures, dishonesty will be a universal means of subsistence, presumption will be substituted for learning. . . . Thus in the Kali age shall decay constantly proceed, until the human race approaches its annihilation.

—VISHNU PURANA

Re: Motiba
Date: 15/06/99 11:57:33
From: mmmp@vsnl.net.in (Shashikant Khara)
To: kamdarm@aol.com (Mira Kamdar)

Chi. Mira,

It would be quite noteworthy as to how Motiba had gained the tremendous power she had to take life in a smooth manner whatever the circumstances she faced, for example to live, with a happy countenance, on a comparatively low income after she married, though she had lived in a quite rich atmosphere all through her childhood.

Her ability to stay calm while taking up the challenges of life came from the religious background she had at her parents place, where going to *jainshala,* Jain school, was as much a part of the routine of daily life as going to normal school.

Motiba's grandmother was very keen on giving Motiba and her cousin Shantaben a religious attitude toward life. The two cousins were brought up together, and both were eventually married into the Kamdar family of Jetpur. But their destinies turned out to be very different. Shantaben's husband passed away after only four months of marriage. According to our Jain

and also our Hindu custom, this was blamed on Shantaben, who
was seen to be an evil entrant into the family. The young
widow's life was made miserable by her in-laws. When things
became unbearable, Shantaben's father, Sri Manibhai Khara, who
was a shy person, asked Sri Muljibhai, my father and also
Motiba's father, for help. Sri Muljibhai went courageously to Jetpur to rescue Shantaben. Shantaben's mother-in-law told him he
could take Shantaben back to Amreli but only if he was willing
to take care of her the rest of her life. He gladly accepted, and
never allowed her to go back to her in-laws in Jetpur.

On the other hand, on the side of Sri Prabhudas Kamdar,
your own grandfather's family, your Motiba was accepted as a
very good person from a very noble family. She was even better
cared for after seven years when she gave birth to a son, Prabhakar, your father, as giving a male heir was accepted as a
grand deed in an Indian family.

In those days, widows could never remarry, and Shantaben
was thinking of devoting her life to religion. All the family
members were encouraging her to become _sadhviji,_ a Jain nun.

Shantaben approached many known Jain gurus of the time,
to choose from whom she should take the _sadhvi_ vows of sacred
life. After a long period of inquiry, she decided to ask Sri Kanjiswami to give her vows, and accept her as a disciple.

Shantaben went to see Sri Kanjiswami in Amreli with Sri
Nanchandbhai Khara, Motiba's and my own uncle, who was
eager to help her in her religious pursuits. To Shantaben's utter
surprise, Sri Kanjiswami said he would not give her _diksha,_ the

vow to become a nun. He asked her not to be hasty in taking
diksha, as he had found the real truth of the enlightenment of
the soul—*samkit* in Gujarati, *samyak darshan* in Hindi and Sanskrit. Shantaben was overjoyed at the revelation of Sri Kanjiswami, who changed the whole course of her life. She became
one of the two most noteworthy disciples of Sri Kanjiswami, the
other being a woman named Champaben.

Shantaben started living with Champaben and both tried
very hard to catch the theoretical basis of Jainism as outlined
in the Jain equivalent of the Christian bible, the *Samaysara,*
and in the sermons of Sri Kanjiswami whom we know as Sri
Guruji Kanjiswami. Meanwhile, Motiba was enjoying her pres-
tige as the mother of a Kamdar son, your father Prabhakarbhai.

A unique incident happened. When your father was about
ten years old, the two cousins, Motiba and Shantaben, met
again at Songad. Shantaben and her co-disciple Champaben
were running an ashram there for *brahmacharinis,* young women
who had taken vows of religious celibacy. At the ashram, the
women studied Jain theology and listened to the sermons Sri
Kanjiswami gave three times every day. They also performed all
our Jain *pujas* at the Digamber Jain temple of Sri Simandhar-
swami at Songad. Motiba had always been very pious, and she
wanted to visit Shantaben and Champaben's ashram.

Now, both these Khara daughters, Baluben (your Motiba)
and Shantaben, grew up in the same house and were married
into the Kamdar family of Jetpur. But, as fate would have it,
Baluben enjoyed reverence and good luck much like the Hindu

god Krishna, whereas Shantaben's fate, widowed so young and
alone in life, was considered to be like that of Sudama, a poor
and anonymous Brahmin. Thus went the belief in the Kamdar
and Khara families. People would say, "Oh, Baluben and
Shantaben began life the same and married into the same family but Baluben has been fortunate like Sri Krishna whereas
Champaben has had bad luck like Sudama."

By the time your Motiba went to Songad, Shantaben's reputation in the Jain world had experienced a stupendous rise. She
was worshipped by all the people we knew. After greeting each
other lovingly after a long time, Baluben remarked to
Shantaben: "Though we are likened to Krishna and Sudama in
our community, I wonder who is Krishna and who is Sudama
now? I am struggling hard enough to maintain my family
chores. I don't even have a glimpse of the path of salvation, yet
you have become the shining star of the people of our clan. I
very fondly declare you as my Krishna and ask you to accept me
as Sudama and to lead me to a life of enlightenment." To
Motiba's utter happiness, Shantaben said: "Let it be so."

Motiba visited Songad often. Sri Kanjiswami had studied the
Samaysara and also the teachings of Sri Rajchandraji of Kathiawar. So many people gathered around him at Songad, and his
fame and depth of knowledge shone like the noonday sun. He
became known as "Gurudev" our holy teacher, and Champaben
and Shantaben became known as "Bensri" and "Ben," respec-
tively. They were very much satisfied each time Motiba visited
Songad trying to pick up the real essence of the Jain religion.

Till the end of her life Motiba remained a devotee of these three great souls, and that gave her the strength to fight the deadly disease cancer and to face a very tortured state of body at the end of her life with a very calm and compassionate attitude.

Chi. Mira, since a long time I wanted to draw your attention to this side of your Motiba. I wish you could put these ideas in whatever manner and whatever chapter you like in your book, and I think it will be a befitting honor to Motiba's soul. I would certainly like the readers to have a glimpse of the background of her most understanding nature.

Thanking You,

Yours,

Shashimama

For most of our lives, contact between family members in India, Southeast Asia, the United States, London, and East Africa—for those are the places where most of us have settled—was sporadic, concentrated around important events such as marriages and deaths; renewed when leisure tours, studies, or business sent someone traveling in an ocean liner or a jet plane. Now we are wired. An e-mail message can be sent at an hour convenient to the sender and read later at an hour convenient to the receiver in a distant time zone. There is no chance of waking someone up with an inopportune telephone call or disturbing their sleep with the whine of a fax machine printing out a message at three o'clock in the morning. And it's practically free. After Shashimama, who now lives in Andra Pradesh on India's east coast, began corresponding with me by e-mail, I forwarded his electronic address to my father, who now lives on the island of Sardinia in the middle of the Mediterranean Sea. Online, the two old friends are once again able to chat with an ease neither has experienced since the days half a century ago when they sat together in a Bombay movie house deconstructing the mysterious details of American custom, dress, and language.

When my father decided to settle in America; marry an Oregon farm girl; and, finally, become an American citizen, he did so in the spirit of earlier generations of immigrants: if he was going to live in the United States, he would not do so as a sojourner. He would become an American. He would not speak to his children in Gujarati, because he wanted us to be "real" Americans, our identities uncompromised by a foreign accent or foreign ways. Giving us American identities was his greatest gift to us: he made us citizens of the richest country in the world, with unlimited opportunities and a quality of life the envy of all the earth. Of course, this American identity was never unproblematic for us. We were always part this and part that, negotiating pathways through fractured portals. Still, at the dawn of a rapidly globalizing century, this is not necessarily a disadvantage. Though we may pine for a lost sense of belonging, our fluid identity allows us to drop into places and fly off to other places and always feel as at home as we will ever feel in any one of them.

There is only one piece of advice I remember verbatim from my childhood. My father used to tell me, "It's best to be in, but not initiated." What he meant was that it is limiting to belong to a single group. The best of all situations is to be able to drop in, speak the lingo, be accepted, but retain all the while an outsider's perspective, and to be able to do this with respect to as many groups as possible. All of Motiba's grandchildren, whether of mixed race or not, whether raised in America or in India, have this ability to some extent. We can function as well in Seattle as in London or Bombay, crossing borders with ease. In a world where the boundary between haves and have-nots, between the electronically connected and the technologically excluded, between those who toil in the knowledge industries and those who simply toil is rapidly replacing national borders as the real frontier of privilege and identity, this ability to be able to function in—yet not wholly be of—any one culture, any one city, or even any one country can be a distinct advantage.

Electronic communication and the Internet are a great boon. They facilitate the existence of diasporic communities such as ours. It is little wonder that there has been an explosion of Internet sites that cater exclusively to the Indian diaspora. From masala.com to chaitime.com, with literally hundreds upon hundreds of other sites in-between, including iaol.com, "Indian Americans Online," there is a growing transnational cyber-community of dispersed Indians and other South Asians.[2] Whether a cook living in Edison, New Jersey, surrounded by subcontinentals, or a lonely *desi* doctor in a small Midwestern town, you can plug in, log on, and connect; read up on the latest news from India; download a couple of Hindi film tracks; join a chat; peruse the marriage adverts; even order Basmati rice for home delivery. And this applies equally well to Indians in England, Africa, Australia, or even India itself. Cyber-India is a country without borders.

For several decades, it was fashionable in America to speak of Asian Americans as the "model minority." Our seemingly quiet, law-abiding ways, our stereotyped devotion to academic excellence and professional success were seized upon as an argument both against affirmative action for less high-achieving groups and for the use of quotas in certain universities where Asians seemed to be qualifying for admission in numbers disproportionately large compared to their share of the demographic puzzle. In some respects, Indian immigrants were the model minority of the model minority, with an exceptionally high median income—well above other Asian groups and even above that of White Americans.[3] Early exclusion of nonprofessionals under formal U.S. immigration policies ensured that the first big wave of Indian immigrants was made up almost exclusively by doctors, engineers, professors, and scientists. The Indian Americans in the 1960s through early 1980s took pride in their success and felt a certain satisfaction that though India itself might be a poor country, Indians could succeed as well if not better than most people when presented with decent opportunities. It was a small group and, by and large, an affluent one, but it remained almost entirely invisible, eclipsed by older and larger groups from other parts of Asia. Asian Indians were, and still are, vastly outnumbered in the United States by East Asians, especially Americans of Chinese and Japanese descent. Whereas in England "Asian" is nearly synonymous with "South Asian," in the United States even today, when American residents of South Asian origin

exceed one million persons and constitute one of the faster growing immigrant groups, "Asian" does not readily conjure anything
related to "Indian"—or Pakistani, or Bangladeshi, or Sri Lankan, or
Nepali—for most people. South Asians in the United States remain
somewhat uncategorizable, sort of Asian American but not "Pacific
Rim"; sometimes very dark skinned and "Black identified" yet not
African American. In 1923, the United States Supreme Court
went so far as to distinguish between the admitted fact that Asian
Indians belonged to the Caucasian race and a firm conviction that
they could not, by any stretch of the imagination, be defined as
"white persons" and, therefore, could not be eligible for natural-
ization under U.S. law.[4]

The confusion over our identity persists within the "community." Immigration from South Asia really began to accelerate at
precisely the same moment the forces of globalization began to
push the United States and the world to redefine transnational
relationships. Yet, paradoxically, the South Asian diaspora has
remained highly tribalized, splintered into hundreds of discrete
groups and subgroups that each, more often than not, feel more in
common with their brethren elsewhere in the country or in the
world than with their next-door neighbors from a different group.
Many members of my family would feel more of a bond with a
Kathiawari Jain they might meet for the first time in Timbuktu than
with the Punjabi, the South Indian, the Pakistani, or the
Bangladeshi who lives next door in the same New Jersey housing
tract. The same is true of many of those same Punjabis, South Indians, Pakistanis, and Bangladeshis. The religious, regional, caste,

and class differences that divide people on the subcontinent are more often than not transported to their new home. One need only cast a cursory glance at the marital ads in *India Abroad* or *India West* to realize how alive these divisions are: "Jat Sikh parents seek professional boy"; "Punjabi Hindu parents invite correspondence from US born/raised MD or professional"; "Sunni Muslim brother looking for match for graduate sister 26 (looks 20)."

A generation of young people only now coming into adulthood may change all that. Many of these individuals were babies or small children when their parents immigrated to America after quotas were done away with in 1965. Others were born here of Indian parents. In either case, they have grown up to be Americans in a way their immigrant parents will never experience nor fully comprehend. This generation has founded dynamic South Asian student organizations on university campuses across the country and started nonprofit groups to address social problems in the community, from the scourge of domestic violence to the plight of taxi drivers—overwhelmingly from South Asia—in New York City. This is a generation where a nice Gujarati girl from Texas can become obsessed with *bhangra*, the wildly popular dance and music style originally from Punjab, spending all her spare time and pocket money preparing to compete in George Washington University's "*Bhangra* Blowout." This annual event attracts participation from literally thousands of college students of diverse South Asian origins from around the entire United States. These young people have transformed a folk dance tradition from one part of India into a pan–South Asian—and very American—phenomenon. They belong to a generation that—whether

born of Muslim, Hindu, Sikh, or Christian parents originally from
Pakistan, India, or Bangladesh—is conscious above all of what they
share as South Asians raised in America.

But though the newest generation of Indian Americans is less
fraught with the old ethnic, regional, caste, and religious divisions
of South Asia than its parents, it is much more conscious of class.
There are the children of doctors or investment bankers denied
nothing by their indulgent and successful parents. The girls are
known as "I.A.P."s, "Indian American Princesses." They ski in Colorado, wear expensive clothes and jewelry, and attend—or aspire
to attend—Ivy League schools. At the same time, there are the
children of working-class immigrants from the Jackson Heights
section of Queens; or San Jose, California, children whose fathers
drive cabs, work in construction, own newspaper stands, or
whose mothers toil on the assembly lines of the silicon chip man-
ufacturers. Living in communities and attending schools where
the dominant population is African American or Hispanic, they
often adopt the baggy pants, knitted caps, and gold chains of an "in
your face" inner-city cool. And then there are the privileged members of the international superclass, the children of India's own
rich, its hereditary rulers still living large off the tattered remains
of their lost princely domains, its great industrial families. These
young people fly in and out of New York, London, and Dubai with
the ease of people who own private residences on different continents. They are as comfortable with repartee in the Hindi they
learned at the Doon School as they are with the American idioms
they picked up at Harvard.

There is even a very precise set of terms to define these various divisions within the Indian-American community. There are the "ABCDs," "American-Born Confused _Desis_" (_desi_ means "a person from the country," in other words, a person from _our_ country, a person from India and, by extension, a person native to South Asia). My cousins have further refined the joke, referring to themselves as "ABCDEFGs"—"American-Born Confused _Desis_ Emigrated From Gujarat." Then there are, as for any immigrant group, the "FOBs," "Fresh Off the Boat," definitely not upper-class people and universally despised for their non-English-speaking, native-dress-wearing, embarrassingly unchic appearance and comportment. Finally, there are the "el-tobs," the "LTOBs" or "Long-Time Off the Boat" Indians. As a saucy Indian-American physician/writer in New York wrote on this subject, "The cool LTOB has a style and ease often missing in geeky FOBs and clueless ABCDs." ABCDs are "torn between a home where sex is a four-letter word and a society where sex is the answer to every problem." As far as clothes are concerned, "FOBs are partial to generic clothing and can be quite an eyesore while most ABCDs still think Express and Limited are designer names. The obvious disparity in style comes to light at cultural melees when the LTOBs are gliding by in chic, ethnic wear by Rohit Bal and the ABCDs have splurged as much on trashy looking sequined _ghagras_ from Khazana."[5] As for the Indian government, it classifies all of us as "NRIs," "Non-Resident Indians," or "PIOs," "Persons of Indian Origin." Even I, born in the United States to an second-generation Danish-American mother, can claim PIO status—and take advantage of the unique investment privileges and visa status that implies with regard to India—purely on the basis that my father, a former Indian citizen born in Rangoon, is of "Indian origin."

Recently, a new kind of immigrant has arrived in the United States from India: the "immigrant entrepreneur." Principally a phenomenon of Silicon Valley, the typical Indian immigrant entrepreneur arrives in this country on an H-1B visa with an advanced degree in electrical engineering, not uncommonly from one of the campuses of the famously excellent Indian Institute of Technology. A few years later, he is CEO of a $400 million high-tech start-up. Seventy-four percent of immigrant engineers and scientists working in the South Bay region are from India or China. Of the region's technology companies started between 1995 and 1998, 29 percent were run by Indian and Chinese chief executives.[6] The influx of Indian immigrants into the successful ranks of information technology entrepreneurs has been likened to a "Curry Brigade,"[7] and the veteran journalist Michael Lewis claims that during the 1990s, the "smell inside a Silicon Valley start-up was of curry."[8] Among the more visible members of the Curry Brigade are Sabeer Bhatia, the founder of Hotmail.com; Vinod Khosla, cofounder of Sun Microsystems and a partner in the powerful venture capital firm Kleiner, Perkins, Caufield and Byers, Co.; and Kanwal S. Rekhi, who, after making over $300 million in Silicon Valley has retired to devote himself to helping other South Asian entrepreneurs make in the valley through an organization known as TIE, The Indus Entrepreneur Group. Then there is Gururaj Deshpande, better known as "Desh" Deshpande, "the richest Indian on earth with a personal worth in excess of $4 bil-

lion,"[9] a fortune he amassed founding such companies as Corel
Networks, Cascade Communications, and Sycamore Networks.

At the same time, the ranks of working-class Indian Americans
are growing as well. With deep divides between the successful and
the struggling, there are more and more stories of gross exploitation of *desi* by *desi* and of Indian-on-Indian violence and crime. A
wealthy landlord in Berkeley, California, one of the "role models"
of the local Indian-American community, was recently accused of
illegally bringing in teenage girls from India to use as personal sex
slaves, as well as other undocumented individuals to toil for little
or no wages on his various properties. The girls, it was alleged, had
been sold to him by their parents in India who could no longer
afford to keep them.[10] While the successful portion of Indian
America is busy building million-dollar fantasy houses in New Jersey more akin to mini–Taj Mahals than to family homes, multiplex
cinemas in California exclusively to screen Bollywood movies, and
lavish temples complete with hand-carved marble friezes by arti-
sans from Rajasthan and priests imported from India to serve the
nonresident faithful in such far-flung areas as Texas and Illinois, the
poorer, less-educated arrivals often face much more grim realities.

In the major urban centers of America—the New York metro-
politan area, Chicago, the San Francisco Bay Area—on any given
Friday or Saturday night, in a rented club, a hotel ballroom, or a posh
restaurant, one-night dance parties are held where young FOBs and
LTOBs along with their middling cousins the ABCDs hip-hop,
bump, and grind their way into the wee hours of the morning. These
parties are organized by diverse groups, ranging from "YIP," "Young

Indian Physicians," to professional party production outfits such as "Down2Party," but they share a common passion for Indopop; Indo-reggae; *bhangra,* of course; and the music of Bally Saghoo, Nitin Sawney, and Cornershop. The celebrities of these events are the DJs, some of whom have national reputations and have recorded their own music mixes on compact disc: DJ Kucha, DJ Rekha, DJ Vishal, DJ Robby, DJ Karma. They get the crowd moving, keep it hopping, chart a rollicking course between Hindi film sound track favorites, remixed oldies with a new rock beat, Indorap, and the latest Asian pop from London. The parties have suggestive names: "Nirvana," "Midnight," "Fantasy," "Infinite." The young organizers post invitations on the web, send out mass e-mailings, pass out postcards at Indian grocery stores and the annual India Day parades. More recently, an entire web site—www.desiparty.com—has been created, listing upcoming parties from New York to Arcadia, California, even London, England. "Dress to Impress," "First one hundred ladies free," "Full bars on both floors," they exhort. "Strictly 21. ID required," "No Violence. Leave the Drama at Home," they warn.

Indian pop culture has become so internationalized that Hollywood and MTV stars are wearing *bindis* on their foreheads and getting *mehndi* done on their hands. A new line of makeup by Covergirl is called "sheer Karma." "Be here. Be sheer. Let your energy show," the ad invites. The model wears saffron-colored handwoven silk trousers and a paisley embroidered turquoise silk tank top. She sports an Indian silver ankle bracelet. Her feet are bare. Multiple bangles encircle her wrists.[11] Indian fashion was featured at the World Economic Forum in Davos, Switzerland, in early 2000, as was the work of the premier Indian-American artist, Natvar Bhavsar. It's hard to know if the current American rage for *chai, bindis, mehndi,* and even *karma* will last. They may prove as ephemeral as Nehru jackets, beads, and transcendental meditation were in the 1960s. But I don't think so. At that time, India was the ultimate orientalized focus for Western boredom with itself. Now India's diaspora population in the West along with India's own vibrant cultural exports are locked in a synergistic relationship, circulating and recirculating sounds, looks, films, and ideas that flow in and out of the world's major urban centers.

* * *

Our family held its first big Indian wedding in America in February 1999. Bharatiphaiba's son Samit, known to all of us as Sam, had met a—what were the chances?—Gujarati girl in medical school and fallen in love. Rakhee's family consists of typical members of the Gujarati diaspora, having immigrated to the United States not from India but from Africa. Rakhee's mother was born in Zimbabwe to Gujarati parents; her father was born in India, but the couple settled in Zambia after their marriage and from there moved to Florida. Sam and Rakhee's wedding was a grand affair, held in the bride's hometown of Orlando. Family members flew in from all over the country. During three days of festivities and ceremonies, everyone dressed in his or her finest silks and brocades and the front desk of the Sheraton where we all stayed was kept busy depositing and retrieving the women's multiple sets of jewelry. The bride and groom, both future doctors, were models of second-generation success. Everyone was proud of them.

In a traditional Hindu wedding ceremony (virtually indistinguishable from a Jain ceremony—and, in any case, Rakhee's family is Hindu), the groom sets out from his home on horseback or in

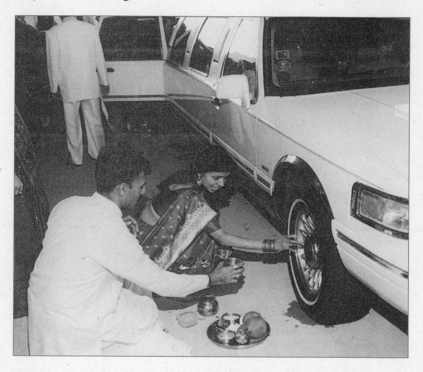

Blessing the limousine that will take Sam from the Sheraton to his waiting bride, Orlando, Florida, 1999.

a horse-drawn carriage to meet his bride at her parents' home. *Puja* is performed at the moment of the groom's departure to ensure a felicitous departure. So it was that the family arranged for Sam to leave the Sheraton in a stretch limousine, decorated with garlands of flowers, with the blessings performed on the car and an auspicious coconut placed so that the front wheel of the car would run over it and break it apart at the moment the vehicle took off. We all caravanned over to the wedding hall, in this case a local Bahia Shrine Temple, rented for the occasion. In the parking lot, Sam was transferred from the limousine to a horse-drawn carriage to make his final approach to his bride in the traditional way.

* * *

It was a delightful wedding, impeccably hosted by Rakhee's family. The bride and groom were resplendent in their gorgeous silks, purchased on a special shopping trip to Bombay by Bharatiphaiba. A *langna mandap* had been erected on the stage for the ceremony, and the entire hall was decorated with garlands of fresh flowers, tables with matching linens for the dinner to follow, a dance floor cleared for the celebration that went on late into the night. People of all ages—old aunties, little kids, cool Gen-Xers, middle-aged parents—we all danced the night away to the irresistible beat of an Indopop musical extravaganza put on by DJ Magic Mike, flown down specially from New York.

Sam's brother Prashant, whom we all call "Pete," has just gotten engaged. His wedding promises to be even more "diasporic" than his brother's. Pete works for Goldman Sachs in London, where he met his fiancée Dimpel Doshi. Dimpel comes from a Gujarati family settled in Singapore. The couple's traditional engagement cere-

Sam and Rakhee under the wedding langna mandap. *Devyani and I look on from the groom's family's side behind Sam.*

mony was performed in Chicago, they will be married in Singapore, and then make their home in London.

It is a shame Motiba did not live long enough to join us at Sam and Rakhee's wedding or to see Prashant engaged. She would have had a wonderful time. I know she would have loved to see how my son, Alexander, has grown, and to meet my daughter, Anjali, but Motiba and Anjali just missed each other, one's death preceding the other's birth by a few months.

* * *

The world Motiba left and the one my children have inherited is fraught with new perils. Despite my own family's success in America, there is evidence of Kaliyuga—the final, degenerative phase of Hindu cosmic time—all around us. India has become an avowed nuclear power, Pakistan as well. Tensions between the two countries, always high, have recently escalated, and the more relations between them deteriorate, the higher the risk that the world will see a twenty-first-century nuclear holocaust in South Asia. Meanwhile, China has become the undisputed powerhouse in Asia, a development that is worrisome for India, which fought a war with China in 1962. India's Minister of Foreign Affairs, Jaswant Singh, warns that India "lives in a dangerous neighborhood,"[12] a reference to China as much as to Pakistan, and has no choice but to build up a "credible, minimum deterrence" that includes nuclear weapons.

According to the World Food Program, India is now home to half of the world's hungry people.[13] The 350 million Indians who still live in absolute poverty equal the country's entire population in 1947, and it is unlikely that any amount of economic growth will improve their lot soon.[14] Meanwhile, India's physical environment continues to degenerate at an accelerating pace under pressure from a population that has now passed the one billion mark. Its major cities are increasingly unliveable, its countryside denuded of trees, its rivers foul with raw sewage and industrial effluent.

These factors continue to make life in the United States an attractive option for a broad spectrum of would-be Indian immigrants. True, a handful of homesick or patriotic individuals have returned to India in recent years to participate, above all, in the explosion in the country's lucrative information technology sector, but most Indians who've immigrated to the United States prefer to remain based here. I write "based here" because, more and more, there is a fluidity to the relationship between Asian Indians in the United States and their counterparts in India and in the rest of the diaspora. Many of the new arrivals are less immigrants than "bridge makers,"[15] maintaining a bicultural, transnational lifestyle and outlook that are facilitated by the revolution in transportation, communication, and information technologies—the very sectors in which many of these individuals work.

In a country where an entire group of Asian Americans, Japanese Americans, was dispossessed and interned during World War II for maintaining what were perceived to be "dual loyalties" and where recent accusations of inappropriate political contributions by Chinese Americans working secretly, it was charged, on behalf of the government of China to influence U.S. political leaders solicited strong emotions on both sides, the development of transnational diasporic communities where biculturalism is celebrated rather than condemned can be troubling. "Why don't they just become American if they're going to live here?" is a common reaction from the native born. But what does it mean to "become American" at the beginning of this new century, in an increasingly interdependent world, in a global economy?

Motiba's descendants in America are among those who will redefine, as each new group of immigrants has done since the country's founding over two centuries ago, what it means to "become an American." For us, now, more and more, it means being at home in the world, or, at least, being at home in different worlds. It may mean putting down roots in the United States, but it also means stretching out branches across national borders.

My cousin Ketan, Dipukaka's eldest son, and his wife Shilpa have just had their first child, a little girl named Priya. Ketan and Shilpa met in school in Bombay. They came here together to do graduate work in electrical engineering at Virginia Tech, and both work in "wireless communications." Ketan's brother Amit is staying with them while he works on a degree in computer science. They live in Seattle, Washington, a city seeking to define itself as the capital of a new trans-Pacific, high-tech economy, and the city where my father got his first real job in America, working for Boeing. My cousins Paresh and Viren, Vinukaka's sons, also live there. With my sister Anna, my brother Pravin, and I all living in Oregon and Washington, the family has returned, without it being planned, to my father's beachhead in America, the Pacific Northwest. Paresh, when not working as a stockbroker, is a passionate mountain climber and snowboarder, as likely to be found scaling Mount Rainier as sitting watching the ticker tape in his Bellevue office. He's just gotten engaged to his best "boarder buddy," a California girl of European descent. Viren, a student, sports a ponytail and plays percussion in an alternative rock-world-music fusion kind of band called "Bakshish."

Shilpa, born in the United States when her father, a structural engineer, was working here for a time before deciding to move back to India, is an American citizen by birth. Ketan is about to become a naturalized citizen after living and working in this country for a number of years. Their daughter Priya, ethnically Indian

A gathering of Pacific Northwest Kamdars.

in every way, is an American citizen by birth and will almost certainly grow up here. I have no doubt that Priya, Motiba's great-grandchild and the first Kamdar born in the twenty-first century, will invent a new identity, a new way of being Indian and American and perhaps something else altogether that we cannot even imagine yet. In any case, she will have an opportunity for self-invention that Motiba could never have dreamed of. As Shashimama's e-mail makes crystal clear, young women in Motiba's day had but two choices: arranged marriage or religious devotion.

* * *

If Motiba accepted her fate, it was because she believed that we are all sojourners, temporarily passing through; here today, gone tomorrow, back again next year or next century, rich one round, poor the next, in an endless cycle of birth, death, and rebirth. Only the *thirthankaras,* the "forders," those rare souls disciplined enough to make their way across the ultimate frontier between existence and *moksha,* liberation, can pretend to any kind of permanent state. The rest of us and all that lives are condemned to err through infinite incarnations, adopting endless, myriad identities.

Acknowledgements

Without the sustained help and support of many people, this book would never have come into existence.

First and foremost, I have to thank my parents, Prabhakar Kamdar and Lois Eagleton, for their unfailing faith in me and their unquestioning and generous support for a project that necessarily revealed much about themselves.

My extended Indian family uncomplainingly submitted themselves to lengthy interviews, repeated queries of all stripes, and badgerings for photographs, recipes, and anecdotes, all of which they gave generously. I want to thank Motiba's children, in addition to my own father—Vinoo Kamdar, Dilip Kamdar, Bharati Bhayani, and Usha Kamdar—for reading the manuscript and for getting back to me with friendly corrections and useful comments. Shashi Khara, my great uncle and Motiba's brother, whose reaction I dared not predict, was an early supporter of the project. He and Motiba's sister-in-law, Dhiraj Khara, and their first cousin Himmat Khara and Himmat's wife Padma all helped me gather information about family history and the history of the various cities in which Kamdars and Kharas have made their homes.

The family of Lataben Desai—Arunbhai, Bhabhi, Atman, and Aditya—as well as Kirit and Ila Kamdar took excellent care of me and my children while I was doing research in Rajkot. Lataben herself, whom I know simply as "Kaki," was my earliest publicist, alerting local journalists to my project and landing an interview for me in the popular Gujarati magazine *Chitralekha* before I'd even started writing the book. Rasik and Rama Parekh in Bombay have always treated me just like a daughter. I must also thank Rasik and Panna Hemani for their warm friendship and hospitality in Delhi, and Rasik's mother for her memories of little girl life in Kathiawar.

In the United States, I must thank Ketan and Shilpa, Sam and Rakhee, Paresh and Sibyl, and Viren for their help and encouragement. Shilpa's mother Ranjan Mehta helped me fine-tune the recipes, feeding me her own delicious concoctions while we worked. My sister Devi and her husband David Cohen, my brother Pravin and my sister Anna all deserve thanks as well for their support. Thanks to Janan Abdo, Jill Johnson, Amanda Barrow, Natvar and Janet Bhavsar, Pam and Larry Dunn, Janice Grubin, Dana Gordon, Robert Harvey, Helene Volat, Bonnie Levinson, Loic Lamoureux, Aradhana Seth, Ganeve Rajkotia, Frederique Belanger, Daniel Fresquet, Jose Dubrueil, Elisabeth Degremont, Jacques Mayoud, Paul Lindenauer, Lindsay Hebberd, Sreenath Sreenivasan, Sundaram Tagore, Swadesh Rana, Michael and Cindy Jones, Anu Teja and so many others for their friendship.

If Ben and Tina Schwarz, two of the most discerning readers I know, had not reacted with wild enthusiasm when I shared with them a hastily dashed off seven-page sketch of an initial anecdote, I would never have undertaken to write the book at all.

Among my colleagues at the World Policy Institute, I must thank James Chace, Steve Schlesinger, Bill Hartung, Armando Martinez,

Belinda Cooper, Philip Gourevitch, and Linda Wrigley. Sherle Schwenninger deserves special thanks for coaching me years ago to begin my transformation into a writer.

Without Amitav Ghosh's help and encouragement, I probably would not have dared to go to Yangon, nor, therefore, been able to write the Rangoon chapter. The people he put me in touch with cared for me as if I was a member of their own family. Unfortunately, for their own protection, they must remain unnamed here. I must express my heartfelt thanks to them and to all the brave and generous people in Yangon and living here in exile who, at some risk, helped me uncover a bit of the history of the Gujarati merchant community in Rangoon. Thanks also to Maureen Aung Thwin for her enthusiastic endorsement of my research on Burma. It is my deepest wish that political circumstances in that country change so that some of the harm inflicted on the people of Burma/Myanmar by the military junta over the last fifty years may begin to be repaired.

Jayabapa Jhala not only encouraged me to pursue this project before any of it had been consigned to paper but sat down with me and gave me a list of potential sources of information on the *kuldevi* his and my family share, Ashapura Devi, and on the history of Kathiawar in general, responding graciously thereafter to my every e-mail query.

I must thank the scholars Mary Callahan, Jerome Bauer, Robert Taylor, and Sarah Maxim for reading parts of the manuscript for historical and factual accuracy.

Victoria Farmer deserves special thanks for promptly referring me to just the right person each time I contacted her desperately looking for someone who could help me with some aspect of the book. I must thank Marshall Bouton, Sumit Ganguly, Pranay Gupte, Kanti Bajpai, and Varun Sahni for their friendship and their support of my work over the years, this book being no exception.

There has been no more devoted enthusiast for this project than Judi Kilachand, who has done everything in her power (and her Rolodex!) to help me. I thank her for her steadfast friendship.

One of the real joys of writing this book has been meeting Panna Naik, perhaps the most celebrated contemporary woman poet in the Gujarati language, who painstakingly checked the Gujarati and Hindi terms for accuracy and compiled the selected glossary.

I am especially and deeply grateful to my agent, Sterling Lord, who has been warmly supportive of this project from the very beginning. From my perspective, he is as much a mentor as anything else, and has brought me along, not a small distance, as a writer during the couple of years I have worked with him. Sterling has always been gracious enough to make me feel as if my writing and my book were the most important of his considerations, when I knew full well that could hardly be the case. It has been my great privilege to have his regard.

My editor, Kate Darnton, has labored tirelessly to improve my efforts, and has done so ruthlessly yet cheerfully, exactly as was required. I doubt many writers these days get the kind of attention Kate lavished on this project, and I feel truly blessed to have had her guiding hand over the manuscript. Peter Osnos is also to be credited with creating a publishing house that, committed to bucking the prevailing "mega-hit, bestseller" trend, would not only take a risk on a book such as this one, but would give it the attention it has received.

Finally, I must thank my husband, Michael Claes, for his love and enduring support throughout, not to mention the meals prepared, the children watched, the laundry done while I was locked up in my office or half a world away in India or Burma doing research. No woman who writes and has children could wish for more from a husband.

To borrow a pronouncement of Panna Naik upon realizing we were connected in ways we had not suspected, it has all seemed *runanubandh*, everything is predestined.

Glossary

Glossary of Gujarati and Hindi Terms

AARTI: Offering prayer with a lighted sacred lamp to God

AGASI: Rooftop terrace

AKHAND ANAND: Endless joy

ALMARI: Armoire

AMIRAAT: Nobility

BAJARI: Millet

BARFI: Sweet made with milk

BHAJIYA: Vegetable fritters made with chickpea flour

BHAKHARI: A kind of Gujarati wheat flatbread

BHANEJ: Literally "sister's son" but also used for daughter's first born

BHANGRA: Panjabi folk dance

BHAVAI: A popular form of folk theater

BHEL PURI: Snack mixture of puffed rice, chickpea noodles, chopped boiled potatoes, coriander chutney, and a sweet sauce of brown sugar and tamarind

BIDI: An indigenous cigarette

BINDI: A round auspicious mark made on the forehead

BRAHMACHARI: One who practices celibacy

BRAHMACHARYA: Celibacy

CHAAS/CHHASH: Buttermilk

CHANA: Chickpeas; garbanzo beans

CHANIYA BOR: A kind of berry

CHANIYO/CHANIA: Petticoat

CHAPATI: A thin, soft, circular flatbread made of whole wheat flour

CHAPPALS: Sandals

CHI: Abbreviation of "Chiramjiva," a salutation meaning "may you have a long life," used by an older person when addressing a younger person. A younger person addressing an elder person replies with the salutation "murabbi," "pujya," "aadarniya," meaning worthy of respect/worship.

CHIKOO: *Acrass sapota*; a brown-fleshed tropical fruit about the size of a kiwi

CHOLI: Woman's blouse or bodice

DAHI: Yogurt

DAL: Lentil soup

DANDIA: Colorfully painted wooden sticks used to perform traditional Gujarati folk dance

DARBAR: Prince

DARSHAN: To take in the sight of, to see with reverence a great or holy individual

DESI: Literally " a person from the country," i.e. a person from India, and now by extension someone of Indian or South Asian origin

DEVDASI: A girl dedicated for life to a temple, religious establishment, or deity

DHARMASHALA: Traveler's or pilgrim's resting house

DHOKLA: A typical Gujarati dish made of a fermented batter of
ground black eyed-peas and rice poured into pans, steamed,
and cut into squares or diamonds

DHOTI: Loincloth; a loose-fitting male garment of muslin
wrapped around the groin and waist

DIKSHA: Initiation

DIWALI: Also known as Dipavali. A grand Indian festival of lights
celebrated during the second half of the Hindu month of
Aaso/Ashvin.

DIWAN: Chief executive of a royal estate

DUDHWALA: Milkman

GANTHIYA: Noodles made from fried chickpea flour

GARAM: Hot

GARASIA: A person, usually a member of a royal family or some
one rewarded for service to a royal family, who holds title to
land given for his and his family's maintenance

GHEE: Clarified butter

GOL: raw sugar; alternately called jaggery

GUL MOHUR: *Poinciana regia.* A tropical flowering tree also known
as the "flame of the forest"

GUSSAWALA: Short-tempered person

HAVELI: Mansion

JARI: Threads of gold or silver embroidered on or woven into fine
silk garments

JINA: Conquering one; victor. The title given to the twenty-four "realized souls" of the Jaina tradition. More specifically, it may refer to Mahavira Tirthankara, the 24th of these.

KAAMBI: Anklet

KACHORI: Small bowl

KADHI: A soup made with yogurt, chickpea flour, and spices

-KAKA: suffix meaning father's brother

-KAKI: suffix meaning father's brother's wife

KAMDAR: Estate manager

KAMDAR SERI: Kamdar lane

KAMEEZ/KAMIZ: A knee-length loose-fitting shirt worn over loose pants called *salwaar* or *shalwar* or over tight-fitting leggings called *churidar*

KAMKHA: Woman's short, backless blouse tied at the back of the neck and torso with strings

KANJIVARAM: A silk sari made in the South Indian town Kanchipuram

KAPDU: A woman's garment

KHAANDAAN: A noble family by birth

KHAKHARA: Roasted thin chapati

KHANDANI: A form of rent

KULDEVI: Clan goddess; family goddess

KULFI: Ice cream dessert made with boiled milk; sugar; and various flavorings such as almonds, saffron, and pistachios

KURTA: Knee-length tunic

LAAJ: Modesty; in Gujarati culture, a woman covering her head and face with her *sari* to show modesty and respect

LAAPSI: A dish of sweetened cracked wheat

LANGNA MANDAP: Decorated canopy under which a traditional Hindu marriage ceremony takes place

LADDU: Sweets made with whole wheat or chickpea flour

LASAN: Garlic

LUNGI: A male garment formed by encircling and tucking a cloth around the waist to cover the lower half of the body

MAAKHAN: Butter

MAHABHARATA: Hindu epic narrating the war between Kauravas and Pandavas

-MAMA: Suffix meaning mother's brother

-MAMI: Suffix meaning mother's brother's wife

-MASA: Suffix meaning mother's sister's husband

-MASI: Suffix meaning mother's sister

MASALA: spices

MATAJI: Mother goddess

MEHNDI: Hindi meaning henna; *mendi* in Gujarati

MEMSAHIB: Term of address for an English or other, generally white, woman, used more commonly before India's independence from England in 1947

METHI: Fenugreek

MOKSHA: Final liberation or salvation of the soul

NARIYALPANI: Coconut water; the liquid from inside a green coconut

NOKAR: Servant

PAALAV: Gujarati term for the last portion of a six-yard *sari* that is draped either over the right shoulder to hang over the bosom

(the traditional Gujarati way) or over the left shoulder to hang
down the back

PAANWALA: *Paan* seller; *paan* consists of a betel nut leaf wrapped
around various herbs and seasonings

PAKORA: Vegetable fritter

PALLU: Hindi term for *paalav* above

PARYUSHAN: The eight-day festival of the Jains beginning from
the twelfth day of the dark (second) half of month of Shravan
and ending on the fourth day of the bright half of Bhadrapada
in Indian calendar

PASTIWALA: Scrap paper collector

PATARA: Wooden chest or trunk, often wheeled and ornamented
with beaten brass panels representing auspicious animals such
as elephants, peacocks, and parrots, used for storing clothes
and jewelry, especially of a woman's dowry

-PHAI/PHOI (BA): Suffix meaning father's sister. Ba, "mother" is
added to show respect

PIYAR: A married woman's parents' home

PRASAAD: Food offered first to a deity, then, having been blessed
and purified, eaten

PRAVACHAN: Lecture

PUJA: Performance of religious rites involved in making offerings
of flowers, leaves, fruits, water, incense, etc.

PUKKA: True

PURDA: Curtain or veil; the practice of keeping women veiled or
away from public view

PURI: Fried, round, wheat bread that puffs up into a spherical shape

RAJAAI: Quilt

RAJAAIWALI: Female quilt maker

RAMAYANA: Hindu epic written by Valmiki narrating the story of
Rama

RANGOLI: An auspicious design of rice powder, paste, or colored
pigments made on the floor or ground

REKADIWALA: Portable food stall; man who transports the stall

ROTLO: Thick millet flatbread made on a terra-cotta griddle

SAASHTAANG DANDWANT PRANAAM: The act of prostrating oneself
with outstretched limbs

SAGADI: An earthenware or iron cookstove

SALWAAR/SHALWAR: Woman's loose-fitting trousers

SAMSARA: Empirical world

SAMYAG DARSHAN: Right faith

SARI: A five- to nine-yard length of cloth draped and folded to
create a woman's dress. The cloth may be cotton; silk; or,
more recently, synthetic nylon or polyester. It is often ornamented with printed, embroidered, or woven designs
and can be richly embellished with jari, silver or gold
threads.

SATI: Self-immolation; woman who burns herself to death on the
funeral pyre of her husband

SATYAGRAHA: Insistence on truth; this term became synonymous
with the Gandhian struggle for India's independence from imperial Great Britain.

SHEERA: Sweet made with whole wheat flour or cream of wheat,
clarified butter, and sugar

SHREEKHAND: Pudding-like sweet made with thickened yogurt, sugar, cardamom, and saffron

SWADESHI: Indigenous; locally or home-made

TAVAA/TAWAA: A large terra-cotta or cast-iron griddle used to make all kinds of Indian bread

TAVI/TAWI: Small terra-cotta or cast-iron griddle used to make all kinds of Indian bread

THALI: Round, rimmed dinner plate made of brass or stainless steel

THEPLA: A kind of Gujarati bread flavored with turmeric and, often, fresh fenugreek leaves

TILAK: An auspicious mark on the forehead made of vermilion or sandal wood paste

TIRTHANKARA: A "forder." One who fords the great divide between the empirical world and moksha. Jains count a total of twenty-four tirthankaras, whom they worship as examples of success at life's principal goal: *moksha*

TOLA: A measure of weight equal to 11.66 grams

UNDHIYU: A stew of steamed winter vegetables

WADA: Doughnut-shaped fritter made with a batter of ground and fermented black-eyed peas

Notes

Kathiawar

1. Harikrishna Lalshankar Dave, *A Short History of Gondal* (Bombay: Edu-cation Society Press, 1889), p. 1.
2. Manekshah S. Commissariat, M.A., I.E.S. (Retd.), *A History of Gujarat: With a Survey of its Monuments and Inscriptions, Vol. II. Mughal Period: From 1573–1758* (Bombay: Orient Longmans, 1957), p. 198.
3. Ibid., p. 197, note 31.
4. Quoted in Manekshah S. Commissariat, *A History of Gujarat, Including a Survey of Its Chief Architectural Monuments and Inscriptions, Vol. I. From A.D. 1297–8 to A.D. 1573* (Bombay: Longmans, Green & Co., 1938), pp. 164–165.
5. Capt. H. Wilberforce-Bell, *The History of Kathiawad From the Earliest Times* (London, 1916; Reprinted New Delhi: Ajay Book Service, 1980), pp. 26–28.
6. Louis Fischer, *The Life of Mahatma Gandhi* (New York: Harper and Brothers, 1950), p. 72.

Rangoon

1. For this and other historical detail in the chapter, I am indebted to the following: Nalini Ranjan Chakravarti, *The Indian Minority in Burma: The Rise and Decline of an Immigrant Community,* Foreword by Hugh Tinker (London: Oxford University Press, 1971); N. Gan-gulee, *Indians in the Empire Overseas: A Survey* (London: New India

Publishing House, 1947); Usha Mahajani, *The Role of Indian Minorities in Burma and Malaya,* Foreword by Pandit H. N. Kunzru (Bombay: Vora & Co., 1960, distributed by the Institute of Pacific Relations, New York); and Hugh Tinker, *The Banyan Tree: Overseas Emigrants from India, Pakistan, and Bangladesh* (Oxford: Oxford University Press, 1977).

2. *India, Burma, Ceylon and South Africa: Information for Travellers and Residents* (London: Thos. Cook & Sons, 1906); and *A Handbook for Travellers in India, Burma and Ceylon* (London: John Murray, 1911).

3. "The most disastrous famine of modern times was brought about in A.D. 1899 by the failure of the rains. . . . Before the middle of January A.D. 1900 less than half the cattle in the province remained alive." Capt. H. Wilberforce-Bell, *The History of Kathiawad From the Earliest Times* (London, 1916; Reprinted New Delhi: Ajay Book Service, 1980), p. 254.

4. See the section on Burma and the map of "Rangoon and environs" in *A Handbook for Travellers,* pp. 441–470.

5. See Chakravarti, *The Indian Minority in Burma;* and Mahajani, *The Role of Indian Minorities in Burma and Malaya,* for detailed descriptions of tensions between Burmese and Indians during this period.

6. For a description of the onset of war in Burma and the attack on Ran-goon from a British point of view, see Alfred Draper, *Dawns Like Thunder: The Retreat From Burma 1942* (London: Leo Cooper, 1987).

7. I thank Mary Callahan, Professor, Jackson School of International Af-fairs, University of Washington, for this detail.

8. Hugh Tinker, "The Forgotten Long March: The Indian Exodus From Burma, 1942," *Journal of Southeast Asian Studies* (Singapore), vol. 6, no. 1 (March 1975), p. 12. In his introduction to Chakravarti's *The Indian Minority in Burma,* Tinker writes: "I too remember the nightmare trek of the Indians out of Burma in 1942. I shall always have a picture in my mind of the trail from Tamu to Palel in the Assam-

Burma borderland, and of the bodies which lay where they fell when exhaustion and disease were too much for their enduring spirits. Some of those bodies were so shrivelled and small." p. viii.

9. Ibid., p. 13.

Bombay

1. Amrit Gangar, "Films From the City of Dreams," in *Bombay: Mosaic of Modern Culture,* Sujata Patel and Alice Thorner, eds. (Bombay: Oxford University Press, 1996), p. 210.

2. Françoise Mallison, "Bombay as the Intellectual Capital of the Gujaratis in the Nineteenth Century," in *Bombay: Mosaic of Modern Culture,* pp. 76–87; and Sonal Shukla, "Gujarati Cultural Revivalism," in *Bombay: Mosaic of Modern Culture,* pp. 88–98.

3. Gangar, "Films From the City of Dreams," pp. 218–220.

4. Sharada Dwivedi and Rahul Mehrotra, *Bombay: The Cities Within* (Bombay: India Book House Pvt. Ltd., 1995), pp. 229–235. The authors include stunning photographs of the interiors and exteriors of some of Bombay's most famous Art Deco cinema houses on these pages.

America

1. The source of immigration numbers cited is the U.S. Census. Information is available at www.census.gov.

On the history of Asian Indian immigration both here and elsewhere in this chapter, the following works were consulted: Lan Cao and Himilce Noras, eds., *Everything You Need to Know About Asian-American History* (New York: Plume, 1996); Roger Daniels, *History of Indian Immigration to the United States* (New York: Asia Society, 1989); Susan Gordon, *Recent American Immigrants: Asian Indians* (New York:

Franklin Watts, 1990); Arthur M. Helweg and Usha Helweg, *An Immigrant Success Story: East Indians in America* (Philadelphia: University of Pennsylvania Press, 1990); Gary R. Hess, "The Forgotten Asian Americans: The East Indian Community in the United States," in *The Asian American: The Historical Experience,* Norris Hundley Jr., ed. (Santa Barbara, CA: Clio Books, 1976); Evelyn Hu-DeHart, ed., *Across the Pacific: Asian Americans and Globalization* (New York: Asia Society/Temple University Press, 1999); Manju Seth, "Asian Indian Americans," pp. 169–198 in *Asian Americans: Contemporary Trends and Issues,* Pyong Gap Min, ed. (Thousand Oaks, CA: Sage Publications, 1995); Ronald Takaki, *Strangers From a Different Shore: A History of Asian Americans,* Revised edition (Boston: Little Brown and Company, 1998).

Kaliyuga

1. *Visnu Purana,* trans. H. H. Wilson, Reprint (Calcutta: Punthi Pustak, 1961), IV, 24 128ff. Quoted in Klaus K. Klostermaier, *A Survey of Hinduism* (Albany: State University of New York Press, 1994), p. 127. "Kaliyuga," literally the "age of strife," is the final age of the endless cycle of Hindu cosmic time, an age which began in 1400 B.C. and in which we will continue to live until a complete collapse of all order in the universe is reached, whereupon the grand cycle will begin anew. The Jains similarly believe that we are living in a period of *avasarpini,* a "downward age." Cf. James Laidlaw, *Riches and Renunciation: Religion, Economy, and Society Among the Jains* (New York: Oxford University Press, 1995), p. 36.

2. I am quite aware of the difference between the terms "Indian" and "South Asian," and to the often-insensitive subversion of the latter by the former; my narrative is, however, a fundamentally Indian one and can only tangentially be related to the more diverse South Asian experience in the United States.

3. See in particular Arthur M. Helweg and Usha Helweg, *An Immigrant*

Success Story: East Indians in America (Philadelphia: University of Pennsylvania Press, 1990).

4. Ronald Takaki, *Strangers From a Different Shore: A History of Asian Americans* (Boston: Little, Brown and Company, 1998) p. 299.

5. Sandhya G. Ganti, "Long Time Off the Boat Desis: The LTOB Species Is Unrelated to ABCDs and FOBs," *Little India*, November 1999, distributed by saja.org, November 6, 1999.

6. Annalee Saxenian, *Silicon Valley's New Immigrant Entrepreneurs* (San Francisco: Public Policy Institute of California, 1999), p. 24.

7. Chidan and Rajghatta, "The Indians Are Coming, The Indians Are Coming: How the Curry Brigade Invaded Silicon Valley: Where Integrated Chip Means Indians, Chinese," *Indian Express*, October–December 1999, distributed by saja.org, December 10, 1999.

8. Michael Lewis, *The New New Thing: A Silicon Valley Story* (New York: W. W. Norton, 2000), p. 116.

9. Arthur J. Pais, "The Invisible Millionaire," *India Today*, November 29, 1999.

10. Debra Levi Holtz, Chuck Squatriglia, Chronicle Staff Writers, "Berkeley Landlord Depicted as Overlord of India Village," *San Francisco Chronicle*, January 22, 2000.

11. Inside front cover, *Good Housekeeping*, March 2000.

12. See Jaswant Singh, *Defending India* (Bangalore, India: Macmillan India, Ltd., 1999).

13. Priyanka Tikoo, "India Is Home to Half the World's Hungry People,"
India-West, February 25, 2000, p. A21.

14. For an eloquent analysis of the persistence of poverty in India, see: Siddharth Dube, *In the Land of Poverty: Memoirs of an Indian Family, 1947–1997* (London: Zed Books, 1998).

15. See the excellent recent book by Evelyn Hu-DeHart, ed., *Across the Pacific: Asian Americans and Globalization* (New York: Asia Society/Temple University Press, 1999).

READERS GUIDE ONLINE

www.penguinputnam.com/guides

OR AVAILABLE AT YOUR LOCAL BOOKSTORE

A Member of Penguin Putnam Inc.

www.penguinputnam.com

Available wherever books are sold